Sartre and Marxism

Sartre and Marxism

Pietro Chiodi

Translated from the Italian by Kate Soper

Humanities Press 1976

This edition first published in 1976
in the United States of America by
Humanities Press Inc.
Atlantic Highlands
New Jersey, N.J. 07716

'Sartre and Marxism' first published in Italy April 1965
© Giangiacomo Feltrinelli, Milan, Italy

This translation © 1976 The Harvester Press Ltd

Library of Congress Cataloging in Publication Data

Chiodi, Pietro.
    Sartre and Marxism.

    (European philosophy and the human sciences)
    Translation of Sartre e il marxismo.
    Bibliography: p.
    Including indexes.
    1. Sartre, Jean Paul, 1905-   2. Existentialism.
3. Dialectical materialism.   I. Title.
B2430.S34C5313   1976   194   76-3778
ISBN 0-391-00590-1

Computer typeset by Input Typesetting Ltd, London
Printed in Great Britain by
Redwood Burn Limited, Trowbridge, Wiltshire

Contents

Translator's Note

Since Chiodi quotes so extensively from Sartre's *Critique de la rasion dialectique,* (Paris, Gallimard, 1960), I had hoped to use and refer to the English translation of Sartre's work, which is forthcoming from New Left Books. Unfortunately, the English version was not available in time. The translation from the main body of the *Critique* is therefore my own, and references to the French are cited thus: (p. 000). I have, however, made use of the English translation by Hazel Barnes (*The Problem of Method,* (London, 1963) of the *Question de mèthode,* which prefaces the *Critique.* References to this work are cited thus: (p. 000, PM).

Kate Soper

Preface

In his autobiographical work, Sartre says of the time when he wrote *La Nausée*, 'I *was* Roquentin: in him I exposed without self-satisfaction the web of my life;' a little further on he says: 'I have changed.' [1] The war, the Resistance and the post-war social and political conflicts played a decisive role in this process of change. In the same book, Sartre speaks of the ties of solidarity with Others in the following terms: 'I have never recovered that naked awareness without recoil of each individual towards all the others, that waking dream, that obscure awareness of the danger of being a Man until 1940, in the *Stalag* XII D.' [2]

To claim that the 'change' Sartre underwent is that which led him from a philosophy of non-commitment to one of commitment would be wholly correct. But it would be both incorrect and misleading to explain this as the simple displacement of existentialism by Marxism. Incorrect because the *Critique de la raison dialectique* contains at least as much existentialism as Marxism and misleading because Sartre would certainly not agree to making every form of Marxism a philosophy of 'commitment' and every form of existentialism one of 'non-commitment. On the contrary, he would have us note that the Lukács, who, in the course of abandoning Stalinist Marxism immediately after the war, branded existentialism as the 'perpetual carnival of fetishized interiority,' is the same as the Lukács who cast Stalinism in its most definitive mould when he described it as 'idealistic voluntarism,' — that is to say, as terroristic pseudo-praxis. [3]

Only if we take for granted the position adopted by Lukács in *Existentialisme ou marxisme?*, and thus agree to a dogmatic identification of existentialism with a philosophy of non-commitment and of Marxism with one of commitment, can we possibly interpret the confrontation theorised in the *Critique* between the two as an integration of existentialism in Marxism. In reducing existentialism to an 'ideology' the *Critique* seems to suggest an interpretation of this kind — while at the same time pointing to the bankruptcy of current Marxism, and committing itself to a restoration of genuine Marxism.

vii

Sartre does not want to revise Marxism, because Marxism is not a matter of 'revising' but of 'doing,' – and of 'doing' precisely because it has been paralysed since the moment of its birth. In fact, by attempting to go beyond Hegelianism without incorporating those existentialist moments which run parallel to, and are inseparable from it, Marxism has ended up by overcoming idealism in the form of idealism itself, and in doing so has ceded place to that monstrosity which Sartre defines as 'materialistic idealism.' So that for Sartre the sole purpose of a meeting between Marxism and existentialism is to make use of the latter as a means to ascend from the 'Marxism of today' towards an authentic Marxism as existantialist realism. We shall have Marxism, let us say, only when its task of inverting the Hegelian dialectic so as to place it upon its feet is fully realised, which means only in the recognition that it has two feet, one of which is existentialism. No progress will be made in overcoming idealism unless both feet are used: it is in this sense that existentialism will 'resolve' itself in Marxism, helping the latter on its way rather than amputating itself from the course of history.

Existentialism, in making subjectivity its theme, has issued in a theory of non-commitment; the Marxism of today, in being the theory of commitment, has issued in an anti-subjectivist terrorism. But, as Marx himself conceived it, commitment was to be understood as the historical transformation brought about by a *multiplicity* of human subjects in the course of, and with a view to, their own de-alienation. Hence the necessity of a meeting between existentialism and Marxism, which will safeguard at one and the same time, both commitment and the 'irreducibility' of the committed.

A project of this kind, however, presupposes that the philosophy of our time is still living the crisis of Hegelianism, and that Marxism is still very far from having accomplished the task which Marx entrusted to it, that of being the heir and supercedent of classical Germany philosophy. If a philosophy is to go beyond Hegel in the direction of founding inter-subjectivity in the historical commitment to a transformation of society along humanist lines, it must first settle accounts with the conceptual apparatus employed by Hegel to theorise both subjectivity and history, – and thus in the first instance with the concept of 'dialectical reason' which precisely expresses the location and the modality of the historical realisation of subjectivity. Looked at in this way, the meeting between existentialism and Marxism which Sartre undertakes to effect takes the form of a *critique* of dialectical reason – a critical re-examination of that dogmatic dialectical reason common to both Hegel's spiritualistic idealism and to the 'materialistic idealism' of pseudo-Marxism. The aim of such a critique is the erection of a Marxist realism whose *critical* platform is provided by the existentialist problematic, that is to say, by means of a vindication of the *finite* nature of the protagonist of the dialectic, the human being.

The issue here is, therefore, the renewal of the *critique of historical reason,* but in a way that will allow us to understand historical reason as *dialectical.* It follows that any recourse to the epochal relativism of Dilthey's historical reason will be considered incompatible with this in that it does not confer on history that *unitary sense* which Sartre holds to be inseparable from a theory of commitment of a Marxist type. (p. 90, PM). The key point in Sartre's critical revision of the dialectic is his altered concept of subjectivity. To that disquieting demand in which the Marx of the *Economic and Philosphical Manuscripts of 1844* concentrates his critique of Hegel, as to who is 'the bearer of the dialectic,' Sartre replies that it is man conceived existentially as *praxis-project.* The critique of historical reason must, in consequence, find its true critical basis in existence understood as praxis-project. The dialectic is founded in existence, is concerned with existence, and renders existence comprehensible. This, at any rate, is the underlying thesis of the first volume of the *Critique.* In the second, as yet unpublished, Sartre proposes to establish 'the profound significance of History' (p. 12 PM), as a direction of development that goes beyond the confrontation of projects. This is a position peculiarly analogous to that which Heidegger was brought to adopt when, as a sequel to the analysis of the exisential project conducted in the first volume of *Being and Time,* he proposed in the second volume to extract from this a clarification of the 'meaning' of being. A task which he failed to realize.

The *Critique* is to be seen, then, as an attempt to restore the dialectic to its critical foundations, taking as the point of departure the existentialist concept of the project. But is an undertaking of this kind possible? It is true that the concept of the 'dialectic' is sufficiently equivocal to leave a certain margin for the riskiest conceptual operations. But in relying upon the connexion between 'dialecticity' and the 'profound significance of History,' Sartre is assuming dialecticity in its strong sense – in a historic-teleological sense – and looked at in this light his undertaking cannot be judged until the second volume of the *Critique* has appeared. Nevertheless, in that Sartre would have the dialectical meaning of history established upon the basis of an existential dialectic, and the dialecticity of existence based in turn upon the 'project' whose theory is developed in the first volume, it is possible in the meantime to derive some important observations from the analysis of the concept of existence-as-project.

Sartre attributes two characteristics to the project as a structure of existence: 1) the project is the relation between subject and object (where 'object' is taken to include both the world of things and Others); 2) the subject-object relation expresses a state of alienation of the subject. In appealing to the concept of existence-as-project Sartre's intention has been to abandon the field of absolute freedom in which he had theorised existence in *Being and Nothingness,* in order to recover the Marxian concept of historical *conditioning.* But by interpreting the project as the alienating relationship of subject to object, he has ended up by making that conditioning into a *state of alienation* (counter to the Marxian principle that conditioning, so far from being a state of alienation, is not a state at all but a constant). Furthermore, he comes to make conditioning — which taken in its Marxian sense should be seen as the constitutive and founding character of the structure of existence in its *entirety* — a characteristic of *only one* of the poles (that of subjectivity) which gives the structure of existence its divided character.

All that remains of existentialism in this conception of the project as a subject-object relation is the character of *ineliminability* of the relation itself; this is certainly an anti-Hegelian doctrine (given that for Hegel the relation is posited only in order to be removed in the final triumph of the Subject), and it is certainly Marxian: but Marxian only when placed within the general framework of Marx's reformulation of the Hegelian concept of the relation — the principle corollary of which is the denial of the coincidence of the relation with alienation. For Marx, alienation is a determinate form of the relation, and not the relation as such, so that the suppression of alienation does not mean the suppression of the relation, but its *transformation.* Here we can trace three related but opposing positions: 1) the Hegelian, according to which alienation must be suppressed, but since alienation and the relation coincide, the suppression of alienation necessitates the suppression of the relation; 2) the Marxian, which, in common with the Hegelian position, demands the suppression of alienation (and herein lies the ultimate reason for the revolutionary continuity between Hegelianism and Marxism), but in denying the coincidence of alienation with the relation, accompanies its demand for the suppression of alienation with the recognition that the relation cannot be suppressed; 3) the proto-existentialist position, which agrees with the Marxian that the relation cannot be suppressed, but in conserving the Hegelian identification of alienation with the relation, implies as a result that alienation is ineliminable.

Scholastic and sclerotic Marxism, the 'Marxism of today,' has retained the original Marxist demand for the elimination of alienation but has sought to satisfy it through devices aimed at the repression of the relation of multiplicity in the name of an absolute unity — which means, in effect, on the basis of the Hegelian presupposition (which provides the justification for political absolutism) according to which alienation can only be suppressed by ridding the social relationship of alterity of all the existential content which adheres in it. For this reason, Sartre considers the Marxism of today to be an 'idealistic voluntarism' — a form of terrorism operating from Hegelian premises. By reinstating the non-suppressible nature of the relation, he aims in the *Critique* to restore Marxism to its original status. But his starting point in this operation is an existentialism which wants to insist on the ineliminability of the relationship of alterity while remaining *within* the confines of the Hegelian premise that this relationship is identical with alienation (of the subject in the object); therefore, he is not in a position to supercede Hegelianism in a way consistent with Marxism. He is not in a position, that is to say, to specify a level at which it would be possible to *suppress alienation while conserving the relation.*

In other words, Sartre has not taken into account the fact that the task of replacing dogmatic Marxism, as yet imprisoned in idealism, demands the aid of an existentialism which has in its turn freed itself of idealistic presuppositions and can thus validate its insistance upon the ineliminable nature of the relation without appeal to the idealistic premise of the coincidence between that relation and alienation — in the last analysis this means without an appeal to the interpretation of the existential project as the alienating relation between subject and object. Unless this is done, the confrontation between existentialism and Marxism will serve only to *galvanize within Marxism those idealistic presuppositions from which it pretends to liberate it,* thus offering what is, on the best hypothesis, merely an *internal revision of idealist Marxism,* rather than establishing a Marxist realism. The presupposition common to Hegel, to idealist Marxism and to the Sartre of the *Critique* is based on what can be considered the fundamental logico-ontological locus of every idealism: the interpretation of human reality as the relation of alienation between subject and object. But this locus is the pure and simple expression of the impossibility of Marx's basic assumption: that it is possible to suppress alienation while conserving the relation. The resulting alternatives that emerge *within* this idealist locus can only acquire, in any instance, a *partially* Marxist, that is, pre-Marxist import. Ultimately they reduce to two: 1) alienation is suppressed by suppressing the relation (the solution of Hegel and of idealist Marxism); or, 2) the relation is preserved by preserving alienation (the solution of an existentialism still imprisoned in idealism).

Sartre's current position represents an attempt to synthesise these two alternatives: to suppress alienation while preserving the relation. Such an attempt is entirely valid, and points to an authentically Marxist supercession of idealism. But Sartre cannot succeed in his task because he wishes to accomplish it while remaining *within* the idealist logico-ontological locus — a locus, which as we have seen, constitutes the pure and simple impossibility of such a synthesis. It is this locus which Sartre makes his own when he interprets the existential project as the subject-object relation. The form that the *impossibility* of the synthesis between that relation and de-alienation takes for him is that of the *'instantaneity'* of de-alienation. This *'instantaneity'* in fact, is the temporal determination of a demand which is being insisted upon in conditions of *impossibility.* (Compare the confrontation between eternity and time in Kierkegaard.)

To conceive the structure of the existential project as that of the subject-object relation, thereby implying that the subject's state is that of alienation, is to present *society* in the form of a confrontation of a multiplicity of projects in a state of necessary alienation. Every man is a project of alienating objectification for every other. Here we have Hegel's thesis regarding the identity between multiplicity and alienation. Hegel, however, was able to suppress alienation in the final suppression of multiplicity by suppressing the subject-object relation in the final unity of the Subject. Sartre, on the other hand, cannot suppress the subject-object relation because its very structure expresses the existentialist impossibility of its being suppressed. For Sartre, de-alienation thus takes on the form of an *impossible* attempt to suppress the alienating multiplicity of human projects in the unity of the projecting subject. This is the task entrusted to the *group* in its role as protagonist of de-alienation. The 'group—in—fusion', or 'as molten' * sets itself to 'snatch man from his *statut*** of alterity,' in such a way that 'the Other (the former Other) is taken to be *the same.*' (pp. 638, 425) But while this task of snatching man from his *statut* of alterity in order to deliver him from alienation is possible for Hegel, it is impossible for Sartre whose existentialism presupposes the impossibility of suppressing the relation of exteriority. The Hegelian demand for the suppression of alterity and the existentialist recognition of its impossibility converge in the Sartrean concept of 'interiorisation' of alterity and of objectivity in general. (p. 424) The effort of the group is directed towards the suppression of alterity and objectivity, but the furthermost point it can attain in this activity is that of *interiorisation* of objectivity and alterity. De-alienation takes place, therefore, only at the *instant* at which objectivity is on the point of its inversion from exterior to interior. Alienation, however, re-enters the heart of the group in the form of interiorised objectivity. So that the group which 'formed itself against alienation [. . .] is no more able to escape it than is the individual, and for this reason falls back into serial passivity.' (pp. 635-36)

Sartre's quarrel with scholastic Marxism is that its theory of alienation renders de-alienation 'too easy' in that it makes it the effect simply of economic change. But the sole alternative to this is not total impossibility

---

* Fr.: 'à chaud'

** On Sartre's use of the term 'statut,' R. D. Laing and D. G. Cooper comment, *Reason and Violence,* (London, 1964), p. 125: 'Once a certain form of relatedness has been constituted, certain general consequences follow from the ontological structure of this particular form of sociality. The term *statut* denotes that array of necessary consequences that follow when one presupposes a particular form of sociality as one's starting-point. Thus a social system having been constituted, its constitution can be conceived as the starting-point for a second dialectical movement, or set of movements, which occurs under the statute or ordinance of the particular system constituted.' (Trans.)

— unless we opt for a literary pantragicism the only advantage of which would be its denunciation of the state of frustration and impotence which characterises revolutionary ideology in France today.

Sartre's thesis that a co-existing multiplicity is incompatible with the process of de-alienation has its gravest consequences in the specific field of *political techniques*. Here is confirmed our view that Sartre's attempt at an existentialist renewal of Marxism has given us only an internal revision of that 'idealistic voluntarism' which acted as the ideological background to Stalinism. Proceeding upon the assumption that multiplicity is as such both alienating and self-alienating, Sartre pours scorn on the very democratic techniques (elections, division of powers, etc.) which were employed in the process of de-Stalinisation itself. When exteriority, interiorised (but not suppressed) by the group-in-fusion, reappears in the group, as it congeals, in the form of a process of internal multiplication, Sartre can only protect the unity of the group by appealing to a *fraternity-of-terror established by a 'chief,' without discrimination between terror and terror,* and without posing *the problem of the limits and conditions* of the exercise of terror itself. Indeed, one understands how Sartre can rebuke Merleau-Ponty for his repudiation of the doctrine that to be in the minority is to be a traitor. Merleau-Ponty has thus some grounds for defining Sartre's position as 'ultra-Bolshevism' and remarking upon the 'painful memories' provoked by Sartre's theory of the *chief*.[4]

Sartre has been correct to recognise as his point of departure the insufficiency of primitive existentialism in the face of the problems posed by social commitment, by history and by objective reason. He has been equally right to recognise that scholastic and dogmatic Marxism, so far from constituting a valid alternative to existentialism, has given rise to 'idealistic' negation of commitment accompanied by a terroristic demand for complicity and servility. But the attempt to recall Marxism to its original inspiration through the agency of existentialism issues in a simple *internal revision* of 'idealist Marxism' because Sartre has conceptualised the existentialist project — which ought to constitute the *critical* basis of the *critique* of dogmatic dialectical reason (both idealist and Stalinist-idealist) — within the idealist schema of the alienated subject-object relation. Hence the idealistic and privatised demand for 'interiorisation' of the object as the condition of de-alienation — a demand as antithetical to Marxism as one could imagine. Sartre believes he has arrived at an anti-idealist position in denying that the object can be effectively 'digested' by the subject — the 'necessity' of the object, even when annulled, would be transferred through interiorisation from object to subject. But if being idealist means 'eating' the object, the fact that afterwards the object sits heavy on the subjective stomach, does not transform idealism into realism.

In actual fact, Sartre continues to move within the categorial schemas of idealism[5]: the object is necessity, the subject freedom; hence it follows that the necessity of the object is necessity without freedom, is *absolute* necessity in the same way that the freedom of the subject is freedom without necessity, *absolute* freedom. And so it is that Sartre can affirm that freedom is the 'necessity of necessity,' that 'freedom and necessity are one' (p. 377), that alienation is 'freedom's destiny in exteriority' (p. 285), that 'the necessity of freedom implies the progressive alienation of freedom in necessity.' (p. 638) The import of all such assertions is the same: that ultimately reality and the absolute are one and the same, whether it is a case of that absolute which comes into being with the subject's alienation in the object, or of that which springs from de-alienation of the object in its subjective interiorisation. Necessity is none other than the mode of determination of the absolute and unconditioned. Here we can see why the myth of 'liberté plenière' (p. 285) reappears in the *Critique* equipped with the whole traditional armoury of freedom as 'necessity of necessity,' as 'destiny', as the 'implication' of its opposite. Only in this case, alienation in objective necessity and de-alienation in subjective necessity arrange themselves historically and chronologically in a sequence of *alternation* rather than as *alternatives*. What remains to be seen is whether a doctrine of this kind is compatible with the revolutionary inspiration of Marxism and, above all, whether such Marxian concepts as 'conditioning', 'praxis', and 'commitment' are compatible with a conception of social reality in which 'the necessity of freedom implies the progressive alienation of freedom in necessity.' (p. 638)

[I]

Existentialism and Marxism

Sartre from 'Being' to 'Doing'

The point has been made, and correctly, that in post-war France, philosophers resolved to change the world rather than limit themselves to its contemplation.[1] In the country that was the birthplace of the Enlightenment, and that had just experienced the horrors of war, this seems the most reasonable and obvious of reactions. All the more so in that on confronting a task of this kind the new *philosophes* could expect to find themselves far from isolated, since Marxism, with its well-established doctrinal structure and its power of political organisation, was set on the same path. But only a few philosophers entered the ranks of the *Partie Communiste Française,* accepting the official interpretation of Marxism. Sartre, who was by this time recognised as the major representative of *philosophie engagée,* was not among them.

Simone de Beauvoir informs us that from his youth Sartre had sympathised with the PCF 'in so far as its negativism agreed with our anarchism,' in accordance with an 'aesthetic of opposition.' On 14 September 1939, Sartre noted in his *carnet*: 'I am now cured of socialism, if I needed to be cured of it.' But in 1941, on creating a Resistance group, he christened it 'Socialism and Freedom.' The group collapsed, and from then on Sartre collaborated with the communists in the *Front National.*[2] In a letter to Brice Parain, written during the war but never sent, Sartre writes: 'As for the political side of the business, you have no cause for alarm: I shall go into this rough-and-tumble on my own; I shall follow no leader, and if anyone wants to follow me, that's up to them. But the most urgent thing is to stop the young men who got into this war at the same age you went into the last one from coming out of it with 'sick consciences.' (Not that this isn't a good thing in itself; but it's most disagreeable for them.) No one, I believe, will be able to do this for them except those members of the older generation who have gone through the war side by side with them.'[3] How accurately, then, Simone de Beauvoir puts it when she writes: 'With the war Sartre had to renounce *being* and resolve to *do.*'[4]

And the 'doing' hardened into reality in the foundation of *Les Temps Modernes,* the most typical of the *engagée* journals of the immediate post-war period in France, and in the creation, in collaboration with David Rousset and Gérard Rosenthal, of the *Rassemblement Démocratique Révolutionnaire* which, in the last analysis, drew its inspiration from Sartre's Resistance slogan 'Socialism and Freedom.' [5] But the collapse of the *Rassemblement* convinced Sartre that one could 'do' nothing without first of all 'settling accounts' with that great revolutionary force inspired by the doctrines of the one who had first upheld that philosophers must change rather than simply contemplate the world. Thus commenced that dialogue with the communists which Sartre summed up in 1957 by saying: 'It is twelve years now that we have been debating with the communists, at first violently, later in friendship.' [6]

Sartre had read *Capital* and the *German Ideology* in 1925, that is, some ten years before reading Husserl, Heidegger and Scheler, but 'understood absolutely nothing' if understanding means 'changing oneself.' (pp. 18, 39, PM) But 'communism' did not just mean the works of Marx and the interpretation given to them by the theoreticians of the PCF; 'communism' also, and above all, meant 'the heavy presence on my horizon of the masses of workers, an enormous, sombre body which *lived* Marxism, which *practiced* it.' (p. 18, PM) If Marxist doctrine constituted a theory of social change, the mass of workers was the force to put it into practice. Sartre's attitude towards 'communism' was consistently characterised by his belief that if change were not taking place this was due to a lack of theory. Responsibility for this lack, however, lay not so much with Marx as with that 'Marxistic' current which ran from the 'economism' of Engels to the 'voluntaristic idealism' of Stalin. What was needed, therefore, was a return to principles, a re-thinking of authentic Marxism, after its perversion in the idealistic dogmatism of Stalinism.

Simone de Beauvoir tells us of Sartre's hopes that the communists might have used the means he offered them for snatching the patrimony of humanism from the bourgeoisie. [7] Sartre was by now convinced that without the communists there was nothing to be 'done,' but that the communists themselves would not be able to 'do' anything so long as they remained entrenched in a Marxism which had lost its vocation of universal humanism. Only existentialism could restore Marxism to that vocation; and, meanwhile, existentialism found a reason for its continuing presence in the decline of Marxism.

Hegelianism, Marxism, Existentialism

This thesis, which forms the basis of the *Critique,* corresponds to something suggested in the very first philosophical text published by Sartre, *The Transcendence of the Ego.* Here one reads:

It has always seemed to me that a working hypothesis as fruitful as historical materialism never needed for a foundation the absurdity which is metaphysical materialism. [8]

It is true that here the question is posed in terms of 'being,' that is, in terms of speculative philosophy, so that its most coherent developments are to be traced in such texts as 'Materialism and Revolution' [9] rather than in writings such as *Les communistes et la paix* [10] or the *Critique;* but it is nonetheless true that in the *Critique* the essential question concerns the foundation of the dialectic, and that the whole work can usefully be regarded as the attempt to interpret this founding *structure* as existential rather than economic. [11]

It is above all in *Question de méthode,* [12] written in 1957 and subsequently incorporated into the *Critique,* to which it forms the preface, that Sartre confronts the problem of the relations existing between existentialism and Marxism. (*Existentialism and Marxism* was in fact the original title of the work.) Sartre begins by observing that philosophy does not exist, only philosoph*ies* – a typically existentialist thesis, which Sartre, however, immediately stands on its head in Hegelian fashion, by saying that those philosophies that exist come to be understood as so many 'totalizations of contemporary Knowledge', and which is ultimately given a Marxist interpretation in that the successive totalizations of Knowledge constitute 'a particular way in which the "rising" class becomes conscious of itself.' (p. 4, PM) The whole of the *Critique* is played out in these three keys with surprising virtuosity and ease. And this is no accident. Because if it is true that Sartre accuses Marxism of having transformed itself into idealism, and that he would use existentialism as a means of recalling it to its recognition of the irreducibility of being to knowing, it is also true that he considers Stalinised Marxism's degeneration into idealism to be the final outcome of a process of corruption (which began with Engel's 'economism') of Marxism's original humanist inspiration. If the movement of the first line of attack is anti-Hegelian, that of the second, by virtue of the weight it places on consciousness, which is in the tradition of Sartre's conception of existence, tends rather towards recovering a good part of the anti-materialist inheritance of Hegelianism.

Sartre proceeds to cite the three living philosophies of the period from the seventeenth century to the present day: the 'moment' of Descartes-Locke, that of Kant-Hegel, and lastly that of Marx. (p. 7, PM) Since there is no going beyond any philosophy so long as man has not gone beyond 'the historical moment it expresses' (p. 7, PM), Marxism is today incapable of being surpassed. Surpassing and revision have no meaning while the present historico-political situation persists. Marxism's domain can only be cultivated, expanded, transformed on a simple level or internally modified: all this is the task of those *'relative* men whom I propose,' says Sartre, 'to call ideologists*.' (p. 8, PM) In the face of Marxism, existentialism is an ideology. It had its birth with Kierkegaard's opposition to Hegelianism, the latter being 'the most ample philosophical totalization.' (p. 8, PM) Kierkegaard was simply an ideologist because he moved 'within a cultural field entirely dominated by Hegelianism.' (p. 11, PM) The significance of this thought lies in its vindication of the irreducibility of lived reality to knowing. This vindication can serve as the base for a 'conservative irrationalism' but it can also be seen as 'the death of absolute idealism': in no case can it be liquidated as a form of 'subjectivism.'

It is 'striking,' says Sartre, that Marxism takes up the same stance in its opposition to Hegel when it insists upon the irreducibility of that existence which is social practice to the knowledge concerned with it. But Marxism effects this in the name of 'concrete man in his objective reality.' (p. 14, PM) So that Kierkegaard is correct in his opposition to Hegel when he denies the reducibility of the real to the known; but Hegel is at the same time correctly opposed to Kierkegaard in maintaining that man is the 'veritable concrete,' whereas for Kierkegaard man ends up by being an 'empty subjectivity.' (p. 12, PM) In this way it becomes easy for Sartre to deduce that 'Marx, rather than Kierkegaard or Hegel, is right, since he asserts with Kierkegaard the specificity of human *existence* and, along with Hegel, takes the concrete man in his objective reality.' (p. 14, PM)

It is quite clear that what we are witnessing here is a recuperation of Hegel which allows existentialist humanism (now confined to 'ideology') to be corrected and redimensioned along Marxist lines. Everything depends on the validity of the assertion that what Hegel meant by man was the 'veritable concrete.'

Existentialism's persistent presence in respect to Marxism

But if existentialism is reduced to an 'idealist protest against idealism' (p. 14, PM), why is it still relevant? Today there are two types of existentialism, says Sartre. Of the first type, as it is exemplified by Jaspers, everything that Marxists say of existentialism can and must be said: that it is the expedient ideology of the anti-Marxist bourgeoisie. In contrast to this, it must be said of Heidegger, who was the principal target of the Marxist polemic, that: 'The case of Heidegger is too complex for me to discuss here.' (p. 15, note, PM) But there is another existentialism, 'which has developed at the margins of Marxism and not against it.' (p. 17, PM) This refers to the existentialism of Sartre himself. Initially it was presented in the form of a reaction against the professorial optimism of pre-war French philosophy, the fundamental defect of which was its anti-dialectical pluralism and its confusion between 'total' and 'individual.'

* Fr.: 'idéologues'

It was the war which shattered the worn structures of our thought — War, Occupation, Resistance, the years which followed. We wanted to fight at the side of the working class; we finally understood that the concrete is history and dialectical action.' (p. 20-21, PM)

Why, asks Sartre, has *this* existentialism 'preserved its autonomy'? Because Marxism has in the meantime come to a halt. Its theory and practice have been severed, producing, on the one hand, an abstract and inalterable knowledge, and, on the other, an empiricism devoid of principles. The schism issued in an 'idealistic violence' which reflected and expressed what was then happening in the USSR. In this connexion it is important to note Sartre's extremist position on the relations of dependence between philosophy and the historical situation: he speaks of the 'necessary reflection' of the latter in the former. (p. 23, PM) The Russian leaders, 'bent on pushing the integration of the group to the limit, feared that the free process of truth, with all the discussions and all the conflicts it involves, would break the unity of combat.' (p. 22, PM) Here we are asked to note that this is not a case of simply providing a *de facto* explanation. When Sartre comes to deal with the group and the sovereignty which is established within it, he will provide a formal justification of these processes. (p. 630)

Marxism, in its state of arrested development, has become an 'idealistic voluntarism' in which the analytical process is reduced to a ritual. What were regulative concepts have become constitutive, giving rise to a 'scholasticism of the totality' which permits the genuine novelty of the facts to escape consideration. So it comes about that we have a bourgeois sociology and psychoanalytic theory which are rich in data but deprived of concepts, side by side with a Marxist Knowledge fossilised in its concepts and deaf to facts. (p. 28, PM)

> In view of this twofold ignorance, existentialism has been able to return and to maintain itself because it reaffirmed the reality of men as Kierkegaard asserted his own reality against Hegel. However, the Dane rejected the Hegelian conception of man and of the real. Existentialism and Marxism, on the contrary, aim at the same object; but Marxism has reabsorbed man into the idea, and existentialism seeks him everywhere *where he is,* at his work, in his home, in the street. (p. 28, PM)

This sclerosis of Marxism is not the product of a natural process of ageing, but of a particular historical situation:

> Far from being exhausted, Marxism is still very young, almost in its infancy; it has scarcely begun to develop. It remains, therefore, the

philosophy of our time. We cannot go beyond it because we have not
gone beyond the circumstances which engendered it. (p. 30, PM)

The task of philosophy today is not, therefore, 'to reject Marxism in the
name of a third path or of an idealistic humanism, but to reconquer man
within Marxism.' (p. 83, PM) This reconquest implies conquering the
entire foundation of Marxist philosophy. One is dealing, therefore, with
an appeal not to irrationalism, but to anti-intellectualism. (p. 173, PM)

> Marx's own Marxism, while indicating the dialectical opposition
> between knowing and being, contained implicitly the demand for an
> existential foundation for the theory. (p. 177, PM)

But the kind of Marxism which, at Warsaw, proposed as a slogan
'Tuberculosis is a fetter on production' has allowed 'the human foundation
to anthropology' to be swallowed up in Knowledge – with the result that
'Marxism will degenerate into a non-human anthropology if it does not
reintegrate man into itself as its foundation' – and this is the reason for the
persistent presence of existentialism, and thus for its particular task. (p.
179, PM)

The dissolution of existentialism and of Marxism

The task of leading Marxism back to its authentic anthropological
foundation hence falls to existentialism. A strange task for what is but an
'ideology' in relation to a 'philosophy.' All the more so in that
'existentialism is anthropology too insofar as anthropology seeks to give
itself a foundation.' (p. 168, PM) This foundation is the *being* of human
reality,' understood, however, not as immutable essence but as
praxis-project. 'The dialectic itself [. . .] appears as History and as
historical Reason only upon the foundation of existence.' (p. 171, PM)
And to that extent 'the comprehension of existence is presented as the
human foundation of Marxist anthropology.' (p. 176, PM)

There is no need, however, to fall prey to the equivocation of believing
that Sartre wants to restore historical materialism to nebulous
'ontologico-existential' foundations. Existentialism by no means
withdraws from history: rather, according to Sartre, it is doubly historical.
Firstly, because it is destined to be absorbed historically into Marxism
when it has become conscious of its own foundation, and secondly,
because Marxism, in its turn, is destined to disappear when the historical
situation which gave it birth has changed. Sartre says, in fact:

> From the day that Marxist thought will have taken on the human
> dimension (that is, the existential project) as the foundation of
> anthropological Knowledge, existentialism will no longer have any
> reason for being. Absorbed, surpassed and conserved by the totalizing

movement of philosophy, it will cease to be a particular inquiry and will become the foundation of all inquiry. The comments which we have made in the course of this present essay [*The Problem of Method*] are directed – to the modest limit of our capacities – toward hastening the moment of that dissolution. (p. 181, PM)

The absorption of existentialism into Marxism does not offer the joyful prospect of its continued existence even at second hand, because Marxism in its turn is bound to disappear:

As soon as there will exist *for everyone* a margin of *real* freedom beyond the production of life, Marxism will have lived out its span; a philosophy of freedom will take its place. But we have no means, no intellectual instrument, no concrete experience which allows us to conceive of this freedom or of this philosophy. (p. 34, PM)

The celebrated passage in *Capital* on the ascent from the reign of necessity to the reign of freedom is here interpreted in terms of an application of ideological historicity to Marxism itself – an interpretation very reminiscent of Gramsci's [13] – and one that encourages the slyest of evaluations of Sartre's theory of the dissolution of existentialism in Marxism: that if truth be told it is an exercise in cultural politics rather than the adoption of a theoretical position. It is quite clear from the passage quoted above that Sartre considers that existentialism will be absorbed into Marxism only when Marxism has installed the existentialist anthropology at its foundation. What Sartre accepts from communism is its demand that limited, 'bourgeois' humanism be replaced by a universal humanism, and that the only way of achieving this is by removing the means of production from the hands of a single class and placing them at the disposal of the entire collectivity. But he continues to hold that the political action this demands can only take place with, as its driving force, an ideology which recognises the existentialist anthropology as its proper foundation. If the demand for this is couched in terms inimical to Marxism, Sartre considers that its effect will be sterile, but if existentialism declares its support for Marxism at the politico-cultural level it will thereby gain a position within Marxism whence it can instigate a transformation of its ideological basis. What counts is not so much reason as a survivalist cunning. Sartre's whole treatment of the relations between existentialism and Marxism can be seen in this light – not to mention the apparently ingenuous declaration that the *Critique* 'could not take place *in our history* before Stalinist idealism had effected its simultaneous sclerosis of epistemological practices and methods.' (p. 141)

Naturally the significance of the entire exercise depends on what interpretation Sartre puts upon 'existentialism' and, consequently, upon 'Marxism.'

[II]

Existence and Project

1. *Sartre between Husserl and Heidegger*

In the 'Conclusion' to *Question de méthode,* Sartre opens the argument in a typically existentialist manner by observing that in the 'ontological region' of living beings, man boasts a 'privileged place' for two specific reasons:
1) because man 'can' be historical, that is to say, he can 'continually define himself by his own *praxis* by means of changes suffered or provoked and their internalisation, and then by the very surpassing of the internalised relations';
2) because man is the existent that we are ourselves; in this case 'the questioner finds himself to be precisely the questioned, or, if you prefer, human reality is the existent whose being is in question in its being.' (pp. 167-8, PM)

That philosophy, insofar as it poses the question of the totality of beings, can only proceed from the consciousness that among these beings man boasts a privileged position in respect to the posing of this question; that this privileged status depends on the fundamentally historical nature of human existence; that this historical nature is such that what is at stake in it is the very essence of man himself; and that, as a result, in posing the question of human reality the researcher and his research are one and the same — all this is to repeat with rigorous exactitude, Heidegger's presentation in *Being and Time* (section 2). So it is not mere chance that in *Question de méthode* Sartre makes Jaspers into the scapegoat for existentialism's deficiencies, while refusing to extend his criticism to Heidegger because 'the case is too complex.' (p. 15, note, PM)

We must understand what is involved here, because in many important respects the *Critique* is a straightforward return to the Heideggerian position after the attack on it in *Being and Nothingness.* We are dealing, of course, with the Heidegger of *Being and Time,* for Sartre rejects the philososophy of the 'late Heidegger', seeing in it a system 'which subordinates the human to what is Other than man' and as a result dissolves man and history in Being. (p. 248) Sartre also reveals his transparent sympathy for the Heidegger of *Being and Time* when he defends him against the accusations of pro-Nazi 'activism' levelled by Lukács, and against Marxist criticism in general:

> Yes, Lukács has the instruments to understand Heidegger, but he will not understand him; for Lukács would have to *read* him, to grasp the meaning of the sentences one by one. And there is no longer any Marxist, to my knowledge, who is still capable of doing this. (p. 38, PM)

It is true that his lack of sympathy for Lukács contributed to the severity of this judgement, but sympathy for Heidegger is also quite transparent.

In *Being and Nothingness,* despite the evident influence of Heidegger, the attitude taken up in regard to his specific positions was that of a rigorous polemic. For instance, with regard to the quite central notion of *Dasein,* Sartre wrote:

> But since the *Dasein* has from the start been deprived of the dimension of consciousness, it can never regain this dimension. Heidegger endows human reality with a self-understanding which is defined as 'ek-static project' of its own possibilities. It is certainly not my intention to deny the existence of this project. How how could there be an understanding which would not in itself be the consciousness (of) being understanding? This ek-static character of human reality will lapse into a thing-like, blind in-itself unless it arises from the consciousness of ek-stasis. In truth the *cogito* must be our point of departure, but we can say of it, parodying a famous saying, that it leads us only on condition that we get out of it. [1]

It is clear here that Sartre is subscribing to the Heideggerian theory of existence as project but, under Husserl's influence, giving it a Cartesian interpretation. Hence he sides against Heidegger in disputing the legitimacy of the quarrel with Husserl the outcome of which was the existentialist secession from the phenomenological school in 1926. In other words, in *Being and Nothingness* Sartre favours an interpretation of the existential project as a project of the *cogito*, while the significance of Heidegger's distance from Husserl lies in his vindication of the pre-eminence of the *sum* over the *cogito*. In *Being and Time* we read:

> If the *cogito sum* is to serve as the point of departure for the existential analytic of *Dasein*, then it needs to be turned around and furthermore its content needs new ontologico-phenomenal confirmation. The *sum* is then asserted first, and indeed in the sense that 'I am in the world.' [2]

On inverting the *cogito ergo sum* we get the *sum ergo cogito:* here the *cogito* is a determination of the *sum,* and as essentially so as anyone might want, but it nonetheless does not exhaust the ontological and phenomenological content of the reality of existence. This content is designated by Heidegger as being-in-the-world, and its basic modalities consist in having a care for others and taking care of the utilisable environment. Now the essential character of the notion of the 'project' offered us in the *Critique* is that of an identification of project with praxis in the Marxist sense. But the Marxian praxis is the equivalent of Heidegger's 'caring': both concepts spring from a polemic against the emphasis placed on consciousness by Hegel and Husserl respectively.

There are other striking analogies between the *Critique* and *Being and Time.* They were both to be works of two volumes, only the first of which has so far been published. Let us first hear what Heidegger intended for the missing volume: 'The analytic of Dasein . . . is to prepare the way for the problematic of fundamental ontology — the question of the meaning of Being in general.' [3] And Sartre says:

> Hitherto we have attempted to ascend to the elementary and formal structures and — at the same time — we have fixed the dialectical bases of a structural anthropology. For the time being we must leave these structures to live freely, to oppose and compose among themselves: the reflexive experience of this still formal adventure will prove the object of our second volume. If truth must be *one* within the growing diversification of interiority, in answering the ultimate question posed by this regressive experience, we shall discover the profound meaning of History and of dialectical rationality. (p. 755)

Both works, then, propose to question the meaning of being in its historicity; in both cases the enquiry is to be carried out in two volumes the first of which deals with the analytico-regressive conditions of the fundamental question; both regard their task as being the elaboration of a 'structural anthropology'; in both cases, the second volume is still missing. Could it be that this last shared aim conceals a common difficulty: that of taking that step from an existential analytic to a theorisation of what Heidegger refers to as the 'meaning of Being,' what Sartre calls the 'profound signification of History' — that leap from small letters to capitals which has never been an easy task for philosophers. Heidegger explicitly recognised its impossibility and, after *Being and Time,* embarked upon a philosophy which does not claim to derive Being from existence, but rather bases itself in Being right from the start. It will be very interesting to see what Sartre makes of the challenge. We can only hope that he does not make us wait as long as Heidegger has. [4]

2. *The 'at stake' as the character of human reality*

If the first characteristic in which man is privileged when compared with other living creatures — his existence, namely, as praxis-project — represents a notable concession to Marx, which Sartre, through the agency of Heidegger, is now prepared to make; the second characteristic, that is to say the identity of the researcher with his research when the object of this is man's being itself, should be seen by contrast as presupposing several of the bitterest points of Sartre's polemic with 'the Marxists'. The choice that Marxism offers today between a voluntaristic praxis devoid of principles or a theory anchored in abstract idealism represents 'the entire loss of meaning of what it is to be man' (p. 83, PM), and is the outcome, according to Sartre, of Marxism's tendency 'to eliminate the questioner from his investigation and to make of the questioned the object of an absolute Knowledge.' (p. 175, PM) This is precisely what happens when 'the very notions which Marxist research uses to describe our historical society — exploitation, alienation, fetishizing, reification, etc. — are those which most immediately refer to existential structures.' (p. 175, PM)

The Marxist concept of 'praxis' can only be grounded in a 'structural *and* historical anthropology' (p. 105)* which in theorising praxis constantly keeps in mind the identity between the researcher and his research. As has already been noted, the positing of the existential analytic as structural analysis and the recognition of the identity within it between the researcher and the researched is in the end all too open a derivation from Heidegger. Yet Sartre resorts to another idea of Heidegger's when he takes the decisive step which establishes the nature for him of the basic connexion theorised by Marxism between praxis and alienation. This is the formula according to which man is a being so made that 'in his being his very being is at stake.' Heidegger made use of this formula in order to stress the fact that in man being neither precedes nor predetermines existence in a way that guarantees it an infallible presence in it, but rather exists as a possibility offered to existence; it is therefore that which is 'at stake' in the project that existence itself makes of itself. Although with the concept of being-in-the-world, Heidegger openly recognised the quality of 'caring' that attaches to the praxis of existence; nevertheless, in interpreting authentic existence as being-for-death, he is removed from the possibility of any dialogue with Marxism. Sartre, by contrast, expels the concept of being-for-death and identifies existence with the praxis that takes place in the actual world. He thus interprets Heidegger's formula in the sense that it is in this praxis-project in the actual world that man's being itself is at stake.

This formula of the 'at stake' is what Sartre appeals to in his support of

---

* I have departed here from Hazel Barnes' translation in *The Problem of Method* in order to preserve Sartre's emphasis. The page reference is to the French text. (Trans.)

the entire Marxist attack on spiritualism and is even used by him to instil that attack with greater dramatic flavour. In the praxis which connects man with nature and with society what is being hazarded is not only the non-spiritual part of human reality; it is man's *being* itself which is 'at stake,' precisely because this being is susceptible to total loss in alienation, reification and mystification. In other words, Sartre sinks the whole social and political content of the Marxist alternative between alienation and reappropriation in a Heideggerian thesis of the essential uncertainty of being. In this way, at least according to Sartre, the concept of alienation preserves the full dramatic quality that existentialism wants it to have by virtue of its religious aspect, without losing any of that other dramatic quality which accrues to it through the Marxist perspective of its possible elimination in a struggle which Marx describes in the *Poverty of Philosophy,* using George Sands' words, as: 'Combat or death: bloody struggle or extinction.'

But the formula of the 'at stake' is also used by Sartre to emend the Marxist corruption of the meaning of human reality. In praxis, man's being is itself 'at stake' because the praxis is project, and the project always includes the co-penetration of researcher and researched, of projecter and projected. Looked at in this light, current 'scholastic Marxism' errs in forgetting that praxis is irreducible to its simple, objective determination. This is the starting point for the whole of Sartre's attack on any economic determinism which tends to strip praxis of its character as project, and the project of its component of auto-projection, consciousness and choice.

So that exploitation, for instance, before being the outcome of a certain economic base, is the *project* of exploitation:

> Economism is wrong because it makes exploitation into a definite effect, and no more than that, whereas as an effect it can only be maintained, and the capitalist process can only develop, if they are supported by a *project of expoitation.* I am fully aware that it is capital which expresses itself through the mouth of the capitalists and which produces them in the form of projects of unconditioned exploitation. But inversely, it is the capitalists who support and produce the capital and who develop industry and the credit system by means of their project of exploitation in order to realise profit. (pp. 687-88)

In contrast to Marx's assertion that the worker is the secret of bourgeois society, Sartre declares that:

> In France, in 1848, the bourgeoisie constitutes itself at first as the secret of the worker; it presents itself to its wage-earners as their necessity of living the impossibility of living. Or, if you like, as their impossibility of struggling against their misery without running the risk

of being exterminated by its ranks. For this reason alone the boss must be ruthless in jettisoning the proletariat from all that is humane if he is not prepared to accept the proletariat doing the same by him. The boss is made executioner, so the worker is the criminal. (p. 713-14)

This makes it quite clear that in the Sartrean schema, class conflict is delivered from economic 'determinism' by being radicalised and dramatised along lines which Sartre himself recognises as Manichean. Class struggle becomes class 'hatred'. It is at this point that the theory of absolute freedom and complete responsibility is resurrected to notable advantage if the polemic is directed against vulgar Marxism's necessaristic determinism, but to great disadvantage to the extent that it psychologises conflict and pays scant heed to the history of modes of production or to the ways in which these condition the process of radicalisation (as, for example, in the case of primitive accumulation in a society undergoing industrialisation). There is much to said — and it will be said later — about a statement such as:

The process of alienation demands that the worker be considered free at the moment of his contract in order that he thereupon be reduced to a commodity. Thus man becomes a commmodity voluntarily: he sells himself. (p. 693)

3. *Project and Conditions*

The project of a 'structural and historical anthropology' the fundamental outcome of which would be the recognition of existence as praxis-project does not include, in fact it excludes, anything such as a 'human essence' or a 'natural humanity.' Sartre's motto is: 'no common *nature* but an always possible communication.' (p. 170, PM) The 'significations' of the communication are not, however, simple psychic or mental entities:

Thus significations come from man and from his project, but they are inscribed everywhere in things and in the order of things. Everything at every instant is always signifying, and significations reveal to us men and relations among men across the structures of our society [. . .] Our comprehension of the Other is never contemplative; it is only a moment of our *praxis,* a way of living — in struggle or in complicity — the concrete, human relation which unites us to him. (p. 156, PM)

Praxis is based in need, 'is born of need.' (p. 170) Even if it must inevitably take the form of labour (p. 246), it does not immediately issue in a transformation: between praxis and transformation the project enters as transcendence. In connecting need and transformation, the project comes to constitute the true and proper structure of existence as praxis:

Sartre and Marxism

The word 'project' originally designates a certain human attitude (one 'makes' projects) which supposes as its foundation the project, an existential structure. (p. 172, PM)

Clearly the 'project' here has very little to do with the 'project' as it came to be understood in *Being and Nothingness,* where it expressed the intentional character of *consciousness* in its absolute freedom.

In the *Critique* not only is the project linked to praxis rather than to consciousness, but it is explicitly presented as 'praxis in "situation".' (p. 126) Situation means conditioning; the conditioned praxis gives an altogether different significance to the notion of possibility from that found in *Being and Nothingness,* because 'the project must of necessity cut across the field of instrumental possibilities. The particular quality of the instruments transforms it more or less profoundly; they condition the objectification.' (p. 112, PM) Need, project, possibility and conditioning become the constitutive elements of the structure of existence. The synchronic and diachronic variation of these elements confers on the structural anthropology its essential 'historical' determination and can make room for the way in which existence is conditioned by virtue of need and possibility without falling into economistic determinism.

Sartre accepts the Marxist principle according to which 'man is the product of his own production,' but only in the sense that 'the structures of a society which is created by human work define for each man an objective situation as a starting point; the truth of a man is the nature of his work, and it is his wages'; the situation as point of departure only has meaning to the extent that it is involved in the process of surpassing towards the possible. It is the surpassing which reveals the situation as the possible situation, and thus as that situation which is but might be otherwise; and 'thus knowing is a moment of *praxis,* even its most fundamental one; but this knowing does not partake of absolute Knowledge.' (p. 92, PM)

The project comes to be defined, then, as 'a double – simultaneous – relationship.' In respect of the given, praxis is negativity. This negativity is defined by Sartre as always being a negation of the negation (p. 92, PM) since it is the negation of that negation which constitutes need; so that the project in the end assumes the character of a restoration of the negated organism. (p. 171) But in this light the project appears as positive relation. It is the prior impulse of the praxis towards objectification in the field of instrumental and objective possibility. So that we have a project which is doubly conditioned: by the past it has come from and by the future it is going towards, and this double conditioning of the intelligent praxis expresses the historical character of human reality:

To say what man 'is' is also to say what he can be – and vice versa. The material conditions of his existence circumscribe the field of his possibilities [. . .] Thus the field of possibles is the goal toward which the agent surpasses his objective situation. And this field in turn depends strictly on the social, historical reality. (p. 93, PM)

4. *The field of the possible and its conditionings*

If the category of the possible is fundamental to every existentialism, we must be prepared for a careful consideration of the way in which the form it takes in the *Critique* differs from that in *Being and Nothingness*. In the latter it opened the way to a theory of the equivalence and unconditioned nature of possibilities; in the former it submits to exigencies opposite in kind. In the *Critique* Sartre says:

> Yet the field of possibles, however reduced it may be, always exists, and we must not think of it as a zone of indetermination, but rather as a strongly structured region which depends upon all of History and which includes its own contradictions. (p. 93, PM)

The field of praxis-project is characterised neither by indeterminacy nor by necessity: it is the field of conditioning. The introduction of the connexion between 'possibility' and 'conditioning' constitutes the most important innovation in Sartre's theory of the possible. In *Being and Nothingness* the problem of the possible was located in the extra-temporal dimension of the relation between the for-itself and the in-itself, and 'the fundamental project of human reality' was 'that of being God.'[5] The impossibility in principle of such a metaphysical project meant in effect the positive denial of all necessity together with the negative denial that consists in assuming that the only alternative to necessity is total indeterminacy; the consequence being that 'all human activities are equivalent (for they all tend to sacrifice man in order that the self-cause may arise), and they are all in principle doomed to failure. Thus it amounts to the same thing whether one gets drunk alone or is a leader of nations.'[6]

In making conditioning determinant of the category of the possible, Sartre is able to retain in the *Critique* the vitality of his polemic against necessaristic determinism without allowing the slightest indulgence to any evasion of the issue in terms of a magico-metaphysical indeterminism. It is on this point that the war must have opened his eyes: it is not the same thing to resist or to collaborate, to keep quiet or turn traitor, to be free or captive. Indeterminism could be the stance of that Beautiful Soul for whom what was 'at stake' in the projection of possibilities was not his own being. But for the man of the *Critique*, whose self is projected in praxis, it is precisely this *being* — including his 'soul' — which is at stake in this project. Praxis, being rooted in needs and in the scarcity of goods available for their satisfaction, reduces the project to the alternatives of loss of self and loss of Others: 'man is a Being through whom (through whose *praxis*) man is reduced to the state of a haunted object.' (p. 749)

It is on this basis that Sartre's declared adherence to historical 'materialism' is to be understood. He says:

> To be still more explicit, we support unreservedly that formulation of *Capital* by which Marx means to define his 'materialism': 'the mode of production of material life generally dominates the development of social, political and intellectual life.' (pp. 33-4, PM)*

In the *Critique* we also find statements of this kind:

> Man is a material being amongst others, and as such enjoys no privileged status. (p. 129)

> The only monism which *starts from the human world* and which *situates* men in Nature, is the monism of materiality. It alone is a realism; it .alone avoids the temptation to contemplate Nature *purely theologically*. (p. 248)

But they should be taken together with others of the following tenor: 'This material being perpetually goes beyond the condition which is made for him.' (p. 150, PM). 'It is the work or the act of the individual which reveals to us the secret of his conditioning.' (p. 152, PM). 'What we call freedom is the irreducibility of the cultural order to the natural order.' (p. 152, PM).

Precisely because he does not interpret Marx's 'materialism' as determinism but as the simple recognition that the basis for the rationality of history as project in situation is the economic, Sartre rejects the dialectical materialism professed until now by official Marxist culture in France, considering it to be a form of 'materialism from outside,' that is to say, a reduction of being to absolute knowledge, and thus, an idealism. To this he counterposes his own, and what he regards as Marx's, materialism 'from the inside,' which resolves itself in the recognition that praxis is always in situation. (pp. 124-26, 129)

5. Existence and Coexistence

By closely binding the project to the need for praxis on the one hand, and to social reciprocity on the other, Sartre has taken a decisive step towards

---

* The English version of this sentence from *Capital* is significantly different. 'The mode of production determines the character of the social, political, and intellectual life generally.' (*Capital*, I, p. 86. note, Lawrence and Wishart, 1974). (Trans.)

embracing a philosophy of 'doing,' of commitment and of change. By denying that the project is will or simple 'passion' in order to endow it with the consistency of a 'structure' (p. 151 PM), Sartre has cut himself off permanently from any lapse into the kind of romantic evasions he at one time entertained in his definition of man as 'useless passion.' Moreover, by conceptualising praxis as praxis in situation, he has withdrawn the project from the metaphysical level of the 'project of being God,' in order to insert it in the field of possibilities which are synchronically and diachronically conditioned by the course of history. This innovation also finds expression in the altered conception of the relations between Hegel and Kierkegaard. In *Being and Nothingness* Sartre asserted that 'to Hegel we ought always to oppose Kierkegaard,' [7] while the line he takes in the *Critique* is that Kierkegaard is correct in his opposition to Hegel from certain standpoints, but that it is Hegel's position which is correct from certain others – and specifically so in its insistence upon the concrete and objective nature of human reality by contrast to Kierkegaard's empty subjectivism. (p. 12, PM)

It is quite clear here that Marx has been an influence in favour of Hegel at the expense of Kierkegaard. But the matter is not as simple as might appear at first sight, since, according to Sartre:

> Marx, rather than Kierkegaard or Hegel, is right, since he asserts with Kierkegaard the specificity of human *existence* and, along with Hegel, takes the concrete man in his objective reality. (p. 14, PM)

It seems legitimate, then, to deduce from this that existence, as it is here conceived by Sartre, grasps within itself both the specificity attributed to it by Kierkegaard (that is, its irreducibility to absolute knowledge) and the objective concreteness attributed to it by Hegel. But it is this conception which gives rise to some of the most serious difficulties in Sartre's latest position.

At the root of the whole matter lies the concept of 'reciprocity' and, even more fundamentally, that of the 'project'. In *Being and Nothingness* Sartre had settled his accounts with Heidegger's concept of *Mitsein,* the salient points of which, he recognised, lay in the presupposition of the original nature of the relationship of alterity, and of its relatedness to the being of man (being-with), rather than simply to consciousness (being-for) – hence its character as a property of human reality insofar as this is being-in-the-world. But he had rejected the validity of the Heideggerian conception because 'the relations of the *Mitsein* can be of absolutely no use to us in resolving the psychological, concrete problem of the recognition of the Other.' [8] In fact, what Heidegger meant by *Mitsein* was a *structure* of being-in-the-world, where 'in-the-world' is understood as *colo, habito, diligo.* Once the question has been turned into a *psychological* problem one can understand why Sartre was unable to solve it except by assuming the *cogito* as 'the only possible point of departure.' In consequence: 'we must ask the For-itself to deliver us to the For-others, we must ask absolute immanence to throw us into absolute transcendence.' [9] But in this case the problem is posed anew in terms of a Hegelian 'recognition' between consciousnesses; and on this basis, the 'we' is bound to alternate between the 'we-subject' and the 'we-object' — which amounts to nothing more than a simple tautological transposition of what is assumed in taking the *cogito* as the point of departure according to the formula: '*being-for*-the-other precedes and founds being-with-the-Other.' [10] So that the we-subject becomes the simple psychological multiplication of the I, and the we-object the effect of objectification on the part of a third. But what is lost in all this is the genuine meaning of Heidegger's concept of *Mitsein*, which is so little an 'abstract' concept that it rather comes to be understood as *Mit-da-sein* — where *da* means the *colo, habito, et diligo* of the *Da-sein* — a meaning which consists in recognizing that the relation to others is no less an original and structural part of being-in-the-world than the relation to the world — the *in-der-Welt-sein* of the *Da-sein* is an *In-der-Welt-mit-Dasein*. Sartre's approach is from the opposite, namely Hegelian, position according to which what is original and structural is not the reciprocity but the unity of absolute consciousness. Roger Garaudy is right in observing that in *Being and Nothingness* we do not find 'the fundamental experience whereby others appear bound together by a solidarity of work, pain, risk and combat.' [11]

6. *'Mitsein' and original reciprocity*

Yet this was an experience which the war and the Resistance had imposed on Sartre too, and the evolution in his philosophy which finds its culmination in the *Critique* stems precisely from that. What effects has it produced on the theory of the *Mitsein*? There is no doubt that here too the *Critique* presents us with a return to the most genuinely Heideggerian positions, which provide a bridge to Marxism. In contrast to *Being and Nothingness*, in fact, the *Critique* takes reciprocity rather than unity as original and structural. This originality has at the same time both ontological and deontological value. It has ontological (and not only 'psychological') value because man is regarded as praxis, labour and struggle, and it is by virtue of proceeding from this praxis that Others *are-there-with*. And it has deontological value because the active force of the humanity which characterises inter-human relations, and which is the objective of the group's revolutionary action, is to bring about society's passage from the state of 'negative reciprocity' to that of 'positive reciprocity,' where the latter is understood as 'that which a man expects of another man when their relation is a human one.' (p. 253)

The concept of *original reciprocity* is, perhaps, the most important innovation contained in the *Critique*. It provides the starting point for three lines of attack developed by Sartre, which we shall analyse briefly. The first is directed against Heidegger. For while it is true that the concept represents a decisive step forward along the path which leads from Hegel to Heidegger, it is nonetheless true that the deontological aspect of reciprocity is lacking in Heidegger because the general bearing of his thought is alien to any normative demand save that invoked by the recognition that being-for-death is the only *true* (and in this sense, authentic: *eigentlich* in the sense of *eigen*) outcome of the existential project. It is clear that a philosophy of 'doing' as opposed to one of mere 'being' cannot hold to this position and still ascribe a normative value to the project in every instance.

In the second place, the concept of reciprocity implies a polemical stance against those 'Marxists' who, as distinct from Marx himself, fail to realise that if they put an original atomism in place of the concept of reciprocity, and look upon inter-human relations as the product of a particular mode of production, they not only pre-empt the possibility of establishing what it is in respect to which negative reciprocity, or alienation, is as it is, but also end up by justifying the atomism of bourgeois humanism, which would, in this event, be rendered unassailable. (p. 179) Every system of production, and every economic relationship in general, presupposes the original, formal structure of reciprocity of which in each instance it represents an historically determined reaction to the effects which the scarcity (*rareté*) of goods provokes in relations of reciprocity. (p. 207)

In the third place, the assumption of reciprocity as the original structure of human reality implies an attack on the Hegelian position according to which the unity of absolute consciousness is raised to the level of original structure and ultimate regulator of existence. The theory of *Being and Nothingness* had been obedient to this dictate in making the form of the project that of being God, that is to say, a project of absolute unification of the for-itself which condemned the relation between consciousnesses to a mortal struggle for reciprocal destruction. This is the position being expressed in the following:

It is therefore useless for human reality to seek to get out of this dilemma: one must either transcend the Other or allow oneself to be transcended by him. The essence of the relations between consciousnesses is not the *Mitsein;* it is conflict. [12]

The *Critique*, by contrast, considers the original formal state to be that of *Mitsein*, and sees the struggle between *men* (and not simply between their consciousnesses) as the effect of scarcity upon reciprocity. While for

Hegel the struggle for annihilation was an end in itself and the object of a mutual pursuit by consciousness, for Sartre 'the end is an objective conquest, or even a creation, in which the destruction of the adversary is only a means.' (p. 192) This demoting of the struggle to the status of means rather than end, to that of external modification (due to scarcity) rather than that of insurpassable structure, and the replacement of 'formal reciprocity' by 'negative' or 'immediate reciprocity,' means that we must interpret 'mediated reciprocity' as that which is to be achieved by the struggle of the group-in-fusion 'to snatch from worked-upon material its inhuman power of mediation between men in order to confer it on each and everyone in the community.' (p. 638)

7. *Reciprocity, Scarcity, Alienation*

For Sartre, then, the problem of the advent of socialist society is the problem of society's passage from a state of unmediated reciprocity to that of mediated reciprocity; but since it is by virtue of scarcity that the original formal reciprocity assumes the form of unmediated reciprocity (p. 208), in which each one sees in the other the source itself of the evil (p. 221), the relation between reciprocity and scarcity plays a fundamental role in the process of constituting socialist society.

This relation is a complex one. In fact it is reciprocity which renders something such as scarcity thinkable (p. 207), but it is scarcity which provides reciprocity with its basis in different historical societies. (p. 201) In this respect the 'Marxists' have been mistaken in not taking into account the 'original' character of reciprocity, deriving it instead from a historical basis in the modes of production. But it is rather the case that the inhuman relation of reciprocity presupposes (and modifies) the human one of reciprocity. (pp. 206-7)

It would seem reasonable enough, then, to suppose that the restoration of the human relation of reciprocity is simply a matter of getting rid of scarcity. And Sartre cherishes something of this kind in his prophecy that Marxism will disappear and be replaced by a 'philosophy of freedom' when 'man is freed from the yoke of scarcity.' (p. 34, PM) But what seems to be involved here is a limit concept in that Sartre regards every human venture as an instance of the relentless struggle against scarcity (p. 201), the disappearance of which would thus mean the disappearance of the human character itself, and of the specificity of human history whose possibility (p. 203) and rationality (p. 133, PM) is founded in scarcity.

This brings us to the key point: Sartre has made a decisive step in taking the relation of reciprocity as the foundation of history and of the universal humanism which Marx placed within the reach of socialist revolution, and he has at the same time recognised the essential nature of the relationship between inter-human reciprocity and the world of things, or of scarcity. These represent two key victories along the road he has decided to follow. By virtue of the first he has freed himself from any 'Marxistic' determinism of the kind which makes inter-human relations the simple products of the 'economic' world and which delineates a 'form' whose lack of a normative function makes it impossible to see how any meaning can be given to something such as 'alienation' or 'reappropriation'. By virtue of the second, he has gone beyond the position of *Being and Nothingness* where inter-human relations were held to be relations of pure consciousness. But he has remained obedient to the dictates of his former stance in granting the relationship of inter-human reciprocity a privileged position relative to the world of things; a privilege which is derived from the fact that the relationship to things, while certainly essential, is only so in a *de facto* way and negative in its function. (p. 246).

But the interpretation of the essentiality of the relationship to things, that is, the relationship of scarcity, as a *necessity of fact and as an exclusively negative factor* means in the last analysis that the basic Hegelian thesis of the coincidence of objectification with alienation has been reclothed in existentialist garb. The only difference being, that while in Hegel the relationship to the object is only provisionally one of necessity and therefore removable along with the alienation that it brings with it, in Sartre the relation to the object *qua* worked-upon material gathers into itself the characteristics of negativity and ineliminability which issue in the concept of permanent alienation. Looked at in this light, Sartre's account of alienation makes no advance on the positions of primitive existentialism, positions which are characterised by a vindication of the non-instrumental nature of action, though it is given its justification within the terms of Hegelian thought.

8. *Group-in-fusion, Unity, De-alienation*

Even if with the theory of the original status of reciprocity, Sartre has taken a decisive step towards conceiving history as the product of men's actions under determinate conditions and has thus freed himself from the Hegelian dogma of the original and ultimate unity of consciousness, he has nevertheless in the end brought himself back within the horizon of the Hegelian myth as a result of his interpretation of the existential structure of the relation of individual men to reciprocity.

The structure of existence, as as we have seen, is the project. In the *Critique* the project is praxis-project, synchronically and diachronically conditioned. The project encompasses, as much in a diachronic as a synchronic sense, two types of structural relation: that to Others (relationship of reciprocity), and that to things (relationship of objectivity). The major achievement of the new position in the *Critique* is the recognition of the essential (and therefore original) nature of the two relationships; by contrast, its weakness lies in its discrimination in favour of the essentiality of reciprocity as direct (and therefore positive) as against the essentiality of things, which is seen as negative.

From this point of view we can understand why the 'ideal' of a society founded on freedom implies the disappearance of the relationship of need to the scarcity of products; and we can also understand why Sartre remarks: 'But we have no means, no intellectual instrument, no concrete experience which allows us to conceive of this freedom or of this philosophy.' (p. 34, PM) The relation to things is the Hegelian objectivity-negativity, but regarded as ineliminable. The most important repercussion that a position of this kind has on Sartre's entire theory of the transition from capitalist to socialist society finds its expression in the following two points: 1) the 'fusion' of inter-human reciprocity in the *unity* of the group; 2) the 'ontological check' which this fusion is destined to meet with. (p. 638)

To understand the first point one must remember that scarcity constitutes the element which gives reciprocity its negative characteristics – hate and struggle. If the negativity of scarcity were to be eliminated, reciprocity would become 'positive' and 'human reciprocity.' What gives reciprocity its inhuman character is the fact that the multiplicity of particular projects on the part of the members of society in a relation of reciprocity take place in the 'field of scarcity' thus giving place to a 'confrontation of projects.' (p. 100, PM) But since the relationship of scarcity, although negative, is nonetheless ineliminable, it follows that reciprocity can only be stripped of its character as conflict of projects, which is what brings about its inhuman character, if the multiplicity of the agents of the projects is suppressed by interpreting reciprocity as a unity of identity. This is why only the 'group-in-fusion' is capable of 'snatching from worked-upon material its inhuman power,' i.e. the group which establishes itself on the basis of a 'project of snatching man from that *statut* of alterity which makes of him a product of his product, in order to transform him, *while molten* and by means of the appropriate practices, into a product of the group' (pp. 638-9); 'in the *we*, multiplicity is not suppressed but disqualified.' (p. 530) In *Being and Nothingness* the 'we' could only be conflict; in the *Critique* the conflict can only be eliminated by eliminating the 'we.' The situation is inverted but remains the same.

The effect of the second point is likewise clear. The group-in-fusion gives the project unity, but this unity is unable to suppress the relation to the object as scarcity, whereby alone it could 'be stabilised' and render the de-alienating action of the group permanent. So that 'that insuperable conflict of individual and community' destines the group-in-fusion to an 'ontological check' whose status is precisely equivalent to the 'instantaneity' of the positive, which is itself the hallmark of primitive existentialism — of an existentialism still moving within the framework of Hegelian categories.

9. *Project, Objectification, Subjectivity*

In the *Phenomenology of Mind* the alienating nature of objectification drives consciousness towards reciprocal destruction, towards unification in the sense of the total elimination of the alienating objectification. With Sartre, the object's character as scarcity drives the existential projects towards reciprocal destruction in a unification which can only be *instantaneous and destined to be checked* because of the *ineliminable* nature of the relationship of objectivity. To both ways of thinking the relationship of objectivity is a negative one.

All this rests on Sartre's assumption that there is an *incompatibility between reciprocity and the relation of objectivity*. And it is on this assumption that the whole of the *Critique* is based. It is here that the theories relating to the collective, the group-in-fusion and de-alienation find their directing principle. But where its influence is most dominating is in the unqualified, and at times disdainful, rejection of the possibility of there being a social base which rests on an 'agreement' between subjects in a relationship of reciprocity. (pp. 188-91) In fact 'the very word "agreement" is in itself aberrant. An agreement supposes, in effect, that individuals or groups, coming from different horizons, and characterised by different sets of attitudes and customs, do arrive at a *minimal* contractual accordance on the basis of their reciprocity [. . .] this is philosophy of History' (p. 527); 'agreement is but "atomisation"' destined to dissolve itself 'in the synthetic unity of the group in combat.' (p. 742)

If we try to go back to the ultimate root of this conception, we are again confronted with the concept of the project. In the *Critique* Sartre no longer attributes the project to the pure consciousness of the for-itself, but considers it to belong to human reality as 'praxis in situation;' all the same — and this is decisive — the project conserves its primitive structure unaltered.

It makes no difference in respect to this structure if in the *Critique* 'the project must of necessity cut across the field of instrumental possibilities [. . .] which condition the objectification', (pp. 111-2, PM); the structural problem is that of the relations which are established within the project between human reality and the two fundamental relations which define it as project: the relation to Others and the relation to things. Or rather, the privileged status which is accorded the relationship to Others at the expense of the relationship to things, which although recognised as essential is confined to pure facticity, derives ultimately from the fact that even the *Critique* continues to conceive the project's structure in terms of an *opposition between subjectivity and objectivity*.

In a conception of this kind — the typically Cartesian one — it is usually not difficult to discern the privileged status given to subjectivity and the corresponding devaluation of the relationship of objectivity. So that human reality becomes a subjectivity condemned to dispersion in an objectivity which is always identified with alienation, with the result that what provides the impetus for overcoming alienation is a magico-idealistic aspiration for flight from this wordly dispersion towards retreat in the nostalgia of original Subjectivity. The unity of the group-in-fusion represents the persistence of this myth which the existentialist demystification condemns to 'instantaneity' and 'check,' but does not succeed in dissolving, hence Sartre's heroic but impotent fury against the object, against the 'evil doings of worked-upon material' (p. 352, note), against the site of 'violence, shadows and witchcraft' (p. 358) where the 'monstrous forces' of our 'servitude' encamp. (pp. 359, 369)

Sartre lumbers himself here with all the baggage of the most traditional arguments of the Beautiful Soul but in a form the more exacerbated by the impossibility of either religious or speculative liberation. Today he appeals for this liberation to 'the working class, which represents in its contradiction the most tenacious and visible effort on the part of men to reconquer themselves as individuals by means of others, that is to say to snatch themselves *from Being* insofar as this is what gives them the *statut* of human *thing* in the midst of other human things which are their inanimate products.' (p. 358) But the working class does not have a project of this kind: it appeals only for a *historical transformation* of relations which appear to be eternal and ineliminable but are, in fact, of neither demonic nor inhuman inspiration. Indeed, it is precisely because they are not that they are susceptible to a process of de-alienation which is *that much more effective for being that much less metaphysical.*

But as long as human reality is conceived as subjective interiority which is externalised and alienated in a project which draws it out of itself towards the object, de-alienation must take on the neoplatonic character of 'interiorisation,' of a 'return' to original subjectivity. And things are not made any better by the fact that this project is forever condemned to 'instantaneity' and to 'check.' Hence the task is that of 'demonstrating the joint necessity of "the internalisation of the external" and the "externalisation of the internal." ' (p. 97, PM)

But then praxis becomes 'a passage from the objective to the objective through subjectification,' and the project 'subjective surpassing of objectivity towards objectivity.' (p. 97, PM) In other words, subjectivity becomes the foundation of the connexions of objectivity.

It is inevitable that subjectivity is given this privileged status when the question of the structural relationship between things is posed in terms of a relationship between subject and object. The great lesson of Heidegger's existential analytic has been forgotten here. Every time the question is posed in *Being and Time* in terms of an opposition between subject and object, it remains within the problematic of the *Vorhandenheit*, for which the conception of human reality and of the world is that of 'things' opposed. If instead one recognises that the genuine problematic for an analysis of the original structure of being-in-the-world is that whose categories relate to possibility, it becomes clear that 'when Dasein directs itself towards something and grasps it, it does not somehow first get out of an inner sphere in which it has been proximally encapsulated, but *its primary kind of Being is such* that it is always "outside" alongside entities which it encounters and which belong to a world already discovered.' (author's emphasis)[13]

[III]

The Dialectic

1. *Realistic Materialism and Idealistic Materialism*

In a letter to Roger Garaudy, the representative of orthodox Marxism in France, Sartre writes:

> Let us understand: Marxism, in being the formal framework of all philosophical thought today, cannot be surpassed. By Marxism I mean historical materialism, which posits an internal dialectic of history, and not dialectical materialism, if by that is meant that metaphysics which fancies it has discovered a dialectic of Nature. This dialectic of Nature *could* even exist, in fact, but we must recognise that we have not even the smallest beginnings of a proof of it. So that dialectical materialism reduces to an empty discourse, as idle as it is pompous, on the physico-chemical and biological sciences; it veils, at any rate in France, an analytic mechanistic theory of the most banal type. By contrast, historical materialism — insofar as it directly seizes upon the origin of every dialectic: the practice of men governed by their materiality — is at the same time the experience which everyone can make (and does make) of his *praxis* and of his alienation, and the reconstructive and constructive method which permits human history to be grasped as a totalization in process. So that thought about existence soon finds itself again thrown into the process of history, and it can only understand it to the extent that dialectical knowledge reveals itself as knowledge of the dialectic.[1]

The reason for Sartre's adherence to historical materialism, and for his rejection of dialectical materialism, is hence quite clear. He rejects the latter because 'the origin of every dialectic' is praxis, and he accepts the former because 'the praxis of men' is 'governed by their materiality.' Sartre's present aim is to provide an 'existentialist thought' which 'recognises itself as Marxist in the sense that it does not ignore the fact that it is rooted in historical materialism.'[2] But 'to be governed,' 'rooted' are expressions which cannot be interpreted in a deterministic sense. 'The dialectic is not a determinism' (p. 73, PM); and human 'conduct, instead of being first clarified by the material situation, can reveal the situation to me.' (p. 154, PM) It is true that 'man is a material being among others, and as such enjoys no privileged status' (p. 129), but it is at the same time true that he enjoys a particular *mode of being,* characterised by his being praxis-project and by his being at stake in his very being. (p. 168, PM) Praxis-project expresses the historical nature of man, because the project, by virtue of inserting itself as negation of the negation between the negation of existence which is need and the positive effect which is the outcome of the project of surpassing, constitutes itself as the ultimate foundation of every historical dialectic. (p. 99, PM)

There are two essential consequences: 1) the foundation of the historical dialectic is the mode of being of existence, its structure; 2) the 'materialistic' dimension of the historical dialectic is made to reside within the projecting praxis as that which conditions it, rather than this praxis being within a presupposed materialist structure which conditions it from without. This is what Sartre means when he defines man as 'a material being with a project.' For him, there are two fundamental types of 'materialism.' There is that which is 'external' or 'transcendental': in regarding man and history as merely a specification of nature, it misinterprets both. It attributes an *a priori* mechanical dialectic – which has no scientific basis – to nature, and then inserts man and nature into this mechanistic trap. (p. 124) This is certainly not the 'materialism' of Marx, who looked for the foundations of the dialectic in the relations between man and man and between men and nature. It is rather a 'materialistic idealism,' whose distance from reality opens the way to dogmatism and Stalinism. (p. 28, PM; p. 126) Opposed to it there is the genuine 'realistic materialism' which alone can give adequate expression to historical existence in its character as 'praxis in situation.' (p. 126)

2. *Determinism, Mechanistic theory, Choice*

When he speaks of 'materialism,' Sartre means that the project, as the structure of human reality and foundation of history, is conditioned in an exhaustive way by the relationship of scarcity. This relationship should be seen as covering a wider field than that of the strictly economic, because there is scarcity of the product, of the instrument, of the worker, of the consumer etc. (p. 225) In this way, historical materialism is confirmed in history but is not its foundation. (p. 134) Economic conditioning expresses the regressive dimension to the project which founds individual and collective history; but what gives history its character as truly human and historical is a progressive impulse in a direction which is not already implicit in the state of things, to which it opposes itself as a form of *response.* (pp. 204-5) The conclusion is that 'without these principles [of economic conditioning] there is no historical rationality. But without living men, there is no history.' (p. 133, PM)

It is from this standpoint that Sartre understands and accepts 'without reservation' the principle found in *Capital:* 'that the mode of production of material life generally dominates the development of social, political and intellectual life.'* But dominates does not mean 'determines mechanistically,' because the surpassing totalization which follows from the project passes through mediations which modify it, and in so doing impede the 'direct reduction' of history to economy. These mediations, which can never be by-passed, are composed of everything which relates to the particularity of existence and to its group relations, to education (infancy), to 'passions' and, in general, to the wealth of that human and historical content which psychoanalysis and sociology take as the object — even if onesidedly — of their researches. (pp. 41, 66, PM) Thus, in his recent book, *Words,* Sartre aims to show the enormous importance of the particularity of his childhood on the development of his life and thought.

Sartre's point is that his quarrel with materialistic determinism is not that of 'American sociology' which is demanding facts that are other than economic when it claims that 'the economic is not entirely determinant.' This claim, says Sartre is 'neither true nor false.' (p. 73, PM) It is not false because it is true that the economic is not entirely determinant, but it is not true because nothing is entirely determinant. The underlying motivation, which gives history its rationality, springs from economic conditioning, but this itself passes through existential mediations which always include modification of the course and influence of the basic conditioning. It is for this reason that Kardiner's discovery that the reactions of the Marchesi islanders to the scarcity of women among them do not square with economic determinism, by no means contradicts historical materialism. Nor does it demonstrate the need for introducing other 'factors.' What it does demonstrate is that economic conditioning, insofar as it defines the field of scarcity, can only be conceived within a framework of a surpassing project the conditions of which are not simply economic. It is mistaken, therefore, to want to account for Valéry in terms of his being 'petit-bourgeois':

> Valéry is a petit-bourgeois intellectual, no doubt about it. But not every petit-bourgeois intellectual is Valéry. The heuristic inadequacy of contemporary Marxism is contained in these two sentences. (p. 56, PM)

* Chiodi's reference is to Sartre's citation in the *Critique* (p. 31) of a sentence from *Capital*. The English version, *Capital,* I, p. 86, note (London, Lawrence and Wishart, 1974) is quite different: 'the mode of production determines the character of the social, political, and intellectual life generally.' (Trans.)

And in regard to Flaubert:

> It is the work or the act of the individual which reveals to us the secret of his conditioning. Flaubert by his choice of writing discloses to us the meaning of his childish fear of death – not the reverse. By misunderstanding these principles, contemporary Marxism has prevented itself from understanding significations and values. (p. 152, PM)

Sartre specifies that 'it would be a mistake to accuse us of introducing the irrational here' (p. 151, PM); the accusation could only come from a mechanistic and reductionist philosophy, which would fall back into 'scientistic determinism.' The dialectical method, by contrast, 'refuses to *reduce,* it follows the reverse procedure. It surpasses by conserving, but the terms of the surpassed contradiction cannot account for either the transcendence itself or the subsequent synthesis.' (p. 151, PM)

On the basis of these assumptions, Sartre rejects the so-called 'Marxist' thesis that 'the basic contradiction,' that is to say, the class struggle, is the only factor which determines and historically orientates the field of possibilities. If we cling to this conception we cannot help but see 'class' as a function of the economic base, therein depriving the struggle of its fundamental character as choice and commitment:

> For us the basic contradiction is only one of the factors which delimit and structure the field of possibles; it is the choice which must be interrogated if one wants to explain them in their detail, to reveal their singularity (that is, the particular aspect in which *in this case* generality is presented), and to understand how they have been lived. (pp. 151-2, PM)

3. *The Dialectic: Hegel versus Kierkegaard*

That Sartre is refusing to make 'materialism' the principle for resolving the existential 'decision' in the 'economic' is clear enough. He interprets it, in fact, as the recognition of the quasi-determinant influence which the economic exercises over the decision which the project incorporates. And it is by reference to this interpretation that Sartre derives his concept of the dialectic.

From a rigorously existentialist point of view the concept of the dialectic would either have had to be repudiated or else have been interpreted as a dialectic of the *aut aut*; in either event the outcome would have been a rigorous refutation of Hegelian reason. This was Sartre's position in *Being and Nothingness.* But it is a position which relegates history and its problems to second place. When, with the advent of the war, the problem of history which had been hounded from the door by the refined intellectuals of the Thirties, re-entered so dramatically through the window, the call to morality, which had already been announced in the concluding pages of *Being and Nothingness,* separated Sartre once and for all from the 'Beautiful Souls' who continued to seek a refuge and an alibi in one or another form of existentialism in order to shield themselves from the horrors of the 'outside world.' Looked at in this perspective, the Second World War had the opposite effect on Sartre's development to that which the first had had on primitive existentialism.

But the problem of history is the problem of inter-existential totalizations, of 'collective' projects and their confrontations, of the 'meaning' and rationality of historical action, and of the incidence upon one or another aspect of this of ideological consciousness and its instruments. But given that this is the case, the attitude to Hegel was bound to change, and starting from the principle of *Being and Nothingness,* where 'to Hegel we ought always to oppose Kierkegaard,' [3] Sartre proceeds to his assertion in the *Critique* that Kierkegaard is right as opposed to Hegel in certain respects, whereas in others Hegel is right as opposed to Kierkegaard. (p. 12, PM)

Kierkegaard is right in refusing to reduce reality to knowledge, but Hegel is right in moving out of 'empty subjectivity' towards the 'true concrete,' that is, towards the individual in his concrete objectification. (p. 12, PM) Hence Sartre's programme for the *Critique*: the elaboration of a theory of the foundation and meaning of history, which does not fall into the Hegelian mistake of reducing historical reality to knowledge. This was also Marx's project; but it very quickly fell prey to the 'cut and dryness' of an 'idealistic' reduction of reality to knowledge. This is why it is not a case of revising Marxism according to some 'revisionist' programme, but of 'doing,' and this is why doing involves a renewed commitment to the irreducibility of the real to knowledge; in other words, it must be founded on existentialist premises. [4]

But then 'doing' Marxism means giving history a meaning which rests on a rationality the particular 'structure' of which is not located in an economic principle reduced to an idea. It is a case, rather, of retracing a 'structure' in existence which functions as the foundation of the historical process. This structure is the project as negation of that negation of existence which is need, and as surpassing totalization in accordance with a dialectic which is neither spiritual nor material, but belongs to existence in the latter's character as original unity of material and spirit, of the given and its surpassing.

4. *Dialectical Knowledge and Knowledge of the Dialectic*

Sartre sets himself the task, then, of tracing a meaning of history which is based on a form of reason whose dialectical totalizations do not presuppose the reduction of reality to that reason itself – which is what happens with Hegel and Hegelianised Marxism (or 'idealistic materialism'). Sartre considers that a task of this kind divides into two profoundly differing lines of research – to which the two volumes of the *Critique* respectively correspond. The first of these we already possess, the second we are still without. The tendency of the first line of research is towards establishing the *foundation of the possibility* of history as the process of dialectical totalizations. The tendency of the second is towards discovering 'the *profound signification* of History and of dialectical rationality.' (p. 755, author's emphasis)

The second line of research presupposes the first because 'dialectical knowledge' relies on 'knowledge of the dialectic' ' for its foundation. The basic task of the *Critique* is that of a 'critique' because it takes the form of an enquiry which dialectical reason demands of itself in respect to the limits and conditions of its validity after the dogma of Hegel and the idealistic interpretations of Marxism. The analogies with Kant's positions are obvious. The second volume proposes to give us a knowledge of historical facts in much the way physics proposed, at the time of Kant, to construct a knowledge of physical facts. Just as in Kant's day, the dogmatic reason which insisted on abstract and *a priori* accounts of existence prevented access to the world of physical facts, so today, access to the world of historical facts is obstructed by the dogmatic reason of idealism which has dissipated the genuine inspiration of Marx's Marxism.

So that if one wants 'to discover the profound signification of History and of the dialectical rationality' as the second volume proposes to do, we shall first have to initiate a critique of historical reason. Dilthey pointed to the necessity of this before Sartre, and it is strange that in the whole of the *Critique* there is no reference to Dilthey's work, especially in view of the enormous influence it had on Heidegger and on the project of *Being and Time* – which is to say, on the project which Sartre now makes his own: that of re-thinking the foundations of history starting from the constitution of man. The explanation for this certainly lies in the fact that Dilthey's historical reason is not a dialectical reason, because for Dilthey, whose line of attack is wholly directed against Hegel, dialectical reason is incompatible with critical reason.

From Sartre's current point of view, looking at Heidegger (and hence at Dilthey) through the filter of dialectical Marxism, the critical reason of Kant and Dilthey remains analytic. That is to say, it rests on atomistic tenets which must result in liberalism at the political level, while dialectical reason is the fruit of the class struggle and constitutes its principal ideological instrument:

The dialectic, as the seizure of practical consciousness on the part of an oppressed class in the struggle against its oppressor, is a reaction created in the oppressed by the divisionist tendency of the oppression [. . .] It is the surpassing of contemplative truth by practical and efficacious truth, and of atomisation (resulting from the serial agreement in spirit) towards the synthetic unity of the group in combat. (p. 742)

So there must be a critique of reason; not, however, of a reason which excludes all dialecticity from history in advance, but rather of a reason which recognises the very substance of itself to be dialecticity. The dialectical aspect of reason, so far from being excluded from this 'critique' in advance, becomes its prime object.

5. *Dialecticity and the Structure of Existence*

Sartre's task, then, in conducting his own critique of historical reason is to establish its dialecticity through criticism itself and not through the dogmatism of Hegelian idealism or pseudo-Marxism. But for any foundation to be critical in this way, it must be characterised by two indispensable features: 1) it must have rediscovered an area of *a priori* validity which can function as its basis; 2) it must refer to the experience which functions as its limit. The establishment of a dialectic which is critical means, therefore, inscribing an area of *a priori* validity but giving it a necessary reference to *experience.* Sartre realises that you cannot speak of dialectical reason without assuming a necessary relationship between reason and the course of historical facts, but he believes it is possible to provide a non-dogmatic foundation for this necessity, a foundation that does not mystify the reference to experience by absorbing what is fact into the *a priori.*

This is the significance of his 'criticism.' The dialectic he seeks is one that is founded *a priori* but is not aprioristic. It is a dialectic 'supple and patient, which espouses movements as they really are' (p. 126, PM), whose principles would be 'heuristic' and 'regulative' (p. 26, PM), and whose method would simultaneously be progressive and regressive. (p. 133, PM) The polemical reference points in founding a criticism of this kind are analogous to those referred to by Kant: on the one hand the dogmatic 'foundation' of dialectical reason (Hegel and idealistic Marxism), on the other the presumption that it has an empirical foundation — of the kind envisaged by Gurvitch's sociological methodology. Where the dogmatic position is valid is in its request for an *a priori* foundation to the dialectic. Its weak point lies in its reduction of reality to knowledge, in other words, in its mystification of experience. What is valid in the empirical position is the demand that the reference to experience be constitutive of the foundation of the dialectic. Its weak point is its denial of any *a priori* constituent. (pp. 117 sqq.)

Sartre's position, if compared to that of Kant, could be defined as the attempt to make the dialectic into an *a priori* regulative principle which nonetheless absorbs within itself the objective cognitive features which Kant attributed to the constitutive intellect, this latter being relegated to analytic reason by Sartre. (p. 136) [6] Sartre realises that if the dialectic is to have validity as 'universal method and universal law of anthropology' (p. 118), it must at the same time be 'a method *and* a movement in the object' in accordance with the following principle:

> We maintain simultaneously that the process of knowledge has a dialectical order, that the movement of the object (whatever it is) is *itself* dialectical and that these two dialectics are in fact one. (p. 119)

But the principle of this unity can neither be an Hegelian type of unity of knowledge, nor a naturalistic type of unity of being such as is hypothesised by dialectical materialism.

On the other hand, this unity cannot be understood as 'a dialectic which imposes itself on facts as the Kantian categories do on phenomena.' (p. 132) For Sartre the necessary unity of the relationship between the *a priori* content of the dialectic and experience must be constructed in such a way that it safeguards both the formal nature of the *a priori* and the autonomy of experience. Sartre traces this unity to its origin in human reality, *because its mode of being consists in its making itself the content of form which is in itself dialectical.* It is in human reality, and in the historical world to which this gives rise insofar as it is originally inter-human, that we shall find, on the one side, the dialectical object of every study of history, and on the other side, the subjective foundation (in the formal-structural sense) of every dialectical knowledge. The fundamental object of the *critique* of dialectical reason is that of tracing the original unity of dialecticity, whether it be of knowledge or of the real, not to Hegel's Knowledge or Engel's Nature, but to the *structure of existence* as praxis-project governed by need.

6. *The Prolegomena to Every Future Anthropology*

The mode of existence of human reality, that is to say its structure as praxis-project, is the 'foundation' of the historical dialectic. It is society, therefore, that is the locus of dialectical experience and understanding. And for Sartre, this is Marxism properly speaking. Society is composed of a multitude of individuals, each one of whom realises his own project-of-being in his relations with Others and in the field of the scarcity of goods relative to needs. The first volume of the *Critique* does not yet confront the problem of the 'profound signification of History and of dialectical rationality' (p. 755); it does not pose, that is, the problem of historical progression as the 'unity' of history, of truth and of intelligibility — as will the second volume. The first volume is exclusively devoted to developing the formal aspect of a critical statement of the problem of the dialectic. It is clear that an enquiry of this kind cannot be based either on idealistic or on materialistic premises, that is on premises which interpret the unity of form and content which is postulated by every dialectical conception, in terms of the factual identity of an absolute principle with itself. What Sartre's formulation of the critique does by contrast is to recognise the structural principle found in human reality as the form of every historico-dialectical structure, and this opens the way to a formal-existential enquiry the object of which is 'to determine the formal conditions of History.' (p. 743)

The first volume, then, proposes to see the dialectic as the conjuncture of 'dialectical possibilities of a purely formal order' (p. 571); the concern, here, however, is not with an empty 'formality,' since the form which supports it is the very dialectical structure of existence, that is to say, the basis of every possible historical 'content.' The concern, rather, is with 'the perfectly abstract logical and dialectical relations which every historical interpretaton will nonetheless have to contain within it as its own intelligibility.' (p. 608) In other words, 'the first volume [. . .] will look exclusively for the intelligible foundations of a structural anthropology — insofar, be it understood, as these synthetic structures constitute the condition itself of an ongoing and constantly orientated totalization.' (p. 156)

> In a word, we are confronting here neither human history, nor sociology, nor ethnography: we shall be aiming, rather, to parody a Kantian title, to establish the bases for the 'Prolegomena to every future anthropology.' (p. 153)

The starting point for these prolegomena is the recognition of the dialectical nature of individual practices whose confrontation in the field of scarcity gives place to the formation of 'gatherings' * which are to be examined in their 'formal intelligibility.' Among these gatherings, particular emphasis is laid on 'series,' 'groups' and 'classes'; in studying 'classes' Sartre will often be referring to the working class, but:

> Our intention is not to define *this* particular class which one calls the proletariat: we aim no further than to discover by means of these examples the constitution of a class, its function of totalization (and of detotalization) and its dialectical intelligibility (its bonds of interiority and exteriority, its internal structures, its relations with other classes etc.) (p. 153)

It is on the basis of this enquiry into 'abstract structures and their functions' (p. 153), into the 'formal frameworks' of individual praxis (p.

* Fr. 'ensembles'

154), 'outside of concrete history' (p. 154), that the major sections of the *Critique* are rendered comprehensible: 1) an investigation into the constitutive dialectic, 'such as it appears in its abstract translucence through the individual praxis' (p. 154); 2) an investigation into the dominance of the anti-dialectic – that is, of the dialectic of passivity which belongs to the practico-inert where this is the field of serial alienation and the result of 'the equivalence of the alienated praxis with worked-upon inertia' (p. 154); 3) an inquiry into the constituted dialectic, with particular reference to the group as representing the sudden resurrection of freedom in opposition to the impotent seriality of the practico-inert. (pp. 154-5)

This third enquiry is conducted in the last part of the *Critique* under the title: *From the Group to History.* It concludes by recognising the formal circularity between series and group, and the 'circular reversibility' of dialectical formations. The task of the second volume will be to crown the edifice of dialectical reason with an enquiry carried out upon History in its concreteness – that is, in its actual reversibility – and thus upon its orientation and profound signification. The first volume will have completed the task of preparation for this if it succeeds through its critique in establishing the necessity of the dialectic – that is, in establishing *a priori* the validity of a non-dogmatic, heuristic dialectic. The prolegomena to every future anthropology will have accomplished its task of preparation if it succeeds 'in establishing *a priori* – and not (as Marxists *believe* they have done) *a posteriori* – the heuristic value of the dialectical method when it is applied to the sciences of man, and in establishing the necessity of reinserting whatever fact it may be that is under consideration, provided it be *human*, in the ongoing totalization and of understanding it from that starting point.' (p. 153)

7. Dialectic, Totality, Totalization

Despite Sartre's deep-rooted and persistent antipathy to Lukács, the influence that *History and Class Consciousness* [7] has exercised on his present thinking is quite clear. Moreover, an analogous influence can be easily traced in Merleau-Ponty, who has devoted one of his most penetrating texts in *The Adventures of the Dialectic* to the impact of Lukács' 'western Marxism.' The influence of Lukács on French existentialism is a beautiful example of what Sartre calls in the *Critique* the 'counterfinality' which history imprints upon the works of man. After accepting the official condemnation (*Pravda*, July 1924) of the theses of *History and Class Consciousness*, Lukács transformed himself into a watchdog of Soviet orthodoxy and took on himself the task of extending its influence to French existentialism by means of his book, *Existentialisme ou marxisme?* (1947); but its effect was wholly negative, and it is easy enough to understand why if one remembers that it was an undilutedly Stalinist tract and contained statements such as 'the attitude to the USSR is becoming the touchstone in all political and ideological problems' [8]; its discourse was all the more repugnant to intellectuals whom the climate of the Resistance had rendered so little inclined to intellectual servility. It was rather the heretical Lukács of *History and Class Consciousness* who was to exercise a significant pro-Marxist influence on French existentialists from Merleau-Ponty to Sartre.

This is easy to understand if we remember that Lukács book, which was published in 1923, had performed the same function for official Soviet Marxism that the French existentialists had set themselves to effect for official French Marxism. In both instances it was a case of opposing a Marxism that had been transformed into a dogmatic materialism with a Marxism of 'Marx in the sense of Marx'; a Marxism which would not follow the revisionist line which had been appropriated by all those who had agreed on the validity of official Marxism's positivist interpretation of Marx. Moreover, in both cases the operation took the form of a return to the Young Marx and of a formulation of authentic Marxism in terms of discussion of the Hegelian dialectic. [9]

Yet a discussion on the dialectic must proceed via a re-examination of the concept of 'totality.' Even in this respect Sartre's line of argument is parallel to that used by Lukács, in that it tends towards re-thinking 'totality' more in the light of the category of 'reciprocity' than in that of 'unity.' A totality of this type is not the self-examination of an original unity, but the outcome of establishing meaning. Referring to the Lukács of 1923, Merleau-Ponty writes: 'when the subject recognises himself in history and history in himself, he does not dominate the whole, as the Hegelian philosopher does, but at least he is engaged in a work of totalization.'[10] The *Critique*, appearing five years after *The Adventures*, bases its entire re-examination of the concept of 'whole' on the opposition of 'totalization' and 'totality.' Sartre says:

> What has made the force and richness of Marxism is the fact that it has been the most radical attempt to clarify the historical process in its totality. For the last twenty years, on the contrary, its shadow has obscured history; this is because it has ceased to live *with history* and because it attempts, through a bureaucratic conservatism, to reduce change to identity. (p. 29, PM)

But this attempt is openly idealistic and derives from the confusion between totality and totalization. Totality as ontological *statut* is simply the outcome of a metaphysical mystification of the *imaginary* horizon which regulates the totalization as the mode of being of human reality insofar as this is project: 'The totality is no more than a regulating principle of the totalization.' (p. 138) The fundamental character of totalization is that of being 'ongoing totalization,' heuristic totalization, whose rules 'furnish their own definitions within the framework of the research' (p. 26, PM) Within the idealistic Marxism of current 'Marxists,' 'the totalizing investigation has given way to a Scholasticism of the totality. The heuristic principle — "to search for the whole in its parts" — has become the terrorist practice of "liquidating the particularity".' (p. 28, PM) Whereas Marx considered the proper method to be to 'ascend from the abstract to the concrete,' for many Marxists 'the aim is not to integrate what is different as such, while preserving it for a relative autonomy, but rather to suppress it.' (p. 48, PM)

8. *The Alternative Dialectics*

The critical re-examination of dialectical reason has thus brought Sartre to the position of conceiving the dialectic as the outcome of the totalizing activity of the individual praxis-project in situation:

> The dialectical movement is not a powerful, unitary force which reveals itself as a divine impulse at the back of History: it is first of all a *result*; it is not the dialectic which forces historical men to live their history through terrible contradictions, but men, such as they are, under the domain of scarcity and necessity, who confront each other in circumstances which History or economy can enumerate but which only dialectical rationality can render intelligible [. . .] The dialectic, if it exists, can only be the totalization of the concrete totalizations brought about by a multiplicity of totalizing singularities (p. 132); and again: if we do not want the dialectic to become a divine law again, a metaphysical fatality, it must come from *individuals* and not from some collection or other of super-individuals. (p. 131)

But how, given that one proceeds from this 'dialectical nominalism' (p. 132), will it be possible to arrive at this discovery of the 'profound signification of history' as the second volume of the *Critique* proposes to do? It would seem very difficult to do more than clarify the circuits of the dialectic in their reversibility, which is the proposed task of the first volume. Sartre is well aware of these difficulties. On the other hand, as he sees it, either one renounces dialectical reason in favour of the analytical reason of bourgeois atomism, or else one must choose between 1) Engel's dogmatic conception of the dialectic, according to which it stands behind all human activity, and necessarily determines it; or, 2) the hyper-empiricist dialectic of Gurvitch, according to which one must look for the dialectic in experience and grant it an existence only within the limits in which one finds it there; or, 3) Stalin's atomistic dialectic, according to which the dialectic is the product of averaging results or, 4) dialectical humanism, according to which the dialectic finds its basis *a priori* in the structure of existence itself.

The last solution, the only possible one, implies a 'contradiction' which must in its turn be lived dialectically: 'man submits to the dialectic to the extent that he makes it, and he makes it to the extent that he submits to it.' (p. 131) But then the dialectic can only reveal itself in an experience which, in order to be critical, must take place 'internally within the *totalization*, and cannot be a contemplative grasping of the totalizing movement.' (p. 140) Every attempt to expel the 'researcher' from the 'researched,' that is to say, from the object of the dialectic, displaces the dialectic from the critical level onto the dogmatic one. This is because it forgets that the identity between dialectical reality and dialectical method, which is required as the very condition of there being dialectical reason, can only reside in the structural unity of existence that consists in the coincidence of researcher and researched.

All the same, there is still the problem of how we make the transition from the dialectic as 'lived totalization' of the individual project to the dialectic as History and meaning of History — to a dialectic, that is to say, which is the effect of the confrontation of projects. One gradually comes to believe that beyond the conscious totalizations of projects, or in spite of them, a general and more profound totalization is being traced in the *Critique* — one that is unconscious and free from the bonds of individual projects, and to which is entrusted the 'meaning' of history — thus 'alienation can modify the *results* of an action but not its profound reality' (p. 91, PM); or else: 'one of the most striking characteristics of our time is the fact that history is made without self-awareness.' (p. 29, PM) Who is the subject of this History? What are the 'devices' by means of which it succeeds in conferring 'meaning'? What is this necessity which is able to impose itself from without upon the dialectical totalizations of individual projects?[11]

[IV]

Necessity

1. *Two Concepts of Necessity*

The two characteristics typical of every existentialist philosophy are: a) the appeal to human finiteness; b) the interpretation of the mode of existence of this finiteness as 'possibility.' The category of the possible thus becomes the basic instrument of all existentialist thought. But notwithstanding this, or even because of it, the category of the necessary has always played the role of *eminence grise* at the heart of every existentialist theory, even to the point of qualifying as the most useful reference point for discriminating between the various forms of existentialism.

When one speaks of possibility in an existentialist context the reference is clearly not to logical possibility, but rather to that of the real: the 'reality' of existence is possibility, the being of man is possibility-of-being. Possibility-of-being means here, 'to be able to be in one or another mode.' There is an alternative set of states or projects in which the being itself of the projector 'is at stake'; this is equivalent to a pure and simple denial of the opposite assertion that the reality of existence (as the mode of existence of man) is necessity — meaning by necessity the impossibility-of-being-other-than-it-is on the part of any given reality.

But in this case, the definition of existence in terms of possibility is equivalent to the definition of existence in terms of auto-projection — that is to say, in terms of a moulding of the self within the natural and social context. This is enough to exclude from the scope of the existential problematic all consideration of attributions of necessity to existence which take the mode of being of existence to be simply presence ('reality' as in-sistence rather than ex-sistence) — as is the case, for example, when it is asked if existence is necessary in itself or else in something other than itself, or, as here, where it is asked whether existence is necessarily possibility (are we, or are we not 'condemned' to freedom?).

But the problem of the relations between existential possibility and necessity does become a very real one for existentialist theory when 'necessity' takes on the meaning of *limit and condition of possibilities* of the existential project. Let us take, for example, the following thesis: For existence as possibility-of-being, there is only one possibility which is precisely that . . . In this case the limit imposed by necessity is extended to the point of removing every alternative: inverted possibility becomes necessity — a mystifying state of affairs which is by no means uncommon in existential philosophy. When Jaspers asserts that 'essential to me as I appear to myself is only that *Somewhere I am unobjectifiably one* with existence as my historic determinacy,' [1] he merely denies the possibility-of-being of existence by identifying situation with a presence which cannot be objectified. In the same way, Sartre, when he states in *Being and Nothingness* that 'freedom is total and infinite [. . .] The only limits which freedom bumps up against at each moment are those which it imposes on itself,' [2] merely reduces freedom to the necessary and non-transcendable *fact* of freedom.

If the 'necessary' has to function as a limit and internal condition on the possible, it will have to establish the possible in its being possible, and not invert it in necessity. Since the possibility-of-being of the possible consists in its granting a place to a field of alternatives offered as choices, it will be inverted into necessity whenever necessity operates in this field in such a way as to render choice impossible. There are three cases in which this can occur: when no, when all, or when only one possibility is offered. In all these cases the field presents itself as the field of the impossibility of choice. But this impossibility is nothing other than the analogue of the opposite necessity.

To the extent that a philosophy of existence would be a philosophy of commitment, that is, a philosophy of self-projection within relations that are objectively transformable, it must revolutionize the category of necessity so as to change its status from that of being an alternative which dissolves in the face of the possible, into being a determination *within* the possible itself insofar as it is a *limiting condition* of the alternatives which constitute this. In the last analysis, Kant's Copernican revolution was a categorical revolution of this kind. The necessity which provides the base of the connexions of the world of science falls within the transcendental possibility of the 'I think,'• which *muss begleiten können,* and not, be it noted, *kannt begleiten müssen.* (*Critique of Pure Reason* section 16). Otherwise, there can be no possible alternatives for a thinking being: man would necessarily always be scientific man, and the dialectic would itself be impossible.

2. *Absolute Necessity and Conditioning Necessity*

Only this kind of rigorous treatment will allow us to delineate the trajectory through which the category of possibility passes from its starting point in *Being and Nothingness* to the point reached in the *Critique.*

One could say in a very general way, that it is a trajectory which departs from a concept of the possible as infinite totality and arrives at the possible as conditioned and limited field. The category of necessity is also transformed along the same lines. In *Being and nothingness* it expresses the metaphysical 'condemnation' of man to absolute freedom; in the *Critique* the set of conditionings which render the project's freedom finite. In *Being and Nothingness* 'the *very impossibility* of continuing in certain directions must be freely constituted,' ' in the *Critique* 'the project must *of necessity* cut across the field of instrumental possibilities' (author's emphasis, p. 111, PM), and this necessity 'transforms it more or less profoundly' because 'the particular quality of the instruments . . . conditions the objectification.' (p. 111, PM) In the first case, necessity expresses the unconditioned nature of a freedom which absorbs *a priori* every condition and every limit, and thus every possible objectification. In the second case, it expresses the limits and conditions of an objectifying freedom which cannot modify the object without its being, in its turn, modified by it. But in this case, the 'past' is not simply the psychic content of memories in respect of which 'I decide absolutely,' ⁴ but is the form that the 'necessary' takes in its nature as internal limit of my very capacities to make a project of objective modification within it.

In *Being and Nothingness* the object entered as the expedient for the necessity of freedom at the heart of a mythical, impersonal, a-historical for-itself to which it was metaphysically attributed. In the *Critique* the object is the bread you have not got; the help that does not arrive in time; it is that in virtue of which man can be reduced to a thing (p. 749); it is all that in the absence or scarcity of which the possibility of existence is itself 'at stake.' (p. 206) Here man is no longer the project of being God but, much more modestly, that of being man — a project which is crossed and threatened from beginning to end by infinite 'necessities.'

This is the perspective within which we must consider the definition of existentialism as 'idealistic protest against idealism' (p. 14, PM); so too its anticipated disappearance in favour of a Marxism which effectively establishes the principle according to which 'there does not exist, as one would like to imagine now and then, simply for convenience, any effect produced automatically by the economic situation. On the contrary, it is men themselves who make their history, but within a given environment which conditions them and on the basis of real, prior conditions.' (Engel's *Letter to Borgius,* 25 Jan. 1894, cit. p. 71, PM)

Correlative with the extent to which Sartre's philosophy has descended from the celestial sphere of idealistic abstraction, necessity has come to lose its abstract and mystificatory character and assumed the role of basic category with which to conceptualise the harshness of the conditions which man, in his task of being man, confronts in things, in Others, and in consequence, in this task itself. It is not surprising, then, to find the

coherence in meaning of the two volumes of the *Critique* summed up in the
following words:

> And when we discover [. . .] beneath the translucence of the free
> individual praxis the bedrock of necessity, we shall hope we have
> discovered the right path. So we can give an idea of what the two
> volumes overall will seek to demonstrate: that *necessity* as the apodeictic
> structure of dialectical experience resides neither in the free
> development of interiority nor in the inert dispersion of exteriority; it
> imposes itself, in the name of an inevitable and irreducible moment, in
> the interiorisation of the exterior, and the exteriorisation of the interior.
> (p. 157)

3. *Dialectical Necessity and Analytical Necessity*

The most serious problem facing a *critique of dialectical reason* is that of
establishing, on the critical bases demanded by the task, the nature of the
relationship between necessity and the dialectic. In fact the term 'dialectic,'
however this is understood, seems inseparable from the idea of a necessary
articulation, whether this is taken as being an articulation of (objective or
verbal) forms, or one of (ideal or historical) contents. This is all the more
so in the case where, as here, the dialectic is understood in the sense of
being the mode of existence of historical reality.

We might pose the question in the form used by Marx in the *Economic
and Philosophical Manuscripts of 1844* where, echoing Hegel, he asks who
is the 'bearer' of the dialectic:

> This process must have a bearer, a subject. But the subject (in Hegel)
> emerges first as a result. This result – the subject knowing itself as
> absolute self-consciousness – is therefore *God, absolute spirit, the
> self-knowing* and *self-manifesting idea.* Real man and real nature become
> mere predicates, symbols of this esoteric, unreal man and of this unreal
> nature. Subject and predicate are therefore related to each other in
> absolute reversal, a *mystical subject-object* or a *subjectivity reaching beyond*
> the *object.*

Sartre makes the very same point against Hegel:

> It is placed from the start, he believes, at the beginning of the end of
> History, which is to say, at that instant of Truth which is death. It is a
> time of judgement because nothing will come afterwards to call in
> question philosophy and its judgement. (p. 120)

Having reduced being to the past, Knowledge becomes the bearer of a dialectic whose necessity is unconditioned. But as far as Sartre is concerned, Marx's 'originality' lies in his having established irrefutably, in opposition to Hegel, that History is *an ongoing process,* that *being remains irreducible to Knowledge.* and that, all the same, the dialectical movement must be preserved *in* being and *in* Knowledge. (p. 121) But this is a position that demands that we re-think the dialectic, and all the more so when we have a positivist empiricism contesting the possibility of its very existence. But this re-thinking did not take place, and the 'Marxists,' in order to come to terms with the positivist attack, extended the dialectical schema *advanced by Hegel* to include the whole of nature, thereby accepting the implicit reduction of being to Knowledge and the interpretation of necessity as external and absolute. Hence the birth of 'idealistic materialism' or 'dialectical materialism,' to which corresponds a dialectical necessity introduced 'from outside' and imposed 'dogmatically' upon man reduced – to use Marx's expression – to a 'simple predicate,' to a 'symbol' of that unreal man fantastically erected in the face of necessary reality which is the bearer of the dialectic, and which is 'Subjectivity reaching beyond the object.'

Sartre maintains, all the same, that the dialectic, while having real man as its bearer, must emerge equipped with necessity. But clearly it is no longer a case of an external necessity in respect of which real man is simply predicated as an object encroached upon and caught up in the necessity of a process which reabsorbs him as simple object. This kind of necessity is merely a 'metaphysical hypothesis,' corresponding to the transference of analytical necessity to the synthetic processes of the 'socio-historical universe.' To make this transfer, Sartre insists, 'is to replace, in the name of a monism, the practical rationality of man engaged in the process of making History, by the blind necessity of antiquity.' (p. 129)

Dialectical necessity 'must not be confused with constraint,' nor even with that process which progressively reduces possibilities to a single one. (p. 282) In consequence, dialectical necessity cannot be employed as a means of prediction or prophecy:

> If, for example, one believes that the proletariat is the future destruction of the bourgeoisie simply by reason of the fact that variable capital is constantly decreasing and fixed capital constantly increasing – hence the productivity of labour is rising while the purchasing power of the working-class on a world scale diminishes, and this is producing crisis upon crisis leading to economic catastrophe for the bourgeoisie – then one ends up by reducing man to a purely anti-dialectical moment of the practico-inert. (p. 731)

The necessity of the so-called 'pitiless play of economic laws' is nothing other than the effect of the specific basis for their relations with each other which men themselves have resolved upon: 'It is not things which are pitiless, but men.' (p. 699) In consequence:

> When a Marxist employs the concept of 'necessity' in order to qualify the relationship between two events internal to the same process, we remain hesitant, even if the attempted synthesis has been perfectly convincing. And this does not mean — on the contrary, in fact — that we deny the necessity of human affairs; it means, simply, that dialectical necessity is, by definition, *something other* than the necessity of analytical Reason. (pp. 134-5)

4. *Necessity as Formal-existential Structure*

The *critical* foundation of dialectical reason which Sartre proposes is inevitably accompanied by a critical revolution in the meaning of 'necessity.' In contrast to the 'hyper-empiricist dialectic' of a Gurvitch — according to which dialectical connexions are to be sought only within the field of specific enquiries, and are recognised as valid only on the basis of these — Sartre maintains that one can speak of a dialectic only if it is possible to proceed to its *a priori* foundation or to establish the necessity of this. But any *a priori* foundation which insists on being *critical* can only provide the foundation for a necessity on 'formal' bases: this means it must exclude as rigorously as possible the absorption of content in a form which typifies the idealist mode of establishing dialectical necessity. From this viewpoint, Sartre considers the term 'idealism' to be equally applicable to the materialism of current 'Marxists' as it is to Hegel's spiritualism.

In opposition to every form of idealism, Sartre would follow Kierkegaard, and Marx too, in refusing to allow the reduction of being to knowledge, of content to form. So that if one wants to provide a critical foundation for the 'necessity' of dialectical reason, that 'necessity' will have itself to be the outcome of a form which recognizes, as did the Kantian one, the autonomy of content, and therefore its capacity for functioning as an element of attestation and of control. But in this case necessity cannot be imposed 'from outside' on the a-critical totality of a unity undifferentiated in respect of its form and content. This is what occurs in Hegel, and even more obviously in Engel's account of the laws of the dialectic, where these in reality are naturalistic inductions corresponding to an empiricism disguised as determinism. The twofold disadvantage of such an account is that it 'kills the dialectic twice over in order to be sure of its death: the first time with the pretence of discovering it in Nature, the second time in suppressing it in society.' (p. 670)

If dialectical necessity is to have a critical foundation it must be a necessity 'from within,' a formal necessity whose *internal* relationship to content expresses the reciprocal conditioning of form and content, and not the unconditioned necessity of an absolute, external principle. Now Sartre holds that the 'site' where the kind of connexion is established between form and content which allows its necessity to express the tissue of conditionings is the structure of existence. This structure is the form of that particular mode of being which is existence. Insofar as it is form, existence is project, the forward impulse of being which lives in the world of need and scarcity, and whose praxis is the negation of that negation — which is given in scarcity — of its own vital presence. This structure is necessary precisely to the extent, but only to the extent, that it is structure, i.e., constitutive form.

The problem now is to see how this formal necessity can be concerned with content while still holding firm to the critico-existential principle of the irreducibility of being to knowledge, of content to form. The Sartrean solution is based on the recognition that the formal structure is at one and the same time the mode of being of human existence — a mode of being, which by virtue of the historical nature provided for it by its structure of praxis project, constitutes the sole possible content of all dialectical knowledge. Dialectical necessity is the necessity which connects form and content from within, in a relation which does not express the reduction of content to unconditioned necessity of form, but is itself, rather, the recognition of the mutual determination between the two. It is thus the recognition of the necessity which attaches to the structure of existence as mode of being of that finite entity which is man.

It is quite clear that Sartre, by way of Heidegger, here joins up again with Dilthey, and with the latter's attempt to establish a *critique of historical reason* on the basis of man's mode of being as finite entity. Dilthey writes:

> The single man, in his individual existence resting upon itself, is a historical being: a being determined by his position in time, by his place in space, by his situation in regard to the cooperative working of cultural systems and communities. [6]

What is missing in Dilthey is the recognition of the pre-eminent status of the economic and of the dialectical nature of historical reason — two factors which for Sartre are indissolubly linked in that he regards the economic determination as the foundation of the very rationality of history. (pp, 126-30, PM)

5. *Dialectic, Religion, Internal-external*

In the light of the above section, Sartre's summary, already quoted, of the purpose of the two volumes of the *Critique* appears more comprehensible: '... *Necessity* as the apodeictic structure of dialectical experience resides neither in the free development of interiority nor in the inert dispersion of exteriority; it imposes itself, in the name of an inevitable and irreducible moment, in the interiorisation of the exterior, and the exteriorisation of the interior.' (p. 157) Dialectical necessity, then, 1) is not the mode of being of a single unconditioned principle whether this is given Hegel's interpretation (as 'free development of interiority') or that of the 'Marxists' (as 'inert dispersion of exteriority'); 2) instead, it is 'structure', and to be precise, 'apodeictic structure of the dialectical experience'; 3) it is the indissoluble connexion between external and internal.

With reference to the first point it is important to note the impossibility for Sartre of interpreting the inversion of the Hegelian dialectic accomplished by Marx in the sense of a transference of dialecticity from 'interiority' to 'exteriority'; this, in fact, is the inversion that the so-called 'Marxists' have wreaked in spite of the authentic spirit of Marx's thought, in which the inversion had the significance of transferring the dialecticity of absolute interiority to man as social being. In this light, Sartre looks upon existentialism as restoring the authentic humanism of Marxism by means of a re-thinking of the dialectic, which the Marxists themselves have failed to carry out, and for lack of which they have ended up with the absurdity of 'dialectical materialism.'

As the second point makes clear, dialecticity is a property of the structure of existence; this structure reveals itself apodeictically in the *experience* of itself as existential self-consciousness. Sartre is convinced that dialecticity is a structural element, but he rejects the idea that this structure is contained in some mythical material; to speak of structure is to speak of relations, and the 'economic,' instead of being the foundation of social relations, constitutes the specific basis they acquire in the field of scarcity and as a result of need.

Thus it follows from the third point, that the extent to which necessity can include experiment is contained in the relational structure of existence and, to be precise, in the relationship which is established within it between 'internal' and 'external.' In this connexion it is of vital importance not to forget that: a) it is one thing to say that the structure of existence is relational; b) it is another to say that this relationality is made extrinsic in the form of a relationship between 'internal' and 'external'; c) it is something else again to say that the relationship between internal and external is made extrinsic in the form of an 'interiorisation of the external' and an 'exteriorisation of the internal.' Contrary to what Sartre maintains, the first point by no means implies the second, and still less the third.

It is surprising that Sartre is prepared to entrust the fate of up-dating a philosophy which to his mind is as important as it is 'worm-eaten' to such antiquated categories as those of the 'internal'/'external' antithesis. It is all the more surprising when the design is to renew the vigour of a philosophy such as Marxism, whose true inspiration is so far removed from any such antithesis. In fact this was one of the points at issue in the whole attack on idealist philosophy which went to constitute Marxism.

It seems, in fact, that what happens as a result is that all the valuable advances made in the *Critique* on the positions of *Being and Nothingness* are gravely compromised. If existence is conceived as the mode of being of a praxis-project which, in Heidegger's phrase, is 'always-already' in the world, what sense is there in speaking of the interiorisation of the external? If sociality is a constitutive character of human reality, what meaning is left in placing the Other in exteriority? And does not the demand for interiorisation of the external prejudice at the level of 'doing' the proclaimed relationality of the existential structure?

6. *Material, Practico-inert, Necessity*

In conceiving the dialectic as bound to the structure of existence, Sartre has subjected the category of necessity to a critical metamorphosis in which it has changed from an unconditioned, extrinsic unity into an intrinsic relation expressing the conditions which constitute the existential and co-existential structure:

> The problem of necessity — which immediately presents itself as a structure of our critical experience — necessarily refers us to the fundamental problem of anthropology, that is, to the problem of the relations between practical organisms and inorganic matter. (p. 158)

The problem of necessity is a problem of internal 'relations' and not one of a methaphysical destiny imposed from beyond history and human reality. The materiality from which necessity takes its body is what Sartre understands as 'fact,' and fact is the limiting condition of the project: 'The necessity of fact cannot be grasped except through (*à travers*) human constructions.' (p. 102)

For Sartre, these 'human constructions' have two fundamental characteristics: 1) they take place in the form of a reciprocal confrontation between projects; 2) they occur in the field of scarcity of 'material.' The one characteristic implies the other to the extent that the confrontation of projects is the effect of scarcity, and to the extent that scarcity is the effect of the confrontation of projects. Nevertheless, Sartre tends to burden scarcity with all the negative elements of the reciprocity. What is involved is not necessarily a mortal struggle, as in Hegel, but it becomes one in the field of scarcity. One might note, all the same, that all that ultimately separates this position from that of Hegel, is the possibility of eliminating scarcity from relations between 'consciousnesses.'

The 'material' whose relationship with the multiplicity of projects is qualified by scarcity is not the mythical, metaphysical entity of those who believe in a dialectics of nature, but is all that which is susceptible to use and transformation through labour:

> The meaning of human labour is that man reduces himself to inorganic materiality in order to act materially on matter and change his material life. It is by means of transubstantiation that the project inscribed by our body in the thing takes on the substantial characteristics of that thing without altogether losing its original qualities. (p. 246)

Here again it is impossible not to point to the old-fashioned nature of the conceptual schema used by Sartre. How can the worker be reduced to inorganic materiality? And what, in this event, would be his initial state? What does it mean to speak of 'transubstantiation' in this context?

The truth is that what we are witnessing here is Sartre's glissade into an interpretation of structural rationality as a dualistic mind-body opposition. This carries with it the imputation of all possible evil to corporeality, whether organic or inorganic. It is not by chance that the passage quoted above is to be found in a context where Sartre recovers the notion of *Être*:

> In losing their human properties, men's projects imprint themselves in Being, their translucence changes to opacity, their tenuousness to density, their volatile lightness to permanence; they become Being in losing their character of lived event. (pp. 245-6)

The Sartrean concept of material defines the field of the 'practico-inert' as the 'realm of the equivalence between alienated praxis and worked-upon inertia.' (p. 154) It is not the bearer of the dialectic, the active motor of history, but simply its 'passive motor' − 'passive' in the double sense of being both non-active and negative. The relational structure of the existential project tends in this way to separate into two branches: on the one hand, there is spirit as interior freedom; on the other, there is material as objective necessity which is connected to spirit by the simple constraint of fact.

Necessity thus loses the critical significance it has in being the internal limiting condition of a project which is project of a finite being who makes history under given conditions and takes on the romantic character of an external object, of a limitation not in the relational sense but in the sense of one which imposes itself as metaphysical negation. If existence is dialectical project and finality, the practico-inert is the field of the anti-dialectic, that is, of the dialectic of inert passivity. This is the counterfinality which dissolves society in seriality and subjects human reciprocity to the dominion of inhumanity, savagery and sadism. Sartre says:

Taken at this level, History presents a terrible and desperate meaning; it appears that, in effect, men are united by this inert and demonic negation which takes their substance (that is, their labour) from them in order to turn it back against everyone in the form of *inert activity* and as totalization by extermination. (p. 200)

It is true that for Sartre there still remains the possibility that at a certain stage in history 'groups' will establish themselves with the deliberate intent of dissolving the reign of the anti-dialectic and of breaking-up the seriality produced by it within human reciprocity; but what is not clear is how these groups can escape the 'instantaneity' of their 'apocalyptic' creation, without falling into a relationship of alienation to the practico-inert, and thus into seriality and dispersion.

7. *Dialectic and Counter-dialectic*

The materiality of the field of the practico-inert, so far from being the foundation of the dialectic, as the idealistic-materialist version of Marxism would have us believe, is the realm of the counter-dialectic:

The field of the practico-inert is not a new moment of a universal dialectic but the pure and simple negation *of dialectics* by means of exteriority and plurality. Quite simply, the negation works not by destruction or dissolution but by deviation and reversal. So that this second moment *of experience* (and not of the dialectic) appears in itself as the anti-dialectic, or, if you like, as the inorganic image, in man and outside of him, of the dialectic as free human activity. (p. 376) [7]

The authentic foundation of the dialectic is the praxis-project; but this praxis is bound to imprint itself upon the inertia of material, thus giving rise to the field of the practico-inert, which, in escaping the finality of the constituting dialectic, becomes available for insertion into heterogeneous dialectical totalizations whose orientation is counter-final relative to the finality of the constitutive process. The effect of this is to render material external to the project and opposed to it as necessity to freedom. The field of the practico-inert is a 'site of violence, of shadows, of witchcraft' (p. 358); it is the 'site' of the appearance 'of necessity at the heart of the free individual praxis'; 'this means that the practico-inert field constitutes itself, within every objective praxis, as the negation of it in favour of the passive activity which is the common structure of collectives and of worked-upon material.' (pp. 358-9)

In confronting the problem of material being the field of the practico-inert, Sartre's concern is with two opposing exigencies; in the first place that of denying to material the dignity of being a bearer of the dialectic, in order to confer this exclusively on human praxes (individual or group); in the second place that of giving a reason for the inversion which individual praxis undergoes in the field of the practico-inert and through which it returns to man as inhuman counter-finality, transforming him from free producer of himself into product of his product. Paradoxically, material gathers within itself passivity and activity, and by a process of 'magic' and 'sorcery' inverts the former in the latter and the latter in the former. The ambiguity of this state of affairs is reflected in the conjuncture of terms with which Sartre describes material: anti-dialectic, counter-dialectic, dialectic of passivity, praxis-made-passive, counter-finality. (p. 154, and note 2)

How is it possible that inert and passive material can act in such a way that man becomes its product? How can inertia be productive, passivity become active? Sartre's reply relies on two related theses: 1) material exists in a definite relationship with human reality which is that of scarcity with respect to needs; 2) the constituting dialectic belongs to a multiplicity of individuals, each one of whom activates it in accordance with *singular* projects of totalization. When the focus of an individual project is a praxis of labour, the object produced in conformity with the project's finality is liable to be engulfed in the project of other individuals. The effect of this is that it is drawn back from the finality of its producer and inserted in opposing totalizations which confer on it its character of counter-finality relative to the finality of its production. But since it is the same constitutive human freedom which is objectified both in labour and in the product of labour, when the project is 'stolen' by the other and inserted by him in a project of counter-finality, the worked-upon material returns to its producer as a negation of his being, as a transformation of this being into 'product of his product.' In this way, then, reciprocity assumes the mode of being of things, and society becomes the basis of a seriality of things — that is to say, a pure and simple negation of man's being. Sartre writes:

> Now this wholly particular situation evidently depends on the multiplicity of individuals co-existing in the field of scarcity. In other words, it is only the Other's free praxis on the basis of material circumstances which is able, by means of worked-upon material, to limit the freedom and effectiveness of my praxis. (p. 360)

And also:

> When particular circumstances allow a praxis to steal the meaning of the *other*, that means only that the object wherein it is objectified takes on a different meaning and a counter-finality (for its producer) in the practical field of the other as a result of the reorganisation of the field in question. (p. 361)

The field of the practico-inert is the place where the inertia of material, gathering into itself the individual dialectical praxis, has the effect of allowing the product of labour to be used by others in virtue of the counter-finality which gives to reciprocity its character of seriality; alienation of the stolen praxis and worked-upon inertia thus take on a common mode of being: thing-ness, reification, loss of the humanity of man and of his product. The 'group in combat' will form in reaction to this process of total alienation of freedom. It represents the sudden resurrection of freedom and of the dialectic as a unitary project, along lines provided by two well-defined objectives, each of which implies the other: passage from the practico-inert to the practico-communal, and dissolution of seriality. (pp. 359, 431)

8. *Absolute Freedom, Material, Necessity*

It is quite clear from all this that Sartre has not succeeded in carrying to its conclusion that critical re-dimensioning of necessity which he saw as being the most important achievement of a *critique of dialectical reason.* It is true that necessity is no longer the external seal of a dialectic whose concern is with man as simple predicate, but it is nonetheless true that in transferring necessity to the position of internal foundation of human and inter-human dialectic he has taken a further step away from his initial aim of making necessity the *conditioning* element of the entire relational structure of existence insofar as this is the mode of being of a finite entity.

From being the limiting and conditioning character of the entire dialectical structure of existence, necessity comes to be attributed, as its particular mode of being, to one of the elements whose relational connexion qualifies the nature of this structure — namely to inorganic material, to nature, to 'things.' In this way the structure breaks up into opposing branches: on the one hand *physis* as the realm of necessity; on the other praxis as *anti-physis,* the realm of freedom. Thus we have lost what was the fundamental gain made by transferring necessity from external to internal: its connexion with the structure as a *whole* as its limiting and founding condition. What is lost, therefore is the awareness of the fact that, from a structuralist point of view, it is impossible to make necessity the exclusive attribute of the relationship to the world, and freedom the exclusive attribute of the relationship of the subject towards himself. If we do so, we confer a privileged ontological status on the relationship of interiority while branding objectivity with the seal of absolute negativity. The relationship to the world, and the necessity which it brings with it, is certainly a limiting condition on freedom, but it is at the same time the basic condition of its finite possibility. Freedom has to be conceived as aspiration towards infinite freedom if the necessity attaching to the relationship to the world is to be seen as a negation of freedom: freedom is *anti-physis* only if *physis* is not a structural element of existence but the impediment of fact to its unconditioned realisation.

The other aspect of attributing necessity only to the objective dimension of the structure is that it ultimately endows subjectivity with the character of *freedom without necessity.* This is the property of the absolute freedom theorised in *Being and Nothingness,* which is a freedom which, as we have seen, for all its being in contradiction to necessity as conditioning, is by no means opposed to that necessity which is absence of conditioning. Pure and absolute freedom is simply the necessity of this absence: it expresses the impossibility of choice being conditioned.

By splitting human reality into *physis* and *anti-physis* and dividing its structure between two diverse and contrary realities or modes of being, all the categorial baggage of *Being and Nothingness* comes back in through the window: the opposition of 'internal' to 'external', of 'interiority' to 'exteriority,' of 'subjectification' to 'objectification.' But above all what is re-introduced is the tacit presupposition of every anti-relational and substantialist dualism from Descartes to the present day – which is that interiority has an *ontologically* privileged status. But this is the most un-Marxist assumption imaginable. In fact, its rejection – in the form of a rejection of its basic corollary, the identification of alienation with objectification – is what directs the whole of Marx's polemic against Hegel.

We must, therefore, in passing judgement on Sartre's undertaking, be careful to distinguish between its intentions and its actual achievements. The former have to do with Sartre's project of conducting a critique of dialectical reason in order to defend it against dogmatic interpretations whether idealistic or crypto-idealistic ('Marxistic'). What a critical re-thinking of the dialectic had to do was endow the inversion of the Hegelian dialectic anticipated by Marx with *critical significance.* This would provide an alternative to the false inversion of the dialectic of spirit in the dialectic of nature. In order to be authentically Marxist the inversion had to attribute the dialectic to human reality conceived existentially as self-projecting structure in relation to the world and to society. But Sartre has ultimately fallen back upon the Hegelian schema because he makes use of the relational structure of human reality which is offered by primitive existentialism – which interprets the relation to the world as necessary only to the extent that it is negative and merely factual. He has thus failed to realise that what constitutes the most important advance common to both Marxism and existentialism is the recognition of the *structural and thus non-negative nature* of the relationship to the world and to Others. A confirmation of this failure is to be found in an idea which to some extent determines the course of the entire *Critique:* the idea that the ideal society is one in which projects take place in a unitary and absolute freedom that follows on the elimination of the factual and negative relationship to the world. But to take up this kind of position is to deny that Hegelianism has any *de facto* justification, while asserting its justification *de jure*.

9. *Complete Freedom and Absolute Necessity*

Let us re-examine the thesis which according to Sartre sums up the content of the two volumes of the *Critique*:

> Necessity, as the apodeictic structure of dialectical experience, resides neither in the free development of interiority nor in the inert dispersion of exteriority; it imposes itself in the name of an inevitable and irreducible moment, in the interiorisation of the exterior, and the exteriorisation of the interior. (p. 157)

Necessity, then, is the mode of being neither of the Idea nor of Material. It is rather the inevitable and irreducible moment of a relation, and to be precise, of that relation which constitutes the structure of existence. Sartre qualifies this structure, however, as the relation between 'internal' and 'external' which consists in the 'interiorisation of the external' and the 'exteriorisation of the internal.'

In the exteriorisation of the internal we have what Sartre claims is 'the first experience of necessity.' The forward dialectical impulse of individual action, when conceived in itself and for itself, outside of any socio-environmental conditioning, is total freedom, is 'full transparency *without necessity*.' (p. 280) But since the totalizing dialectic of any particular project occurs a) in the field of the practico-inert, on whose inertia it imprints itself as a 'seal'; b) contemporaneously with others' projects, what happens is that, through the combined action of a) and b), the object in which the particular act acquired body ends up by being something other than what was projected. And this is not because of any constraint on it or through any failure to effect the proposed end, since 'the first practical experience of necessity occurs in the unconstrained activity of the individual, and to the extent to which the final outcome, although conforming to what was anticipated, reveals itself at the same time as radically other.' (p. 282) The cause of this 'theft of the end' is not some inadequacy in the means to carry through any undertaking in its capacity as 'isolated activity,' nor a failure of some kind to implement it. It is due rather to the fact that labour, impressing itself upon inert materiality as a seal, is susceptible to a process of absorption in other projects and counter-projects which invert it at the expense of its agent. It forces the agent to submit to this in the form of interiorisation of exteriority – his interior freedom is dissolved in seriality as interiorised exteriority. From this derives the 'bewitching field of counter-finality,' the nature of which Sartre illustrates by means of two historical examples: the counter-finality which resulted from the import of American gold into Spain in the sixteenth century, and that resulting from the enormous deforestation in China. In both cases disastrous effects were the outcome of a multiplicity of projects in serial opposition.

In the last analysis, necessity is 'freedom's destiny in exteriority,' where what is meant by exteriority is not 'the external connexions of inorganic material,' since 'there is *exteriority* to the extent to which the produced use-value, insofar as it is materiality, becomes a part of other fields of interiority.' (pp. 283-4) Nowhere is the point made more clearly than here that the re-thinking of necessity as internal to the dialectic ends up in an interpretation of this internal quality as a partial and relative quality: partial because necessity attaches only to the exteriority pole of the existential structure; relative because it is extrinsically related to the pole of interiority which is taken to be absolute freedom; thus, necessity *'c'est la négation de la liberté au sein de la liberté plenière, soutenue par la liberté elle-même et proportionée à la plénitude même de cette liberté.'* (p. 285)

10. *The Identity of Freedom and Necessity*

This is not the point at which to discuss the nature of the relationship between objectification and alienation implied by this type of conception of the relations between subjectivity and objectification. Instead, we must first clarify the relationship between freedom and necessity which derives from it.

Necessity is first experienced when total freedom sees the product of its self-objectification in the field of the practico-inert absorbed in the projects of Others. These projects have the effect of restoring its product to it in a form which no longer embodies the finality of its original intention. Constrained to recognise itself in something other than its own intentions, freedom itself becomes other than itself, interiorising exteriority as the negative modality of the original reciprocity. As exteriority produced and submitted to in the same instant, necessity becomes the norm of every relation between things and between men who have been reduced to the same reciprocal exteriority that dominates things. Under the reign of necessity total freedom is destined to exteriority, and things – and men reduced to things – are submerged in a stringent uniformity whose rule is established by the 'simultaneous recognition of the same as Other and of the Other as same.' (p. 282)

But for Sartre the human adventure does not end here for it does not end with the shipwreck of the individual constituting dialectic on the bewitched seas of the anti-dialectical counter-finality of the practico-inert. It does not end here because freedom can find its sudden resurrection in the dialectic constituted by the group-in-fusion. When this happens the field of inertia and of practico-inert seriality finds itself

contained between two radical negations: that which the individual action meets with in itself, in that it still adheres to its product as *its negation*; and that of the union of groups which establishes itself among the collectives themselves as the practical denial of seriality. If, then, one can give the name of dialectic to this material field of the anti-dialectic, it is precisely because of this double negation. In it, each person's action loses itself to the advantage of the monstrous forces which preserve, in the inertia of the inorganic and of exteriority, a power of action and of unification attached to a false interiority. (p. 359)

The group, so far from being born of the necessity of practico-inert material — as a certain decadent form of Marxism believes — is born in opposition to this necessity, in its two exteriorised and interiorised forms. In fact the group-in-fusion, while being 'the project of snatching from worked-upon material its inhuman power of mediation between men' is at the same time 'the project of snatching man from his *statut* of alterity, which makes of him a product of his product.' (pp. 638-9)

What, asks Sartre, are we to make, then, of this necessity of the practico-inert and of this seriality, when freedom suddenly arises at the heart of them. Let us allow that:

This new structure of experience presents itself as a reversal of the practico-inert field, which is to say, that the nerve of *practical unity* is freedom's appearance as the necessity of necessity, or, if you prefer, as its inflexible recurrence. To the extent, in fact, that individuals in a given environment are directly called in question, at the heart of practico-inert necessity, by the impossibility of living their radical unity, (in reappropriating to themselves this impossibility itself as the possibility of dying humanely, that is to say, in reaffirming man through his own death) there is an inflexible negation of this impossibility ('To live a life of labour or to die fighting'); so that the group constitutes itself as the radical impossibility of the impossibility of living which threatens serial multiplicity. (p. 377)

The necessity attaching to the practico-inert creates a situation for man which is characterised by the impossibility of living humanely. In the face of this there are only three ways out: to die an inhuman death, to die a human death in combat, or to survive as a member of the group in combat in order to negate this negation of the self by the practico-inert and by seriality. In this last event, the necessity of the practico-inert and of its interiorisation in necessity is suppressed, and we have a sudden resurrection of freedom.

A new dialectic is then born which finds its expression in the 'inflexible negation' of the impossibility of living a life determined by the necessity of the practico-inert. But this negation — insofar as it is negation of the negation (p. 359) — takes the form of a 'reversal' of the negated necessity; this 'reversal' is 'the necessity of necessity' because *there continues to be necessity*: the difference being that now it is a case of the necessity of freedom, of a necessity such that under it 'freedom and necessity are one.' (p. 377)

This is the decisive point of the whole of the *Critique.* The practico-inert is negation of man. The re-affirmation of man takes the form of a negation of this negation. But the negation of the negation remains a negation, and since the negation of man has the categorial structure of necessity, the negation of this negation will conserve this structure and will take the form of necessity (of freedom) as negation of necessity (of servitude). Perhaps Sartre has not taken note of Feuerbach's observation that in the Hegelian dialectic the negation of a dialectical figure always occurs in the form of the figure negated — for here the negation of necessity still takes place within the form of necessity:

> In the same way that in the field of alteration, experience exposes necessity as the imperative limit which imposes itself from within upon freedom (insofar as this is stolen by exteriority), so too, the reversal of the practical movement and its reappearance as the negation of necessity are constituted as the violent destiny of necessity itself. (p. 428)

Let us put this in political rather than formal language. The necessity of the practico-inert, which submits man to the violence of the series, is overthrown by a group acting in violence against violence, that is to say, in an exercise of violence. *Violence against necessity transforms itself into the necessity of violence.* So that the group knows no other principle of internal cohesion except that of violence directed towards the external and towards its own members. The basis for this is the Hegelian dialectical principle according to which the negation of the negation occurs in the form of the negation. In other words, supercession is always at the same time conservation. Sartre could hardly say so more explicitly:

> This common freedom draws its violence not only from the violent negation which gave rise to it, but also from the realm of *necessity which it has surpassed but still conserved within itself,* and which threatens perpetually to arise again in the form of an insidious petrification, i.e. as the relapse into serial formation. (pp. 428-9, author's emphasis)

The most striking aspect of this conception is that there is no case in which *freedom of the individual* exists as such. In the constituent dialectic the individual is witness to the theft of his freedom in the necessary alteration of his product. In the constituted dialectic, that is, in the formation of the group, and even more in the techniques for its maintenance, the individual must sacrifice his freedom to the freedom of the group. Thus, whether it is a case of necessity being servitude or of its being revolt and combat, there is no place for freedom as an attribute of the individual. In fact 'the necessity of freedom implies the progressive alienation of freedom in necessity.' (p. 638) Freedom from alienation in the practico-inert is possible only in the form of alienation of that freedom in the group. In *Being and Nothingness* Sartre theorises absolute freedom; in the *Critique,* the recognition that this freedom does not exist issues in a negation of freedom as such. In both cases the assumption is that freedom can only be absolute freedom. But the genuine alternative to absolute freedom is not its negation, but rather freedom in the form of a conditioned freedom, freedom as that order of conditionings in which the structure of existence consists.

[v]

State and Society

1. *Dialectical Criticism and the 'Organic' Conception*

Since Sartre has reintroduced the idea that dialectical reason provides the foundation of being and of historical knowledge, it might seem reasonable to suppose that he is also assuming an organic conception of society of the kind found in Hegel's dialectical conception of history. On the contrary, Sartre rejects all metaphysical and organic interpretations of the 'collective,' affirming that 'there are only men and real relations between men.' (p. 76, PM) This is readily understood if we keep in mind the fact that the proposed re-assumption of dialectical reason takes place within the framework of a corresponding 'critical' revision of its dialecticity. This revision leads Sartre to reject both the theological characterisation of the dialectic as 'celestial law which imposes itself on the Universe,' and its Hegelian character as 'metaphysical force which by itself engenders the historical process.' He sees it instead as simply *resulting* from the confrontation of projects.' (pp. 99-100, PM)

If one abstracts from the question of this 'resulting,' that is, from the issue of its verifiability and, above all, from that of its eligibility to be called 'dialectic,' in order to concentrate exclusively on the idea that it is a 'confrontation of projects' which constitutes the 'real relations between men,' it is quite clear that any critical analysis of Sartre's theory of society demands that we place it in the framework of political theory. This means, within the context of that political thought which between the seventeenth and the eighteenth centuries assumed the form of a 'struggle for reason.'

There is justification, therefore, for the introduction of Hobbes and Rousseau into discussions of the *Critique*. G. Lichtheim writes: 'To start from the non-metaphysical end, Sartre's political philosophy is substantially that of Hobbes, though his language is that of Heidegger.' [1]; and G. Lapassade: 'It could be Rousseau [. . .], though by way of Hegel and Marx, who is the real inspiration at the root of Sartre's thought.' [2] Such remarks are extremely persuasive in the sense that Sartre's enquiry takes place within the arena of the historico-theoretical critique of reason.

Every specification which we might attempt, therefore, and thus every reference to this or that thinker who has operated in this context, creates the most intricate problems and calls for extreme caution in dealing with them. We must not forget that the overall aim of the *Critique* in presenting us with a Marxism that has been re-thought in the light of existentialism, is to elaborate a dialectical conception that is critical and freed of the dogma of its Hegelian and pseudo-Marxist forms. But that does not imply a return to the analytical reason of the Enlightenment, which Sartre considers to be an instrument of 'atomisation,' forged by the bourgeois class to the detriment of the proletariat. (p. 742) In the last analysis, the task which Sartre sets himself is that of meeting the exigencies imposed by analytic reason in the course of a critical re-thinking of dialectical reason — or, to put it another way, of employing the critical content of analytic reason in order to re-think dialectical reason along genuine lines. Transferred to the field of politics, the task becomes that of freeing the Marxist conception of society from every organic conception inherited from Hegel. This means putting individuals at the forefront because they are the exclusive protagonists of the synchronic and diachronic fabric of social relations.

From this standpoint every reference to Hobbes or Rousseau must be made with extreme caution, particularly in the case of Rousseau whose theoretical alignment vis-a-vis both Hegel and Marx is so difficult to specify that it encourages the antithetical attempt to see Rousseau as directly anticipating the communism which Marx, in the *Critique of the Gotha Programme,* opposes to socialism as the 'first phase' of the new society.[3]

2. 'Reciprocity' and 'Human Nature'

Perhaps the most useful thread to guide us out of this maze is that provided by the notion of 'reciprocity.' It has been noted how this has come to the foregound historically as an alternative to the concept of 'subordination' which provides the schema for the organic conceptions of the traditional theological approach. It appears, for example, in Hobbes, Locke and Rousseau and can thus serve as a useful reference point for Sartre's thought, where it is placed at the root of his own conception of political society and given two precise functions: a) a structural one; and, b) a normative one.

In its structural aspect, reciprocity is 'original reciprocity,' 'inter-individual structure,' 'fundamental bond' (pp. 181-88), and it is from this standpoint that Sartre develops his polemic both with the 'molecular solipsism' of traditional liberalism and with a certain form of Marxism which denies human relations their original character in favour of seeing them as the product at the historical level of development of the economic. By assuming the atomistic and anti-formalist theses of liberalism, this 'half-baked' Marxism fails to realise that it clears the path for bourgeois individualism. (p. 179)

In its normative aspect, Sartre distinguishes between original reciprocity as 'negative' and as 'positive' reciprocity — that is, between unmediated reciprocity, or reciprocity of conflict, and mediated, or cooperative reciprocity. From this point of view the struggle for socialism is presented as the commitment to transform unmediated reciprocity into mediated reciprocity on the basis of original reciprocity. Unmediated reciprocity is struggle without quarter given. It is an 'inhuman relation' which presupposes, however, the 'human relation' of reciprocity, which it modifies owing to the fact that reciprocity is realised in the field and on the foundation of unmediated scarcity of the means of life. (p. 207) From this point of view, original and structural reciprocity is the normative principle which underpins the rearrangement of the field of scarcity in view of the fact that its capacity for de-humanising human relations of reciprocity has been eliminated. Under the normative aspect 'reciprocity is that which a man expects of another man, when their relationship is a human one' (p. 253); it presides over the struggle which the group initiates 'in order to snatch from worked-upon material its inhuman power of mediation between men, and thence bestow it to each and everyone in the community.' (p. 638)

So one needs to be very circumspect in establishing any comparison between Hobbes and Sartre. The state of *bellum omnium contra omnes* does not for Sartre correspond to the original structure of human reality, but rather to that modality it acquires when the practico-inert is taken as the mediating factor of relations between men. Even when Sartre describes these unmediated relations in terms of a ruthless struggle and as a project of annihilation — to the point where the society he depicts has been compared to a 'concentration camp' [4] — he always qualifies them in terms of their being relations of 'inhumanity,' that is to say, as incompatible with 'human nature.' He says:

When I say that man exists as Other when he bears the features of inhuman man, this must obviously be taken to hold true for all the human occupants of the social field under consideration, for Others as for themselves. In other words, every one of them *is* inhuman man for all the Others, considers all the Others as inhuman men and really treats the Other with inhumanity [...] However, we must understand the true sense of these remarks, that is, we must see them in terms of there being no human *nature*. Until this point, at least, in our prehistory, scarcity, whatever from it has taken, has dominated every praxis. So that we must, at the same time, understand that man's inhumanity does not stem from his nature, which, far from excluding his humanity, can only be grasped in terms of it, *but rather* that as long as scarcity reigns, there will be a structure of inhumanity in *every man and in all,* and this amounts to nothing more than the material negation insofar as it is interiorised. (pp. 206-7)

3. *Sartre, Hobbes and Marx*

In reality, if there is a return to Hobbes, it passes through Marxism and is loaded with the 'revolutionary' power which Marx's thought opposes to the Hobbesian naturalistic descriptivism. Between Hobbes and Sartre there is the Marx of the *Theses on Feuerbach* for whom 'the chief defect of all hitherto existing materialism' lies in its failure to take account of the 'active side' of human reality insofar as this is transformative praxis. The denial of the existence of a human nature, which in *Existentialism is a Humanism* is still determined by the dictates of a theory of absolute freedom, is conceived in the *Critique* in the light of the possibility of commitment to transforming the inhuman into the human. From this point of view the *Critique* is indeed the ethical treatment we were promised at the end of *Being and Nothingness.*

In other words, Sartre recognises that a philosophy of commitment and change cannot conceptualise alienation as the original and natural state of man:

> We have to make the choice: man is either first himself or first Other than himself. If one opts for the second alternative one is quite simply a victim and accomplice of real alienation. But alienation does not exist *unless man is first of all action*; it is freedom which founds servitude; it is the direct bond of interioritiy which originally characterises human relations, which founds the human relation of exteriority. (p. 248)

While for Hobbes there is only a *natural history* of human relations, for Sartre there is a pre-history which precedes a history which is non-natural; there is a dialectic of culture which supersedes the dialectic of nature; there is an *anti-physis* of the 'reign of man over nature' in general. (p. 377) Sartre makes it clear, however, how this obligatory character of human reality cannot be conceived as a 'historical' or 'logical' reality, *pre*-existent or *sub*sistent to a natural state of inhumanity. All the same:

> ... man can be enslaved only if he is free. But for historical man who *knows* himself and *comprehends* himself, this practical freedom is grasped only as the permanent, concrete condition of his servitude, that is across that servitude and by means of it as that which makes it possible, as its foundation. (p. 180, PM)

The question whether man is by nature a 'political animal' or not is not an alternative Sartre recognises. Because here 'nature' means an original and permanent state, whereas for Sartre human reciprocity *is not an original state because it is not a state,* and it is not permanent because originality, not being a state, has none of the characteristics of permanence. The originality of human reciprocity expresses a *structural normative dimension* which places it beyond the alternatives of being a reciprocity either of love or of conflict. Hobbes' doctrine, for which natural human reciprocity is conflict, is accommodated by Sartre within an interpretation of 'state of nature' as one compatible with its transformation into a state of reciprocity susceptible to anti-natural characteristics, that is, on the basis of denying there can be a state of nature whose originality has the character of permanence. In other words, for Sartre the reciprocity of conflict not only poses the problem of its being surpassed in fact (as containment and repression of it), but also the problem of its 'foundation' in right as revolutionary *reappropriation.*

The difference between the two positions can ultimately be clarified in the light of the two different notions of 'reason' that are being employed. Hobbes' reason is basically calculative, while Sartre's is dialectical. The former is not in a position to surpass the natural quality of the reciprocal state of war, but at the most can only control it by recourse to a principle of 'force majeure.' The latter is an historical reason which recognises in 'scarcity' the contingent cause of the universal state of war and proposes to eliminate it on the basis of a project inspired by right (original reciprocity) and not by mere force as institutionalised right. It is true that there is a good deal of equivocation on Sartre's part as to the possibility of this project being definitively realised; all the same, the question remains firmly posed as one of right and not of fact.

4. *Sartre as Intermediate between Locke and Marx*

To Sartre's normative and formal concept of reciprocity we can usefully oppose the analogous concepts found in Locke and Rousseau. For Locke the relation of reciprocity is formal in the sense that it is neither necessarily one of love nor one of war. In order for it to become a relation of conflict (war) some change (hence a removable factor) must intervene. The analogies between this view and Sartre's are obvious. For Hobbes, original reciprocity is necessarily conflict; for Locke and Sartre, it becomes so by virtue of, respectively, an unreasoned recourse to force and the scarcity of goods. But these are negative factors eliminable in civil society. It is on this terrain, however, that the most serious divergencies arise between Locke's position and Sartre's. In Sartre they have a double origin, existentialist and Marxist.

Those of existentialist origin are connected to the problem of the possibility of a complete and definitive removal of scarcity – that is, of dispensing with the factor that transforms original reciprocity into reciprocity of conflict. As we have more than once stressed, the issue is far from clear in the *Critique*. It is obvious that to the extent that scarcity is not totally and definitively eliminated, it tends to assume the naturalistic characteristics of the Hobbesian position, which in this way would affiliate itself to the proto-existentialist theory of the ineliminability of alienation.

The differences that are of Marxist origin are none other than the fundamental differences between 'bourgeois' and socialist ideology. On the ideological level, in fact, Sartre fully accepts Marx's critique of liberalism as ideological mystification insofar as it is 'partial humanism' or 'class humanism.' Even if Sartre does not accept the formal definition of class provided by Marxism, and still less the Marxist theory of the formation of classes, he nonetheless accepts the ideological function which Marx ascribes to the class struggle. Even if Sartre regards the being-of-class as seriality and practico-inert impotence (p. 640), he yet holds that capitalist exploitation will only be confronted when the apocalypse of a 'group in combat' resolves the inert seriality of classes. (p. 691) The group does not deny, but assumes and radicalizes, the function Marxism attributed to class.

On the more strictly political level, Sartre accepts the inversion of the relations between civil society and State which results from the Marxist critique of the Hegelian philosophy of Right, just as he accepts the Marxian critique of the mystifying disjunction between *bourgeois* and *citizen* which is presupposed in the formalistic egalitarianism of the bourgeois State. And, moreover, he accepts the Marxian theory of the State as a product of 'class' — or 'group' in Sartre's terminology — and thus the purely factual status of the sovereignty it expresses. Thus 'the idea of a diffused, popular sovereignty which would be incarnated in the sovereign is a mystification' (p. 609), and 'the State is neither legitimate nor illegitimate.' (p. 609) Sovereignty always appertains to a group in combat which dissolves or determines series from outside (hetero-determination). For this reason there never is, nor can there ever be, a 'dictatorship of the proletariat' since 'the idea itself is absurd, a bastard compromise between the active sovereign group and passive seriality.' (p. 630) The problem of democracy as a problem of freedom can never be posed except in the form of a 'progressive withering away of the State.' (p. 630)

But for Marx, the complete withering away of the State presupposes the complete removal of alienation. Sartre's oscillation between Hobbes and Marx is, therefore, a function of the existentialist theory of alienation. Marx accepts the Hobbesian theory of the State as absolute power, but he goes beyond it with the demand for its dissolution. Sartre elaborates a notion of original reciprocity of a Lockean type, but conceives it in a Marxist fashion as a reciprocity of power over definite products in the field of scarcity, and defines access to this reciprocity of goods as necessarily conditional upon the self-constitution of struggling groups. He thus ends up by dissociating reciprocity and State, in such a way that his vacillation as to whether or not scarcity is eliminable has the effect of making him vacillate between an absolute Hobbesian State and a Marxist dissolution of the State. But this type of vacillation cannot help but strike decisively at the very notion itself of reciprocity.

5. *Sartre as Intermediate between Heidegger and Marx*

In his comparison of Rousseau and Sartre, George Lapassade is right to point to the profound analogy between Sartre's concept of the group, and Rousseau's of the people. [6] But what is more important to indicate, in our opinion, is the fact that the classical aporias of the relation between the Will of All and the General Will in Rousseau anticipate in an obvious way those that characterise the relationship in Sartre between series and group. At heart the two thinkers move in a common intermediate zone between liberalism and socialism: in Rousseau's case because, in moving from a liberal conception of reciprocity, he proceeds to a concept of social unity that rests on the establishment of genuine equality; in Sartre's case because he regresses from the position of interpreting unity as the integral whole of communist society, and arrives at a recognition of social multiplicity in its original 'pre-social' reciprocity.

According to Sartre, the first characteristic society assumes as a result of social reciprocity being realised historically *in the field of scarcity* is that of non-homogeneity; Society identifies neither with the group nor with the grouping of groups because the serial collectives also form part of it. In society the original relationship of reciprocity has already collapsed in the face of the two fundamental modalities which scarcity introduces into social multiplicity: the 'series' as interiorisation of the alterity either of struggle or of indifference, and the 'group' as seriality in fusion, as positive reciprocity of cooperation whose aim is the dissolution of seriality through the removal of the de-humanising power of the practico-inert. In consequence, the 'fundamental internal relation' of historical society is not the homogeneous one of reciprocity, but a *relationship between group and series.*

The seriality of the collective is the social form assumed by the inhuman relationship produced by reciprocity when it constitutes itself in the field and upon the foundation of the practico-inert. The being of the collective is the non-being of humanity. (p. 79, PM) The social relationship presupposed by reciprocity is realised here on the foundation provided by things — that is to say, on the basis provided by the practico-inert as the locus of counter-finality and reflection of the products of human labour. Marx and Heidegger encounter each other here because all Heidegger's investigations — and those of existentialism generally — on the subject of banality, levelling and de-personalisation are seen by Sartre in a light that suggests a Marxist origin in that he regards these phenomena as the consequence of the alienated relationship between man and the products of his activity. Reciprocity assumes the form of serial uniformity between the members of the social body because each one is other than himself to the extent that he yields up his distinctive being to the uniformity of things. Sartre writes:

> In pure reciprocity, what is Other than me *is also the same.* In reciprocity *modified by scarcity,* the same appears to us as counter-man to the extent that *this same man* appears as radically Other (that is to say, as bearing the threat of our death). Or, if you like, we understand by and large his ends (they are the same as ours), his means (identical to ours), the dialectical structures of his acts, but we understand them as if they were the characters of *another species,* that of our demonic double. In reality nothing — neither big game nor microbes — can be more terrible for man than an intelligent, cruel, carnivorous species which is able to understand and display human intelligence and whose aim is precisely the destruction of man. This species is clearly our own as it manifests itself for each man among others in the environment of scarcity. (p. 208)

At this 'Manichean' level, Others are 'a complicity against me' (p. 184) which can only be combatted with violence, concealed or overt. It has been observed that in the *Critique* Sartre 'remains faithful to the motto chosen twenty years or so ago for *Huis-clos:* Hell is other people' [7]; it does not seem so when one remembers that 'reciprocity is that which man expects of another when their relation is a human one.' (p. 253) Reciprocity becomes hell only in the context of scarcity and of the practical passivity which the structure of the practico-inert takes on; the hell of the *Critique* is *l'enfer tournant du champ de passivité pratique.* (p. 279)

6. *Sovereignty, Democracy, Stalinism*

The most important corollary to this conception of the collective is that it 'has *no quality* allowing it to confer sovereignty nor any structure which offers the possibility of so doing.' (pp. 607-8) Whence derives Sartre's denial that parliamentary democracy and political elections can be a source of sovereignty. Indeed, at this point Sartre takes what is a disconcerting though well-trodden path, for he is led to say that sovereignty and legitimacy are the *de facto* properties of the group-in-fusion insofar as this represents redemption from the seriality of the inert collectivity:

> In a certain way, in the environment of alterity, the mere fact that the group exists outside of [the collectives] and in its synthetic unity, means that it has already obtained a legitimate foundation. [. . .] The group is legitimate because it is a product of itself alone [. . .] the group is *as such* legitimate. (p. 607)

Or:

> Sovereignty is far from ascending from the collective to the sovereign;
> it is from the sovereign [. . .] that legitimacy derives in order to then
> descend and modify the collectives without changing their structure of
> passivity. (p. 609)

The collective submits to the sovereignty which the group exercises over it
by means of hetero-determination and in virtue of the 'passivity of the
masses.' (p. 624) This is the case even with the electoral system:

> An electoral system, of whatever kind, establishes a gathering of
> electors as passive matter of hetero-conditioning; and the poll of votes
> no more represents the *wish* of the country than the Top Twenty list of
> records represents the *taste* of the buyers. The only possible way in
> which the 'wish' of the masses can be manifested is in their
> revolutionary re-grouping against the inertia of institutions and against
> this sovereignty which relies on their impotence. The ballot may,
> indeed, produce some changes – of an insignificant kind – in the
> composition of the sovereign body; it can *in no case* claim to modify a
> government's politics (except in the case where circumstances which
> accompanied it are of themselves such as to bring about a modification).
> (p. 624, note)

Such assumptions are at the root of Sartre's present evaluation of
internal events in the Soviet Union. His judgement of Stalin and on
Stalinism is very different from that he expressed at the time of the
Hungarian revolt. It draws its particularity from the fact that Sartre
would today claim that the basis for evaluating such phenomena as the
'dictatorship of the proletariat' is dialectical reason itself: 'the
"dictatorship of the proletariat" is an optimistic phrase coined too hastily
as a result of ignorance of the formal laws of dialectical reason.' (p. 629)
This is all too reminiscent of Hegel's attitude towards Napoleon: formal
deduction is the justification of simple fact. Sartre says, in fact:

> Historical experience has undeniably revealed that the first moment of a
> socialist society in process of construction could not be – when we
> consider it still on the abstract level of power – anything but the
> indissoluble aggregate of bureaucracy, terror and the cult of personality.
> (p. 630)

The first thing to be noted here is that 'historical experience' merely
demonstrates what has happened and not that which 'could not be
anything else,' at least not unless one allows the supposed validity of the

'formal laws of dialectical reason' to intervene in the form of some *necessitas ex machina.* So one can say:

> It is *true* that Stalin was the Party and the State. Or rather, that the Party and the State were Stalin. But Stalin's violence translates, through a specific process, into the contradictory violence of two dialectics . . . . (p. 630)

Yet Sartre is not prophesying the perpetuation or restoration of Stalinism. He recognizes the existence in the socialist world today of 'the objective demand for de-bureaucratisation, decentralisation and democratisation,' but he affirms that 'we must take this last term to mean the appeal to the sovereign to abandon gradually the *monopoly of the group*' (p. 629) – in short, a species of enlightened despotism. But as regards the advent of socialism in other States, 'the socialisation that is going on in half of the world will produce this new revolution in another conjuncture and through a historical totalization that is different from that which characterised the revolution of 1917.' (p. 630) The end point of the process, however, remains the Marxist one of the 'withering away of the State.' (p. 630)

7. *From Series to Group*

The second fundamental modality which reciprocity can assume is the group. In the series, reciprocity is unmediated in the sense that it is delivered up to the false mediation of the object. This is the field of the practico-inert and the dominion of counter-finality which the worked-upon product introduces into its naturally unmediated state. Unmediated reciprocity resolves itself in a pitiless struggle to the death, and the social relations which derive from that struggle bear the emblem of violence and negativity. If no other kind of alternative were offered to human society, there would be neither history nor historical dialectic, and the reign of violence and brute necessity would hold sway over the entire realm of human existence.

But original reciprocity offers man a second possibility, that of its becoming mediated, or group, reciprocity. The group represents 'the sudden resurrection of freedom' in opposition to the reign of necessity imposed by things. (p. 425) The group produces an ontological state of society which is a complete inversion of collective seriality. There were two characteristics of seriality: 1) the inhuman predominance of worked-upon material over the social reality of man; 2) the *statut* of oppositional alterity between man and man.

With the constitution of the group, both these characteristics dissolve in the 'apocalyptic' process in which 'the group establishes itself as the radical impossibility of the impossibility of living which threatens serial multiplicity.' (p. 377) The group is that unforeseen and violent revolutionary conflagration which occurs when the serial situation of abuse and exploitation has reached the limit of endurance. Its slogan is that coined by Marx himself: 'to live a life of labour or to die fighting.' (p. 377) In antithesis to the typical features of the series, the group promotes: 1) the dissolution of the inhumanity of worked-upon material; 2) the establishment of 'pure freedom, liberating men from alterity.' (p. 639) To achieve these aims, the group must carry out two tasks: 1) 'it must snatch from worked-upon material its inhuman power of mediation between men in order to confer power on each and everyone in the community, and thus establish itself, insofar as it is structured, as the means whereby the materiality of the practical field (things and collectives) is placed again in the hands of free, *communised praxis* (the oath, etc.)'; 2) 'Snatch man from the *statut* of alterity which makes of him a product of his product, in order to transform him, "when molten" and by means of the appropriate procedures, into a *product of the group* – that is, insofar as the group is freedom – into a *product of himself.*' (pp. 638-9)

In studying collectives Marxism has made the mistake of treating them as 'things,' and of not studying them at all the levels of their existence. (p. 77, PM) Collectives do not have any organic or metaphysical composition, nor even the unity of consensus. The series has merely the unity of flight, a parasitical unity; as regards the group, on the other hand, one cannot even say that it 'is' without its already being in process of being totalized. (pp. 429-31)

Typical examples of the constitution of a group are the insurrection of the *Saint-Antoine* quarter of Paris on 13 and 14 July 1789, or else the sudden inversion which takes place when a collection of persons in seriality are charged by the police and thereupon transform themselves into a revolutionary group in assault against these police. (p. 415-18) The collective is by contrast exemplified in the queue of persons *waiting for* a bus. The group has the maximum of praxis and the minimum of inertia; the collective has the maximum of inertia and the minimum of praxis (which transfers it into *exis*). (p. 307) The whole of Sartre's analysis of the group is conducted in the form of an implicit polemic with the Marxist tendency to see social phenomena as a function of economic conditions. (p. 181) It is true that there is a circular relationship between series and group, and for that reason the group's constitution is the absorption of the serial elements. But it is also true that the realm of the practico-inert (which the series presupposes) does not possess the status of an original dialectic, but rather establishes the reign of the anti-dialectic. Any initiative, therefore, is always founded on man's mode of being, on existence as project and freedom.

8. *Class*

The dialectical experience culminates in the recognition that the concrete reality of social life is made up of the double circularity which leads from series to group and from group to series. (pp. 741-2) The second circularity represents what Sartre calls the 'ontological check' on the group which destines it to dissolution once more in seriality. (p. 638) But what place is given to class, which is the principle category for the collective in Marxist analysis of social reality, in this double circularity, and what is its historical function?

Sartre specifies that he too intends 'to situate man in his class and in the conflicts which oppose it to other classes, on the basis of the mode and the relations of production,' but he maintains that this is possible only 'on the basis of existence.' (p. 108) But it is precisely by starting from existence that Sartre has established that dialectic whose 'experience' has culminated in the theory of double circularity between series and group upon which he founds his notion of class. It is a term, therefore, for Sartre, which designates a seondary and derived formation relative to series and group. The circular relationship between group and series begins with society's original relationship to an environment of scarcity – which is to say, in a context *prior* to that of the history of capitalism within which Marxism elaborates its ideas of class and class struggle:

> Marx has revealed the material conditions for the appearance of *Capital,* a social force which ends up by imposing itself on individuals as an anti-social force. But it is a question of gaining concrete experience of the general and dialectical conditions which produce in the relations of man with matter a definite reversal as the moment of a combined process [. . .] It is within this complex of dialectical relations that the possibility of the capitalist process is established. (p. 224)

Classes are formations having relevance in a wider economic context than that of capitalism to which they immediately refer. At the basis of the relative scarcity, from which they derive their origin, there is a primitive scarcity, which is the true and proper object of political economy:

> All this amounts to saying that in granting scarcity its importance one is not reverting to some pre-Marxist theory of the pre-eminence of the factor of 'consumption' but rather exposing the negativity which is the implicit motor of the historical dialectic and which gives it its intelligibility. (p. 225, note) [8]

In taking scarcity as the original context of all social formations, Sartre is drawn into a polemic both with Engels, and with Marxism in general, over the origin of classes. These arise, according to Sartre, not from the fact that production always yields a surplus, but rather from the fact that it is always deficient. This being so, in the field of scarcity, 'an unproductive group can only be established on condition that the rest, as a whole, is deprived of subsistence, the consequence being that one of the fundamental functions of this group becomes that of choosing which of the superfluous elements to eliminate.' (p. 222) Thus 'if one agrees with Marx and Engels about the class struggle — that is the negation of some by the work of others, or, in other words, pure and simple negation — then one grants that they have all that is needed to understand History. But we still need to discover the *starting point* of the negation.' (p. 223)

So class, insofar as it is the product of capitalist exploitation, does not possess the unity of a group but is in the *statut* of serial dispersion and passivity:

> Class, as a collective, becomes a material thing made up of men insofar as it constitutes itself as a negation of man and as a serial impossibility of denying that negation. This impossibility makes class into a necessity of fact: it is the destiny one cannot change. It is not a practical solidarity but, on the contrary, the absolute unity of destinies that results from the lack of solidarity. (p. 353)

Essentially, therefore, class has the *statut* of the series and of 'series totalised by series' (p. 356); its only link with the revolutionary group or group-in-combat is provided by the double circularity which binds series and group in such a way that 'the organized praxis of the group in combat has its upsurge at the heart itself of the practico-inert, in the opaque materiality of impotence and inertia, as the surpassing of *this* materiality.' (p. 357). As a result:

> ... the proletariat, in being at one and the same time Destiny and Negation of Destiny, constitutes *in its very form* a moving and contradictory reality, or, if one prefers, it is *all the time,* and in proportions defined by the historical situation, a group praxis (or, for the most part, a multiplicity of group activities) gnawing away at the inert unity of a common-being-of-class. (p. 357)

In being the *statut* of being-of-class imposed by capitalist exploitation, class will never be able to constitute itself as the source of initiative and struggle. In fact 'its serial and practio-inert *statut* could not produce a class *struggle* if the permanent possibility of dissolving series was not at everyone's disposition; we have witnessed the formation of a preliminary and abstract indication of this possible unity in the development of class interest. All the same, the transformation of class into actual group, is never in any way realised, not even during a period of revolution.' (p. 644) The working class is a collective whose serial and practico-inert unity is the effect of submission to the external presence of the object which capitalism establishes as its internal unity — which is to say, by the fact that the sum total of the means of production is in the hands of Others. Revolutionary transformation can get rid of the bases for this seriality, but only on condition that its relation to seriality is that of the group dissolving it.

9. *Binary and Ternary Relations*

The dissolution of the series in the group-in-fusion is what Sartre, following Malraux's *L'espoir,* defines as 'apocalypse.' (p. 391) The group-in-fusion is the 'singular incarnation of a common people' insofar as it realises the 're-interiorisation of reciprocity' and is 'the immediate opposite of alterity.' (p. 391) The example which Sartre provides at some length is that of the Paris quarter of Saint-Antoine, serialised for centuries by that practico-inert object which is the Bastille, and which it rose to a man to destroy, when, caught between cannon fire on the one side and Royalist troops closing in on the quarter on the other, it confronted the *impossibility of enduring the impossibility of living*; so that freedom reveals itself as the necessity of dissolving necessity (p. 390), and the Bastille 'becomes the common interest, insofar as it *can and must,* at one fell swoop, be disarmed and made the source of supply of arms, and, if possible, also the base against the enemy on the West. The urgency is due to the scarcity of time: the enemy has not yet arrived, but could do so at any moment. The operation defines itself for each participant with the urgency of a sudden discovery of a terrible and common freedom.' (p. 394)

Sartre concludes from this that revolt is born in things but not begotten by them, since it is only inscribed in them as 'an inert idea.' The decisive thrust comes from the threat exerted by other groups and by the projects they have for utilising things. (p. 394) Nevertheless, both the threat and the self-determination of the response to it are possible only on the structural basis provided by the elemental bonds of reciprocity which underlie both collective and group formations.

From the window, unseen, I am looking at two workers, neither of whom has seen the other. Each one of us projects the world from the standpoint of his own unifying praxis. The effect of reciprocity is such that no meeting can occur between us except on the basis of each one of us being constituted as the unifying *third* in respect to the other two: 'Every centre places itself, in respect to the Other, as a centre of flight, as *other* unification.' (p. 186) It is not a case of something subjective, since the entire objective world is caught up in reciprocity thus understood. The first effect it has is to render each person an object in respect to the praxis-project of the other. Its second is to impose the necessity of mediation by a third in order that reciprocity may establish itself. The mediating third, however, may find himself in one of two positions: either that of being the one *against* whom a relationship is established on the basis of the predominance, in reciprocity, of the non-mediation of material in the field of scarcity; or, that of being the one *on whose basis* the group establishes itself as the struggle against the predominance of material in constituting the relation of reciprocity. (p. 187) But in each case 'the binary formation, as the immediate relation of man to man, is the necessary foundation of every ternary relationship; inversely, however, the latter, as the mediation of man with men, is the basis on which reciprocity recognises itself as reciprocal bond.' (p. 189)

10. *Reciprocity as Sameness*

The mediating third is also present and operative in the seriality of the collective, but in a levelling and neutralising capacity:

> The third is absorbed in seriality because its *a priori* structure is that of the Other, of the Other of each and of all; so that its internal-external relation of free alterity in regard to reciprocity loses itself in serial alterity. (p. 398)

But when the collective encounters a crisis as a result of the insurgence of a group-in-fusion, individual praxis, hitherto subjected to seriality, takes on the character of a 'communal and organised act' possessed of given ends and a strategy and organisation for attaining them. (p. 401) Praxis no longer renders the individual other than himself, since 'the contagion of seriality is such that when it liquidates itself in restoring the passive moment to freedom, his praxis belongs to the individual as his *own*, as the free development on the part of one member of the action of the whole group in formation (and, in consequence, of each one insofar as the common unity serves as the mediation between thirds and each one).' (pp. 401-402) 'At this point,' says Sartre 'the individual is *sovereign*, that is he becomes, through the change in praxis, the organiser of the common praxis.' (p. 401)

Then comes the example, which in its reference to 'flight' and to the indefinite '*on*,' clearly reveals its origin:

> Only just now he was fleeing, because one (*on*) was fleeing; now he is crying 'stop!' because he is stopping, and it is one and the same thing to stop and to give the order to stop, since the action develops in him and in everyone by virtue of the imperative organisation of its moments. (p. 401-2)

This unification of multiplicity should not be confused with the analogous unifications which the third accomplishes in regard to the *objective* multiplicity of the bus queue or the *subjective* multiplicity of those who rescue me from a mountain. By contrast, the group which arises as *my* group is the synthetic surpassing of both the object and subject groups of my field of praxis. The group-in-fusion is neither my object nor my subject but 'the "comunitary"* structure of my act,' my 'group existence' (p. 403), in which reciprocity takes the form of being 'the one for the other and the one by virtue of the other simultaneously' (p. 404).

Sartre makes it clear at this point that 'the error common to many sociologists' lies in 'taking the group as a binary relation (individual-community) when it is actually a question of a tertiary relation,' that is, of one that is mediated in the sense that 'I seize the group as my communal reality, and, simultaneously, as the mediation between me and every other third,' in such a way that 'the relation between third and third has nothing further to do with alterity': this is 'mediated reciprocity.' (p. 104) Sartre cites as an example the arrival of a new combatant within a group of insurgents: '*by this fact*, the group is enlarged in me* and in the Other, by virtue of me and by virtue of the Other, in me by virtue of the Other, and in the Other by virtue of me.' (p. 405) The Other 'comes to the group as I come to it: he is *the same* as me.' (p. 406)

In the group, mediation is accomplished not by an object but by a praxis, and I no longer seize upon the Other as the interiorisation of my objectivity. This praxis is not inertia but an 'act': the act of stopping in the course of flight, or the contemplation of an assault. Here the action is no longer simply undergone, nor is its quantity determinant (as it is, for example, with the fluctuations of the market relative to a given serial multiplicity), 'here, by contrast, what I rediscover is the action as human, and the quantity as instrumentality.' (p. 407) Here, more numerous no longer means weaker, but stronger, because my action multiplies itself everywhere while remaining everywhere the same. In this way 'reciprocity at the heart of the group *produces the group* as recipient of it to the same extent to which the group permits reciprocity in making it its mediation.' (pp. 407-8)

But the reciprocity which typifies the group, in addition to mediating between group and third, is the mediation between every third in the group and all the other thirds. Looked at in this way, I am both totalized and totalizing, and the 'password' is given by me and by others in the self-same instant — it 'circulates' as a 'vehicle of sovereignty': 'To the Bastille!' (pp. 408-10) The plurality of syntheses involved is therefore no

---

* Fr: '*la structure communautaire*' (the sense being 'structure wherein my act is the communal act' (Trans.)

* Fr.: 'en moi'; i.e. by virtue of the addition of me to it. Sartre's example is subjective. (Trans.)

more than an apparent obstacle to the establishment of group unity: in fact 'when each one is the free originator of his own conduct, he rediscovers it in the Other not as its *being-Other* but as his *own freedom*' (p. 418); which does not mean that the plurality of totalizations on the part of the thirds no longer takes place, but 'this multiplicity negates itself in each of the acts which constitutes it' (p. 418); 'in a word, the unity and unification from within of the plurality of totalizations is the *from within* which denies this plurality as being a co-existence of distinct acts, and which affirms the existence of the collective action as unique.' (p. 424)

11. *Terror and Threat*

The passage from collective to group is a 'possible' passage in the sense that the reversal of any order is possible in time; it is even, under certain conditions, inevitable, and in this sense, necessary. As soon as the pressure begins to let up, the *chances* of a dispersive remassification increase. This is the birth of the for-itself of the group, its own objectification through contemplation of itself: the crowd visits the conquered Bastille. (p. 435) Whereupon various possibilities are open to the group. For example, it can gather itself in a passive synthesis of the practico-inert ('the monument to the dead'), or it can dissolve itself in a new collective seriality. However, when the group discovers itself as *group in danger,* it makes an *object of itself,* in the sense that its members preoccupy themselves with the issue of its *permanence.* This cannot fail to influence the evolution of its practical structure and ontological *statut.* Its attention and commitment are directed towards safeguarding its constitutive elements – which now perforce become separate (guards are dispersed here and there); 'when freedom makes itself the communal praxis of establishing the permanence of the group by way of producing by itself its own inertia in mediated reciprocity, this new *statut* is called *the oath.*' (p. 439). A typical example is that of the Pallacord.

Sartre is insistent that the oath has nothing in common with the *social contract.* He makes it clear – and this is extremely important – that 'in no sense is it a question here of finding some kind of foundation for this or that society – later on we shall see the complete absurdity of such an exercise – but of illuminating the nature of the necessary passage from an unmediated form, in danger of dissolving itself, to another form of group, a form which is reflexive, but permanent.' (p. 439) The negative possibility which the oath is designed to remedy 'is the possibility of each becoming – by reason of the other third, and in respect to the other third, by reason of himself and in respect to himself – *Other.* Hence with the password 'Let us swear!' each one demands an objective guarantee from the other third that he will never become the Other: he who gives me that guarantee by that same act protects me – in respect of the issue at stake – from the danger that *Being-Other will come to me from the Other.*' (p. 440)

But already concealed at the root of this request for an oath is the dissolution of the constitutive *ubiquity* of the group's reciprocity, and what takes its place instead is the *exigence* of being a party to it; but 'exigence' is a condition imposed by the practico-inert, and with its appearance mediated reciprocity contaminates itself with alterity and permanence. *Reflexive fear* thus becomes the dominant and pervasive emotion; it is the fear of not having enough fear of the enemy once more taking the offensive. So the project arises of 'replacing by a real fear produced by the group itself, an external fear which is removed from it [. . .] And this fear in being the free product of the group and the corrective action taken by freedom against serial dissolution [. . .] is Terror.' (p. 448)

Terror is the violence of freedom against necessity; it is no longer directed at the necessity of the external, alienating object, but towards the group itself, in order to preserve it from the threat of dissolution by the object's seriality. The oath installs Terror as an armed guard over the pledge that has been voluntarily sworn. Violence becomes the safeguard of the common freedom. Sartre does not pose the problem of the *limits* and *control* of violence within the group, because violence is itself *free* and 'it little matters that certain elements of the community, historically, and under definite circumstances, have confiscated it for their own benefit.' (p. 48) The oath installs 'for the first time man's position as *absolute* power of man over man.' (author's emphasis, p. 449) It seems, then, that human reality cannot escape the alternatives of either the sameness of group unity or the dispersion of seriality. In both cases violence has sovereign rule, whether directed against the dispersive necessity of the object or against the self-dispersing necessity of the group.

In addition to the two forms of reciprocity already examined, the oath introduces a third. The first form was that of the unmediated reciprocity of seriality, the second the mediated one of sameness and ubiquity of the group-in-fusion. Now we have an intermediate reciprocity arising: that in which sameness is dispelled, but alterity has not yet taken on serial form, because 'this being-Other is in every third the *same* Being-Other as his neighbour's. (p. 451)

Having started by conceiving society in terms of the romantic ideal of a unity of subjects, as violence and victory over the object, Sartre ends up by making this violence internal to society as the only way of protecting the unity of its members. Terror, however, is not equipped to function as an instrument of discrimination in regard to the political conduct of the group's members. Here Sartre encounters the fundamental insufficiency of every theory of violence: its incapacity to discriminate. He says: 'and all forms of behaviour among communal individuals (fraternity, love, friendship no less than anger and lynching) draw their terrible power from Terror itself.' (p. 455) Terror is not the instrument of fraternity but its foundation: 'The traitors, in effect, are the minority, by definition.' (p. 456)

12. *Organisation, Function, Institution, Sovereignty, Dictatorship*

The group is threatened by dispersion, however, not only because the fear produced by the external threat diminishes, but also because of the necessary differentiation in its functions when the group loses the fluid homogeneity of fusion. When this happens not even the Sacred, as 'fundamental structure of Terror' (p. 457), is a sufficient bastion against the tendency to seriality; and *organisation* becomes a submerged presence at its ceremonies, services and rituals.

> The word 'organisation' designates at one and the same time both the internal action by which a group defines its structures, and the group itself as structured activity exercised, in the practical field, on worked-upon material and on other groups. (p. 460)

Function is born of organisation; in the last analysis it is based on Terror, because it is no more than the inversion of the prohibition against doing something. (p. 463)

So it is that the organic individual reappears as isolated agent; what he is as individual is negated in the common individuality of the group and reappears as a function internal to it. But at this stage the primitive context of alienation is superseded. As with a football team, there is a division of functions but all of them are directed towards a common end. Alterity, says Sartre, following Lévi-Strauss, vanishes as nature and is reborn as culture. (p. 475) Here, reciprocity has been worked upon, contrived. It operates as a protection against centrifugality. It is, at least partially, interiorised inertia, the formation of structure (in Lévi-Strauss' sense). But in no case will it take the form of an 'agreement.' 'The very word "agreement" is aberrant.' (p. 527) Agreement is an 'agreement among spirits,' but, in truth, 'there are no spirits': we would be dealing in a mere 'philosophy of History.' (p. 527)

In the group which is organised on the basis of a fraternity-of-Terror every third tends to make himself a *regulative third,* in a relation to the group of immanence-transcendence — that is, he assumes the function of a regulator. This gives rise to a demand for a sovereign power which will act as integral totalization. (p. 563) By its nature, sovereignty is not only *absolute* but *total.* (p. 564) At the heart of the group, however, it encounters its own *limit* in the fact that 'the bond is not univocal but reciprocal, because the third as regulator integrates himself in the group to the extent that his regulating action integrates me.' (p. 564) Thus, sovereignty finds its actual limit in reciprocity: totalization is accompanied by constant detotalization on bases provided by reciprocity.

This insurpassable conflict between individual and community, which oppose each other, define themselves in terms of the one against the other, and refer each one to the other as its profound truth, is naturally betrayed by new contradictions within the organised group; and these contradictions are expressed in a new transformation of the group; the organisation is transformed into a hierarchy, the oath gives birth to the institution. (p. 567)

At this level the group is established as *institutionalised group*. This means that 'its "organs," functions and power are institutionalised, that within the framework of these institutions, the community will attempt to give itself a new type of unity by way of institutionalising sovereignty, and that the common individual transforms himself into an institutional individual.' (p. 573) The institution is a retrogressive step towards the re-emergence of seriality in the group:

> *The being of the institution,* as a geometrical site of the intersections between collective and community, is the *non-being* of the group that produces itself as the bond between its members. (p. 583) But the institutional system as exteriority of inertia, necessarily reverts to *authority* as the means of its reinteriorisation, and *authority*, as the power over all powers and over all thirds through those powers is itself established by the system as the institutional guarantee of institutions. (p. 586)

The result is that the 'chief' is at one and the same time produced in the group and produces the group which has produced him. He is born and survives on the basis of 'historical circumstances' (p. 586); the chief upholds institutions in the same measure that he produces them. (p. 588) He receives his sovereign authority from the group for whom he is the ultimate and constitutional ruler. The State, as the supreme institution, 'can in no case be understood as the product or expression of the totality of social individuals or of their majority, since this majority is *in every case* serial and such that it is unable to express its needs and state its claims except by liquidating itself as series in favour of a large group (which suddenly confronts authority, or renders it inoperative *in every instance*).' (p. 609) For this reason, the idea of popular sovereignty is a mystification, and the State is neither legitimate nor illegitimate. In its institutional structure, the State represents the extreme limit of group serialisation. It expresses the power of a group and of a class (as a group) and as such 'cannot assume the functions of a mediator between exploited and exploiting classes. The State is a determination of the dominant class and this determination is conditioned by the class struggle.' (pp. 611-12)

So the circle closes. Its renewal can only be entrusted to the struggling groups which constitute themselves at the heart of the exploited class. In this way, the dialectical experience culminates in the recognition of a double circularity between series and group, at the base of which lies the 'ontological check' of the interdependence between freedom and necessity. (pp. 638, 640-2)

[VI]

Alienation

1. *The Conditions of Possibility of the Concept of Alienation*

Our analysis of the various aspects of Sartre's thought has, so far, constantly confronted us with alternatives which depend on the interpretation of the role played in his theory by the concept of alienation. The theory of alienation performs a central and enigmatic function in the *Critique*. The reasons for its centrality are clear enough. In any attempt to combine existentialism and Marxism no other concept could better function at the same time both as an element of cohesion and as one of discrimination. The reasons for its enigmatic quality are more complex and are more concerned with what is being presupposed in such an attempt, than with the attempt itself.

We shall place our examination of Sartre's position in the context of the reference points provided historically by contractualist, Hegelian, existentialist and Marxist theory. From the conceptual point of view, we shall proceed on the basis of certain preliminary specifications, which in merely expressing the formal conditions under which it is possible to formulate the concept of alienation, cannot be charged with being methodologically unjustified assumptions. The *first* of these specifies that the subject of alienation must be conceived as having the *capacity* to lose his own being, while nonetheless eventually reappropriating it. It therefore seems nonsensical to speak of alienation while adhering to any conception of reality for which the subject is by definition guaranteed *coincidence* with his own being. *In the second place,* it would seem that alienation, insofar as it makes one *other* than a subject, presupposes that we allow the existence of *real* alterity; i.e., its concept is incompatible with a conception of alterity as simple 'appearance' (of identity). *In the third place* it seems impossible to conceive of any subject being in a state of alienation who is allowed to possess the quality of *absolute* spontaneity; in other words, the idea of alienation seems indissolubly linked with that of a variable but ineliminable coefficient of adversity to which the subject must submit. Naturally, such a coefficient must behave in a way that is compatible in its modality with the first stated condition, in the sense that there will be no case in which it will be able to acquire the kind of status that would allow it to univocally determine, or render stable and permanent, the 'reality' of the subject in question. In other words, the constraint it exercises must be strong enough to account for the loss of self on the part of the subject, but not so strong as to make its reappropriation impossible. *In the fourth place* it would seem that the idea of alienation is incompatible with anything that is seen as *positive* since, in this case, the demand for de-alienation would lose all sense. To sum up: we can give the following definition of alienation: it is the *negative* process by which a subject makes himself other than himself by virtue of a *constraint* which is capable of being removed on the initiative of the subject himself. The most important corollary would seem to be that in every context in which these *conditions of possibility* for the use of the concept of alienation are not respected, that use is a mystification.

If we re-read those points in the *Economic and Philosophical Manuscripts of 1844* where Marx summarises his denunciation of the 'mystificatory' nature of the Hegelian theory of alienation [1], we can easily see that *the first* of the points made above corresponds in Marx to point (6) of his critique of Hegel: 'That consciousness [. . .] being thus *at home with itself* in its *other-being as such* — as will be explained further on — that, granted the process of alienation must have a bearer,' a 'subject,' in Hegel, 'the subject first emerges as a result. This result — the subject knowing itself as absolute self-consciousness — is therefore *God, Absolute, Spirit*, the *self-knowing and self-manifesting Idea.* Real man and real nature become mere predicates — symbols of this esoteric, unreal man and of this unreal nature [. . .] The *absolute subject* as a *process,* as *subject alienating* itself and returning from alienation into itself, but at the same time retracting this alienation into itself, and the subject as this process a pure *restless* revolving within itself.' But the 'revolution' and the 'restlessness' are the traditional symbols of the coincidence of being with itself. *To the second* of the points corresponds point (1) of Marx's critique of Hegel: 'that the object as such presents itself to consciousness as something vanishing' — for the reason that, as Marx makes clear further on, 'the object is only the *semblance* of an object, a piece of mystification, which in its essence, however, is nothing else but knowing itself.' *To the third* point there corresponds Marx's point (2), in explaining which Marx says: 'Man as an objective, sensuous being is therefore a *suffering* being, and because he feels what he suffers, a *passionate* being'; and immediately afterwards: 'Man is not merely a natural being: he is a *human* natural being.' *To the fourth* of the above points corresponds Marx's point (5) where it is said that in Hegelian theory 'the negative of the object, its annulling of itself, has *positive* significance; consciousness *knows* this nullity of the object because it alienates *itself,* for in this alienation it *knows* itself as object, or, for the sake of the indivisible unity of *being-for-itself*, the object as itself; or else, as it is put more concisely in point (3): 'this externalisation of consciousness has not merely a *negative* but a *positive* significance.'

2. *Kierkegaard and Marx in Opposition to Hegel*

According to Marx, the Hegelian theory of alienation is itself the product of a double alienation: of real man in consciousness and of the consciousness of real man in absolute consciousness. But. Marx makes it clear that at this point the discourse on alienation necessarily becomes mystificatory because it contradicts the conditions of its own possibility. [2]

Kierkegaard also attacks the Hegelian mystification. Nor is it true — as has been authoritively claimed [3] even recently — that his polemic did not go beyond the interests of a 'writer on religious affairs.' Kierkegaard did not confine himself to an emotional vindication of the rights of the individual in respect to the Hegelian dialectic, but in his criticisms of Hegel's dialectic, and of the idea of alienation implied by it, he raised a fundamental objection the import of which is identical to that of Marx's point which we have just examined; that is that the Hegelian system is constructed on a level of abstraction and on the basis of assumptions which make it impossible to employ any concepts implying 'transition,' 'negation,' 'mediation,' or such temporal terms as 'thereupon,' 'when,' 'this is like becoming . . . ,' etc. In the *Concept of Dread* Kierkegaard writes:

> While Hegel and the Hegelian school startle the world by the mighty thought of the presuppositionless beginning of philosophy, [. . .] no embarrassment is felt at employing the terms 'transition,' 'negation' and 'mediation,' i.e. the principles of movement in Hegelian thought, in such a way that no place is definitely assigned to them in the systematic progression [. . .] Negation, transition, mediation are three masked men of suspicious appearance, the secret agents (*agentia*) which provoke all movements. Hegel would hardly call them 'hot heads,' for it is by his sovereign permission they carry on their game so brazenly that even in logic terms and expressions are employed which are drawn from the observation of transition in time; 'thereupon,' 'when,' 'this is like being,' 'this is like becoming,' etc. [4]

Marx and Kierkegaard both denounce: 1) the mystificatory nature of the Hegelian *procedure* in that this is a transference of problems from the concrete to the abstract ('He has only found the abstract, logical, speculative expression for the movement of history,' [5] says Marx; 'The word transition cannot be anything but a witty conceit in logic. It belongs to the sphere of historical freedom, for transition is a *state,* and it is actual,' [6] says Kierkegaard); 2) the mystificatory *use* in Hegel of the notions of 'real' and 'concrete' at an abstract level which renders it in contradiction with the very possibility of thinking them.

De-mystification of the Hegelian procedure thus takes analogous forms in both thinkers: 1) it replaces the abstract by the concrete (remember, says Kierkegaard, that 'first comes life and then theory. And then, also, there usually comes a third thing: an attempt to create life with theory, or else the illusion of living life itself again in theory, even of thus living it again in an enhanced form' [7]; an 'illusion' which corresponds exactly to Hegel's error — whose exposure, according to Marx in the *1844 Manuscripts,* was 'Feuerbach's greatest achievement' — and which consists in regarding the 'positive' as that 'absolute positive' which results from the 'negation of the negation'; the 'absolute positive' is rather the pure and simple abstract absolute, the absolute illusorily made potent by the ideal-dialectical process which presupposes — and does not eliminate — alienation, while the authentic positive is the 'positive resting on itself and positively founded on itself,' that is, the positive which is anterior and not posterior to the alienating abstraction.); 2) it reinstalls the conceptual articulation of the 'theory' within the set of conditions which make possible the non-mystificatory use of such concepts as 'alienation,' 'transition,' 'time' — concepts which the theory availed itself of only by detaching them from the living and historical concrete.

It is not by chance, therefore, that the most important interpretations of both Marx and Kierkegaard alike started within and continued to move along a common horizon which was precisely that of the limits within which the two thinkers advanced their anti-Hegelian polemic in answer to the need for de-mystification, and which thus delimit a methodologically coherent territory.

3. *Alienation as the Possibility of Existence*

These, then, are the considerations we have put forward by way of legitimating our procedure in the analysis of Sartre's concept of alienation, a procedure which addresses itself to the following question: to what extent does the marriage between existentialism and Marxism proposed in the *Critique* represent an advance on the most important of the positions agreed to by both Kierkegaard and Marx as crucial to the demystification of the concept of alienation? In other words, to what extent does the *Critique*: a) transfer the concept from the level of Hegelian abstraction to that of the socio-historical concrete; and, b) restore it to the theoretical context of the real conditions of possibility of this concrete? Or, if we want to transfer our enquiries from the methodological ground to that of their objective verification, we can ask whether in the *Critique*: 1) the 'subject,' the bearer of alienation, is so conceived as to be capable of both losing, and eventually recovering, his own being; 2) 'alterity' is regarded as real or as simply apparent; 3) the coercive factor is conceived in a way that allows for alienation and de-alienation to take place at the same time; 4) alienation is a wholly negative state.

We shall proceed by examining these four conditions of objective verification, in order to then go on to the problem of the implications of the methodological bases which support them. It should be recognised that the whole of the *Critique* tends towards satisfying the first condition. It constantly returns to the theme, whose line of attack is hostile to both Hegel and Engels, of alienation being attributable only to a subject conceived as having the *capacity* to lose, and after losing, the *capacity* to regain, his own being. Sartre says:

> What contemporary Marxists have forgotten is that man, alienated, mystified, reified, etc., still remains a man. When Marx speaks of reification, he does not mean to show that we are transformed into things but that we are men condemned to live humanly the condition of material things. (p. 104, note, PM)

And again:

> Furthermore, in order for notions like reification and alienation to assume their full meaning, it would have been necessary for the questioner and the questioned to be made one. What must be the nature of human relations in order for these relations to be capable of appearing in certain definite societies as the relations of things to each other? If the reification of human relations is possible, it is because these relations, even if reified, are fundamentally distinct from the relations of things. (p. 177, PM)

The reference to the identity between the questioner and the object of his questions does not allude to some interior dimension of the research but is a precise reference to Part 2 of *Being and Time,* where the mode of being of man came to be established as the being in which being is itself 'at stake.' What Sartre means, then, is that only a being who has the kind of relationship with his own being such that that being is itself in question, is susceptible to a condition such as 'alienation.' Sartre says:

> The very notions which Marxist research employs to describe our historical society – exploitation, alienation, fetishizing, reification, etc. – are precisely those which most immediately refer to existential structures. (p. 175, PM)

The reference to Heidegger should not mislead anyone into thinking that any indulgence is being implied on Sartre's part towards the late Heidegger. On the contrary, Sartre is being guided here by the demand for demystification of the concept of alienation and this intervenes as a criterion of discrimination to the detriment of the stance finally adopted by Heidegger.

> How, then, can *praxis* be founded, if it is not to be seen except as an inessential moment of a radically inhuman process? How can it be presented as real and material totalization if it is Being as a whole which is totalized in it and through it? Man would then become what Walter Biemal, in his notes on Heidegger, calls 'the bearer of the Opening to Being' [. . .] But every philosophy which subordinates the human to something Other than man, whether it be existentialist idealism or Marxism, has as its foundation and consequence a hatred of man: History has proved it in both instances. We have to make a choice: man is either first himself or first Other than himself. If one opts for the second alternative one is quite simply a victim and accomplice of real alienation. But alienation does not exist *unless* man is *first of all action*; it is freedom which founds servitude. (p. 248)

Freedom 'founds' servitude in the sense that alienation is 'an *a priori* possibility of human praxis,' (p. 154) where the 'a priori,' that is freedom as including the possibility of its alienation, does not have the significance of a 'primary' logical or ontological status. There has never been a moment in which existence realised itself in a state of ontological pre-alienation, and in any case, a non-alienated species of infra-structure which gives rise to alienated states is inconceivable.

> This hypothesis is absurd. To be sure, man can be enslaved only if he is free. But for historical man who *knows* himself and *comprehends* himself, this practical freedom is grasped only as the permanent, concrete condition of his servitude; that is, across that servitude and by means of it as that which makes it possible, as its foundation. (p. 180, PM)

Alienation, then, can only be a concern of existence (and not of Being, however this is conceived) — that is, of a mode of being whose structural foundation is such that it includes the constant possibility of losing its own being.

4. *Alterity and Alienation*

If the loss of self in other is to be something real and consistent, if, that is, alienation is not to give rise to a mystified and mystifying problem, alterity has to be a real state and not just a state in which the self finds an identity to itself in the mirror of sundry historical disguises (as if by a 'secret agent' as Kierkegaard would say).

Now if it is true that in the *Critique* the protagonist of alienation is the individual existing in his relations with society and with nature, it is also true that these relations are genuine relations of alterity because the other and things are irreducible realities. Therefore, Sartre is in line with the Marxist and existentialist demystification of the concept of alienation. Furthermore, he accuses a 'certain simplistic Marxism' of having restricted the relations of alterity which give rise to alienation, to relations with nature and with men, while forgetting the field of 'primitive alienation,' which, while it finds expression through the other forms of alienation, is independent of them to the point of functioning as their 'foundation,' viz., the relation of man to his own action insofar as it becomes other than what he intended it to be, or alienation as counter-finality. (p. 202)

In order for an action to become other than intended, and thus for it to assume the features of counter-finality, it must inscribe itself in the practico-inert of worked-upon material and as a result become liable to another's using it to his own contrary ends. In this aspect, alienation is a 'theft of the end.' (p. 158, PM) The establishment of strict and ineliminable relations between existence, project and end in relation to the problems of alienation and its mystification, define 'the position of true Marxism and of existentialism' as against the causalist and metaphysical positions of 'numerous American sociologists and some French Marxists.' (pp. 158-9, PM) It should be noted that this being-made-other on the part of the action is not connected to any possible mistakes or constraints affecting the course of its execution; it applies to the completely successful action, which to the extent that it succeeds, is inscribed in material and exists at the disposal of other projects. So that man's 'elementary experience of necessity' is that of a 'retroactive power which gnaws away at my freedom starting from the final objectification and going right back to the initial decision; a power which nonetheless has its source in freedom; it is the negation of freedom at the heart of complete freedom; it is sustained by freedom itself and proportionate to the very completeness of this freedom.' (p. 285)

There are three elements, then, which for Sartre are constituent of alienation: 1) existence as project in pursuit of ends; 2) the worked-upon material of the practico-inert (in the field of scarcity) as that which makes the project effective but at the same time disperses it and gives others a mandate over its disposal; 3) the presence of others' projects. Alienation arises as the effect of coexistence in the field of scarcity which turns the practico-inert into the site of 'monstrous forces of the inorganic and of exteriority.' (p. 359) But the two external factors, Others and material, do not have equal weight for Sartre. In fact material, though operating as this 'site,' intervenes only in a function subordinate to that of the other and principal factor, which is the other man: first and foremost because material as such is not the active element of the inversion in counter-finality which affects the individual praxis; and secondly, because material appears only in the context of scarcity, a context which at least in principle is merely contingent. (p. 202)

It is therefore in the field of co-existence – that is, in the co-presence within the social environment of a multiplicity of projects – that we must look for the ultimate foundation of alienation and thus reveal the possibility, and eventual techniques, of the process of de-alienation.

5. *Alienation, Reciprocity and Unity*

We have already had occasion to note the way in which co-existence as the substance of social life is supported, according to Sartre, by an original structure which he defines as 'reciprocity.' In realising itself in the field of scarcity, reciprocity can assume either a positive or a negative form. In the positive form, it gives rise to the exchange of goods or to communal enterprise, in the negative form to struggle. But this always passes through the mediation of material and thus does not have its foundation in a reciprocity merely of consciousness, as Hegel believed. (p. 192)

Reciprocity is, in the first place, a normative structure – something that man has to realise in order for him to have a future, but it does not possess any ontological status and thus 'does not protect men against reification and alienation, although fundamentally opposed to these.' (p. 191) All the same, the interpretation of reciprocity in the *Critique* radically determines its interpretation of alienation.

Reciprocity, as normative structure and structure of potentialities, represents the satisfaction, at the social level, of the primary and fundamental condition of any conception of a phenomenon such as alienation. That is, it complies with the necessity that the subject of alienation should be such as to include within his being the possibility of losing and of re-acquiring that being. Since the subject of alienation is existence in its being as co-existence, this latter must possess a structure which is at the same time open both to negative possibilities and to the recognition of their negativity. The Sartrean reciprocity incorporates both characteristics: it is structure in the two senses of negative possibility and positive norm, and it is not so in a sense which would exclude either characteristic; that is, it is not a structure in an organic or ontological sense.

But the problem is not exhausted at this point. Rather, it begins precisely here, where the issue at stake is that of determining the mode of being of the elements that come into play in reciprocity, i.e., the mode of existence of singular entities. It is clear, in fact, that this mode of being qualifies and specifies the nature of reciprocity. In a general way it is defined in the *Critique* as that of the 'project,' or 'praxis-project.' However, throughout the whole discussion concerning reciprocity, Sartre presents the 'project' in terms of a subject-object relationship. This gives

rise to two important questions: 1) the extent to which the interpretation
of the existence-project in terms of a subject-object relationship constitutes
a legitimate operation from either the existentialist or the Marxist point of
view; 2) the extent to which the notion of reciprocity can preserve the
functions attributed to it by Sartre once the elements of reciprocity are
distributed between them in a relationship of the subject-object type.

With regard to the first question, it should be noted that every
interpretation of human reality in terms of a subject-object relation accords
the subjective pole a privileged status and reduces reality itself to an aspect
of the relationship of knowledge. It is not by chance that what we are
dealing with here is the traditional schema of the idealist formulation, nor
that it has its ultimate corollary in the identification between
objectification and alienation. If one wants to follow Marx, in his
refutation of this identity, one must dispense with the problematic which
necessarily goes along with it. It is not by chance that the existential
analytic has always rejected this identification, since it considers the
opposition between subject and object to be a *secondary and derived*
phenomenon whose validity is confined to the institutive field of particular
(cognitive) relations. Human reality is not first subject and then object. It
is not even a relationship between a subject and an object of
contemporaneous origin, because it is co-presence of alterities which have
to be recognised in what they are, either men or things, and not objectified
from the standpoint of a relationship implying ontological privilege to the
subjective pole.

With regard to the second question, it should be noted that if
reciprocity has a place among elements whose mode of being is that of a
subject-object relation, then the relation of reciprocity will not be able to
avoid taking the form of a subject-object relationship. In consequence, for
each and every member, all other members and reciprocity itself become
an object for a subject. But in this case, the project of himself which every
member undertakes in the form of an objectification of his own
subjectivity, will involve a totalization of the totality of all other members
and of reciprocity itself. If this totalization is to have its own origin and
foundation in the subjectivity of the individual member, it will have to lay
claim to erecting this subjectivity upon the constitutive and normative
principle of reciprocity itself, but that is equivalent to a pure and
straightforward negation of that principle both in its structural and in its
normative aspects. Reciprocity only has an institutive and normative
meaning if it implies that the individual recognises in the moment of his
project the real alterity of every other member in regard to the
compossibility of their projects. If this is not the case, reciprocity always
and in every case becomes negative reciprocity or the reciprocity of
struggle, either in Hegel's or Hobbes' sense, and is resoluble only in its
dissolution in the unity of the absolute State or absolute Knowledge.

And this is the route which Sartre follows. He starts by recognising that reciprocity is 'that which a man expects of another man when their relation is a human one.' (p. 253) But then conceiving the human elements in the reciprocal relation as subjects objectifying themselves in a context of scarcity, i.e., in accordance with egocentric totalizations, he ends up by making reciprocity negative in every instance. As a result, positive and de-alienating reciprocity can only be attained through the unity of the group as *sameness of its members,* as that 'fusion' and 'apocalypse' in which 'every third grasps the Other as the same.' (p. 425) Positive reciprocity is equivalent, therefore, to the negation of reciprocity in this sameness. Whence stems the view that multiplicity is condemned to be the inauthenticity of seriality — whence also the relegation of 'agreement' to the impotence of dispersal and alienation, the rejection of electoral procedures as mystification, and the theorisation of the 'chief' as guarantor of the unity of the group.

6. *Objectification and Alienation*

In *Being and Nothingness* Sartre writes: 'My freedom is alienated in the presence of the Other's pure subjectivity which founds my objectivity'; [8] and in the *Critique:* 'alienation, in being the real and rigorous process internal to the system, produces itself in *alterity* and by virtue of it.' (p. 644) Objectification, as that which is carried out by a subject, is in every case a source of alienation. And if we look closely at the matter, it is so under two different aspects: as the externalisation of self on the part of the subject who is alienated by his objectification of himself in something other, and as a result of a work of objectification which the subject carries out to the detriment of others. In *Being and Nothingness* the first aspect is dominant, in the *Critique,* the second. We can understand the reason for this if we reflect on the equivalence presented in the later work between the instituted praxis and objectification, not to mention the primary role granted in it to the mediation of worked-upon material.

But here we have to clarify Sartre's position on a decisive point. As long as he maintains that alienation is founded as a possibility in the relationship of alterity, there is nothing to take exception to. In this case he does no more than affirm one of the fundamental conditions of the possibility of alienation itself by way of denouncing the Hegelian and pseudo-Marxist mystification which tends to make alienation the product of the development of a single principle, whether spiritual or material. The demystification consists in this case in restoring the phenomenon of alienation to the field of its real possibility and that means to the complex of relations which constitute the social world. But when Sartre maintains that alienation is bound to alterity *to the extent to which alterity is equivalent to objectification,* his discourse comes to be implicitly conducted in a Hegelian key, and alterity, instead of foundation of possibility, becomes the necessitating element of alienation in the objective.

There is a passage in the *Critique* where Sartre explicitly poses the problem of the relations between his theory of alienation and those of Hegel and of Marx. After having put forward the thesis that the theft of the end wreaked by Others to the detriment of the action in which the individual objectifies himself, is the fundamental source of alienation, and having presented the experience of such a theft as the first experience of necessity (i.e., of the irreparable nature of this loss through theft), he says:

The man who looks upon his work, who recognises it as his in every way, and yet at the same time does not recognise it at all; who can say both: 'That isn't what I wanted' and 'I understand that it's what I made and that I couldn't have made it any other,' the man who is cast back upon his pre-fabricated being by his own free praxis and who recognises himself in the former as in the latter, this is the man who grasps, in an immediate dialectical movement, necessity as *freedom's destiny in exteriority.* Shall we say that this is a form of alienation? Certainly, since *it returns to him as Other.* All the same, we must make a distinction: alienation in the Marxist sense of the term begins with exploitation. So shall we revert to Hegel, who makes alienation a permanent feature of objectification, whatever form the latter takes? Yes and no. We should, in fact, bear in mind that the original relationship of the praxis as totalization to materiality as passivity obliges man to objectify himself in an environment which is not his own and to present an inorganic totality as his own objective reality. It is the relationship of interiority to exteriority which originally constitutes the praxis as the organism's relation to its material environment; and there is no doubt that man — from the moment at which his aim ceases to be that of simply reproducing his life and becomes that of producing the sum of goods that allow the reproduction of life — discovers himself as *Other* in the world of objectivity, totalized matter, as inert objectification perpetuating itself through inertia, is, in effect, *a non-man* and even, if you like, a *counter-man.* Each one of us spends his life inscribing in things his evil-doing image, which fascinates and misleads him if he tries to understand himself *in it,* although he is all the time none other than the totalizing movement which ends in *this* objectification. (p. 285)

Here alienation is presented as the necessary relationship (that of 'destiny') between freedom and exteriority. The relation between man and the world of things and others is presented as 'a relation between interiority and exteriority,' whose outcome is to accord a metaphysical privilege to interiority on the model of the privilege given to the for-itself relative to the in-itself in *Being and Nothingness.* It is the typically Cartesian position of the radical heterogeneity of exteriority and interiority functioning as the ground for privileging the latter. On this basis, Sartre can affirm that man 'discovers himself as Other in the world of objectivity': objectivity is as such alteration and alienation. [9]

7. *Existentialism, Marxism and Hegelianism*

The fundamental tendency of the Marxist theory of alienation is towards the possibility of its removal. If this were not so, revolutionary praxis and the project of restoring man to his humanity would lose all sense. That is, it presupposes that the on-going existence and ineliminability of the relation of alterity remain compatible with de-alienation, which would not be possible if alterity, objectification and alienation coincided with each other. But this thesis that alienation is eliminable should not be confused with another, often presented alongside it but in no way implied by it, that the *definitive* elimination of alienation is the elimination of the capitalist mode of production. This is by no means to suggest that this latter thesis is not Marxist but simply that it is not necessarily implied by the former, with two consequences: 1) that to accept the former does not imply accepting the latter; 2) that the rejection of the latter does not involve abandoning the former.

That is — if one is convinced that the second thesis cannot be sustained, if, that is, one is convinced that alienation will not be automatically and definitively eliminated once capitalist relations of production have been eliminated — that by no means demands a rejection of the first thesis and with it a more or less disguised return to the Hegelian theory of the coincidence between alienation and objectification. This is because the rejection of the second thesis simply means abandoning the conviction that alienation can be definitively eliminated at one fell stroke; it does not mean abandoning the idea that it is eliminable, nor above all, the commitment to eliminating it. But the return to the thesis that alienation is identical with objectification implies that alienation is ineliminable and thus that every de-alienating praxis is meaningless.

It is not easy to clarify the position of existentialism in regard to this problem because there is no univocal point of reference, as there is for Marx. It is absolutely impossible to account for contemporary existentialism merely in terms of its performing a Kierkegaardian function. Speaking in the most general way, one can say that primitive existentialism has denied the Hegelian reduction of alterity to objectivity and has thus denied the possibility of a conclusive removal of alienation in a final process of re-absorption of objectivity by the Subject; but in spite of this anti-Hegelianism, it has adhered to, and even reinforced, the Hegelian thesis to the effect that alienation is *historically* ineliminable, which means that, at least in this respect, existentialism has remained a prisoner of Hegelianism. Moreover, it also means that if existentialism is to be definitively liberated from Hegelianism it must be by way of a re-thinking of Marxism — a re-thinking that must be carried out, however, in the light of the existentialist warning as to the mystificatory nature of the Hegelian doctrine that alienation can be *conclusively* removed. This is a doctrine that has its precise equivalent in the second thesis illustrated above according to which the elimination of the capitalist mode of production would involve the conclusive and definitive elimination of alienation.

Nevertheless, Sartre shows a way to the confluence of existentialism and Marxism which is a valid one — but only on condition that the re-thinking of the two positions, so far from implying a return to the residual Hegelian elements they have in common, is rather directed towards a fusion of the conditions which each of these philosophies has established in its turn as essential to the elimination of such residues. Just before he died Merleau-Ponty wrote that the moment had come for studying Marx as a 'classic'; the same can certainly be said for Hegel. In fact, Merleau-Ponty did not mean 'classic' in the sense of something perfectly finished or in the sense of its being a model. An edifice is 'classic' when it is a collection of superb ruins, when it has *proved capable* of surviving and becoming 'epoch making' precisely because its structure is dissipated in the 'relics' and themes its own life has provided, when it is no longer occupied by its owner and therefore closed to strangers but thrown open to all by the very fact of its triumphant collapse into ruin. It thereupon becomes the property of each and everyone to take from or make of it what he will, entrusting to others who come after to do the same.

8. *The Possibility and Impossibility of De-alienation*

The most serious charge to be made against the theory of alienation expounded in the *Critique* is precisely that it has proceeded to re-think Marxism (after the sclerosis of Stalinism) in terms of an existentialism which is constructed in such a way that it reproduces within Marxism the Hegelian identification of alienation with objectification against which the Marxist critique was so explicitly and rigorously directed. What Sartre has focused on in the Marxist theory of alienation is the, for him unacceptable, thesis of its definitive removal. Having considered this thesis, as part of the articulated unity of the Marxist edifice, to be inseparable from the anti-Hegelian insistence on the hard and fast difference between objectification and alienation, he has been led to reject this latter condition as part and parcel of his rejection of the former thesis. He thus falls back into the Hegelian position of claiming that there is the closest possible tie between objectification and alienation. In reality, however, the theory of the 'easy' and definitive eliminability of alienation is a suggestion in Marx which derives from the Hegelian identification of objectification with alienation and from the consequent possibility of eschatological resolution of the object in the subject.

But Sartre's recourse to the identification of alienation with objectification is weighed down by further consequences which stem from the existentialist context in which his theory operates – a context characterised by the fact that in it objectification coincides with real alterity. For existentialism in general the relationship of alterity is a relation between ineliminable realities and not one between a subject and an object at the mercy of that subject. So that if, in Hegelian fashion, one makes objectification one with alienation, while at the same time presuming, in existentialist fashion, that objectivity and real alterity coincide, alienation is deprived of the possibility of its ultimate removal – which it preserves in Hegel, where objectivity is in the last analysis 'semblance' – and assumes instead the irreducible character of alterity. Then the subject is placed in a position of not-being-able-not-to-objectify-himself in an alterity, which, by the very fact of its being objectification, is alienation demanding removal and by the very fact of its being real alterity is irremovable alienation. This is the significance of Sartre's words:

> Each one of us spends his life inscribing in things his evil-doing image, which fascinates and misleads him if he tries to understand himself *in it*, athough he is all the time none other than the totalizing movement which ends in *this* objectification. (p. 285)

The *paradoxical* nature of the human situation is thus defined in the *Critique* by the co-presence of the demand for de-alienation and the impossibility of that de-alienation. This *zero point* is what Sartre defines as *necessity* or *destiny*: 'freedom's destiny in exteriority.' A conception of this kind will inevitably have important consequences for Sartre's theory of society, sovereignty and State.

9. *Reciprocity, Objectification, Class*

The first thing to be noted is that the fundamental form of alienation as 'theft of the end' implies the simultaneous presence of two factors: worked-upon material in which the objectification of the subject inscribes itself; and the other person, who in turn objectifies himself and thus involves the worked-upon material of the first subject in a totalizing project of his own, thus inverting the finality of his work in counter-finality, in a finality directed against its original author. Clearly the second factor, though being the determinate one in the social environment, presupposes the first, which is the real and true stimulus.

All the same, from the social standpoint, the determining element is the presence of the Other. Hence the *Critique's* pervasive tendency to identify alienation with multiplicity. This is in reality one of the most cumbersome elements of the Hegelian inheritance which Sartre arrives at through primitive existentialism and its contempt for the 'crowd' (which is then the Hegelian *formlose Masse*). In conceiving existence as 'freedom's destiny in exteriority,' as self-objectifying/self-alienating interiority in omni-comprehensive totalizations, Sartre has no alternative but to interpret reciprocity as a struggle carried on in alienation. As long as multiplicity persists, alienation will persist in the dispersion of exteriority and of reciprocal struggle. Hence Sartre defines multiplicity as seriality, and seriality as a destiny of impotence and alienation.

Sartre draws several conclusions from this, two of them contrary to Marxism: 1) alienation is as old as the twin factors producing it (social alterity and worked-upon material); it does not appear only at the stage of capitalist exploitation; 2) class as a community of the 'status quo' is purely serial and incapable of functioning as the protagonist in the process of de-alienation. Two other conclusions are of Marxist inspiration, and therefore directed against the bourgeoisie: 1) social multiplicity, in so far as it is seriality, can constitute neither the origin nor the foundation of sovereignty; 2) historical progress is entrusted to groups, which after having liquidated the serial impotence of the classes within which they form, are struggling to liquidate their exploitation by other groups.

Sartre's polemic against the Marxist conception of class as capable of functioning as historical agent, or directly as the protagonist of history, derives not only from his devaluation of the economic and material structure on which class rests, in consequence of which it is instead the individual (and the group as unity) whom he makes suitable to function as the bearer of the historical dialectic, but also — and perhaps above all — from the profound devaluation within his theory of all that which is collectivity, multiplicity, seriality — that is, of all that which possesses a dimension of submission, of being-object, of exteriority. The effect of his conception of *reciprocity as reciprocal objectification on the part of subjects destined to interiority* is the identification of alienation with objectification. *De-alienation thus becomes possible only through the suppression of objectification, which in being a feature of the reciprocal relation of multiplicity, can only be suppressed through the suppression of multiplicity itself.*

As a result, Sartre presents alienation as 'mediated relation to the other and to the instruments of labour, on the serial terrain and as the serial mode of co-existence' (p. 154); and de-alienation as the ultimate objective of the group in its 'double undertaking' of 'snatching from worked-upon material its inhuman power' and of 'snatching man from his *statut* of alterity, which makes of him a product of his product, in order to transform him, *when molten* and by means of the appropriate procedures, into a *product of the group* — that is, as long as the group is freedom, into a product of himself. (pp. 638-9)

10. *Group, Reciprocity, Unity, Sameness*

The establishment of the group in combat as 'group-in-fusion' is the apocalyptic moment in which, in the dissolution of objectification, alienation disappears. In the series the object stands in opposition as the crushing element of human multiplicity; in the group-in-fusion it is *interiorised* as the common objective. When this occurs, unification is no longer imposed from outside because 'unity is unification *from within* of the plurality of totalizations. It is *from within* that it denies this plurality as a co-existence of distinct acts and affirms the uniqueness of collective activity.' (p. 424) And further on: 'This re-interiorisation of the multiplicity as transition from discontinuous quantity to intensity, results in the dissolution of *number* as relation of exteriority between discrete elements (between singular totalizations) [. . .] Thus, the group, to the extent that it re-absorbs number, is non-quantifiable multiplicity.' (p. 424) And again: 'in the we the multiple is not suppressed but disqualified.' (p. 530) So that 'what was formerly Other appears as the *same*' (p. 425) and *reciprocity* reveals itself in what it really is: 'ubiquity as a unity simultaneously excluding both the multiple and the identical' (p. 530), where the identity excluded is the simple negation of the undifferentiated multiplicity of series.

But the most striking aspect of this theorization of authentic multiplicity in terms of its being sameness and ubiquity lies in the political application Sartre gives it. That the unity of the group in combat is realised 'from within' means that 'each (synthesis) asserts itself *here* in freedom as *the* ongoing totalization and establishes in practical terms all the others as *it-self* (either by posing as regulative, or by receiving its own order from some other third, which is to say, by freely producing the same and unique order *here)*. On the other hand, the interiorisation of practical unity brings with it, as we have seen, the interiorisation of multiplicity, which becomes the *means of* common action.' (p. 424) There are two serious political implications in this: 1) the first lies in the equivalent status accorded the personal totalization and the totalization carried out by 'any third, whoever it may be'; 2) the second lies in the use to which unified multiplicity is put in common action. These are, indeed, the traditional corollaries to any political theory those appeal is to the function of unity in mass, and the function of efficiency in unity.

In the group-in-fusion alterity disappears and with it the possibility of alienation: 'And similarly for this third the action of the group, as a total praxis, is not primarily "other action" or alienation in the totality, but it is the action of everyone insofar as it is freely itself, both for him and for any other third.' (p. 418) And again:

> This new and crucial structure of mediated reciprocity can be characterised as follows: *in the third I see myself coming to the group,* and what I see is only lived objectivity. Hitherto, the objectivity of an act appeared *to the Others* or was reflected for me in the object produced. In the group-in-fusion, the third is my interiorised objectivity. (p. 406)

Nowhere else is Sartre so explicit: the source of alienation as seriality and remission in things is provided by 'objectivity' in its 'appearing to Others' and in its self-reflection in the 'produced object.' De-alienation, therefore, implies interiorisation of objectivity in the extra-individual unity of the group for which objectivity is none other than the interiority of the group within itself, the 'objective' as internal finality.

11. *The Instant and Zero Point of Alienation*

It is more than clear from what we have said so far how de-alienation is tied to the persistence of the group. In the group, multiplicity 'negates itself in each of the acts which constitute it' (p. 418), but this fundamental condition of de-alienation is not only wanting in any permanent character it also includes the dialectical conditions of its own dissolution. The group, says Sartre, 'is formed against alienation, insofar as the latter replaces the free practical field of the individual by the field of the practico-inert; but it is not in a position to escape alienation any more than the individual is, and for this reason, it falls back into seriality.' (pp. 634-6)

As de-alienation sprang from the interiorisation of objectivity, the return to alienation takes place in the form of 'entire transition into the objectified being.' (p. 636) In this way, the group 'which arose in order to dissolve series in the living synthesis of a community finds the barrier to its spatio-temporal development in the insurpassable *statut* of organic individuality and finds its being, outside itself, in the passive determinations of organic exteriority which it wanted to suppress.' (p. 635)

What this means, simply, is that de-alienation has the temporal dimension of an *instant;* it is the *zero point* of the paradoxical confrontation between freedom and necessity. The group 'is not in a position to escape alienation any more than is the individual' because it submits to 'the insurpassable *statut* of organic individuality.' As we have seen, this *statut* constitutes the original foundation of alienation in that it consigns the individual to 'freedom's destiny in exteriority.' De-alienation could be definitive if Sartre was moving on a level that was purely and simply Hegelian; then the group's interiorisation of objectivity in its own unity would have the character of definitive de-alienation which consciousness acquires in Hegel when in its own unity it realises the interiorisaton of every instance of alienation by the object. But as we have already had occasion to make clear, while Sartre's conception of the relations between man and external reality in terms of an objectifying subject is Hegelian, he anchors objectification to the existentialist concept of alterity as the irreducible real, with the result that the pull of the group towards de-alienation meets with an insuperable resistence in the ineliminability of the organic alterity of worked-upon material. There is a zero point at which the maximum de-alienating force of the group-in-fusion encounters the minimum, but irreducible, resistence of the practico-inert alterity. This is the starting point for a gradual process of inversion wherein the group, passing from the oath, through organisation to institution, falls back into the alienation of series.

12. *The Circular and the Tragic in History*

Sartre would have us note that the enquiry conducted in the first volume of the *Critique* has a 'formal' character, while the problem of the 'profound meaning of History' is to be deferred to the second volume. On the basis of the first volume, however, one cannot help noting the strongly pessimistic, and in this aspect anti-Hegelian and anti-Marxist, conception of history it offers us. Even if the group carries its power of fusion to the point of unity, the wall of alienation cannot be scaled and the circularity which extends from the series to the group will join up with the circularity which carries the group back to series, in an inexorable process of double circularity. (pp. 636–40)

This notion of 'circularity,' even if held to by Sartre 'in the context of frameworks, curvatures, structures and formal conditions which constitute the *milieu formel* in which concrete history must necessarily produce itself ' (p. 637), operates at a level which in a certain sense is beyond that of optimism or pessimism in that it reinstates a tragic conception of history very close to that given us by a Heidegger or a Löwith. [10]

There is something 'insuperable' in the sequence of human history, a 'destiny' which attaches to the exteriority of freedom, a necessity adhering in the *statut* of *insurpassability* and *return*. [11] Says Sartre:

> This insurpassable conflict between individual and community, which oppose each other, define themselves in terms of the one against the other, and refer each one to the other as its profound truth, is naturally betrayed by new contradictions within the organised group; and these contradictions are expressed in a new transformation of the group; the organisation is transformed into a hierarchy; the oath gives birth to the institution. (p. 567)

This insurpassable element in the *statut* of relations between man and the concrete situation in which he makes history is consistently expressed by Sartre in terms of 'necessity':

> *Necessity* as the apodeictic structure of dialectical experience resides neither in the free development of interiority nor in the inert dispersion of exteriority; it imposes itself, in the name of an inevitable moment, in the interiorisation of the external and the exteriorisation of the internal. (p. 157)

Obviously this is not a case of 'metaphysical' necessity, susceptible to material content and thus able to be used in prediction. (pp. 129, 134) Here the necessity is 'formal' in the sense that it concerns the structure of existence as relation between interiorisation and exteriorisation. The foundation of every necessitating element within this structure lies in the fact that interiority cannot remove itself from its relationship to exteriority.

In the double circularity between series and group, 'necessity,' as the ineliminable presence of objective alterity, takes two consecutive forms: 1) in the establishment of the group it is the necessity of eliminating the necessity imposed by the objective alterity of the practico-inert (i.e., the impossibility of accepting the impossible conditions of life imposed by determinate socio-economic conditions) (p. 377); 2) the necessity that the group again dissolves in the process which, by way of organisation and institutionalisation, leads to series; this process has its necessity in the confrontation with the non-eliminated (because ineliminable) alterity of the alienating permanence of the practico-inert. (p. 638)

The insuperable presence of the practico-inert (which is reducible but not to the point of elimination) is the original necessity which gives rise to the necessity of establishing the group and, at the same time, to its 'ontological check.' The group interiorises the objective necessity, but not being able to annul it (because the object is not simple 'appearance' or 'nullity' as Marx accuses Hegel of making it), the group submits to the accumulative process of 'petrification' carried out by the interiorised necessity within it, and in this way the double circularity closes ' to the extent itself that the necessity of freedom implies the progressive alienation of freedom in necessity.' (p. 638) The practico-inert infects the entire process with necessity: it first introduces the necessity of setting up the group; then, because the group as far as possible resists its resolution into series, it forces the freedom which animates it to alienate itself progressively in necessity in the form of a progressive petrification. The double circularity is therefore made up of two movements: the first of ever more intense de-alienation through the fusion of series in group, and the second of ever more intense re-alienation through the petrification of group in series. At the centre, the zero point, lies the instant of paradoxical confrontation between alienation and de-alienation. The whole process is regulated by a necessity for which the definitive ineliminability of the practico-inert is its 'bedrock,' its eternal epicentre.

13. *Necessity, Terror, Complete Freedom*

The political consequences of such a conception are as clear as they are serious. Freedom here becomes possible only in the *'instantaneity'* and unity of the group, which means that *it is unthinkable as a permanent institution.* Beyond the apocalypse of the fusion, necessity reigns. In political terms, this necessity becomes extrinsic in the form of violence — either the violence of the group-in-fusion against external necessity (the impossibility of living under certain conditions), or the violence of the group's retreat under the impact of interiorised necessity, which takes the form of progressive serialisation. In the first case, the violence is violence directed against the violence of *oppression*; in the second case it is the *fraternity-of-terror.* (p. 689)

Human multiplicity is freed of alienation only in the 'instant' of its negation in the unity of the group, a negation which takes an instrumental form in that it effects the interiorisation of the object. Outside this instant, there is nothing but alienation: either alienation in the objective necessity of the practico-inert or alienation in the subjective necessity of the group's unity. In order to escape the necessity of the practico-inert and its alienation, man has no other alternative but to entrust himself to the organised unity of the group, thus alienating himself in it. In this way 'the necessity of freedom implies the progressive alienation of freedom in necessity.' (p. 638) In order to escape violence in the form of oppression, man's only recourse is to violence in the form of the fraternity-of-terror, where terror is 'itself the bond of fraternity,' (p. 689) In order to avoid alienating himself in the slavery of the practico-inert and its series, he must transform himself into 'communal individual' and submit to 'the alienation of freedom in his very praxis itself.' (p. 470)

At this point Sartre's thought manifests one of the features of the theory of alienation which Marx had isolated as belonging to the Hegelian point of view, which is that alienation, besides being negative, is also positive; the alienation which is positive is the alienation in freedom, in the group as *liberté plenière.* (p. 285) Man has no alternative but to choose between alienation in things and alienation in the group, between the dictatorship of things and the 'dictatorship of Freedom.' (p. 744) Reciprocity as *peaceful coexistence* finds no place in the *Critique.*

Sartre's latest theory does not allow for a consolidated yet at the same time positive multiplicity. Positive reciprocity is coincident with the dissolution of the many in the unity of the group; all other multiplicity is negative reciprocity. So that for the group which is in the process of congelation the maintenance of its unity is the justification for the terror on which it bases fraternity; it is a terror which neither *discriminates between its acts* nor confronts the *problem of their limits* except in terms of the 'right of violence which each has over the other.' (p. 456) Above all, it fails to contemplate the possibility of opposition: 'the traitors, in fact, are the minority by definition.' (p. 456) This viewpoint on minorities, which Merleau-Ponty in *Humanisme et terreur* regarded as the necessary presupposition of his attempt to justify the Moscow trials (an attempt subsequently and decisively abandoned) is reiterated by Sartre in the text dedicated to the memory of his late friend. In 'Merleau-Ponty vivant' we read:

> In reality, with this tiny phrase which made so much noise that everyone today accepts it as a fundamental truth, and which has a universal value beyond the limits assigned to it by its author, Merleau-Ponty has done nothing more but apply what the war had taught him to other circumstances: we are not to be judged merely on the basis of our intentions. [12]

'What the war had taught him . . . .' Perhaps the *Critique* contains many things that the Algerian war had taught Sartre; perhaps the reformulation of Marxism in terms of scarcity, misery and starvation − and thus of Manichean hatred − has its roots in a historico-political context which is not that of the Soviet Union, despite the fact that Sartre has espoused Khruschev's cause. [13] A further reflection of such an attitude can be found in Sartre's autobiographical declaration in 'Merleau-Ponty vivant' where, referring to the events of 1950, he says: 'To the bourgeoisie I have consecrated a hatred that will come to an end only when I do.' [14]

Perhaps the weakest of the arguments supporting Sartre's theory of the group as unity is the assumption that unity induces a level of efficiency superior to that which multiplicity can attain by any 'agreement,' 'consent' or 'contract.' But history has repeatedly given the lie to this assumption. Not to mention the fact, moreover, that Sartre's integral unity is an abstract ideal. For it is not limited to the hypothesis of an objective unity of intent but postulates a subjective unity of individuals in a communal individual, an integral fusion. In the group in combat 'there is not *one* understanding, nor *ten,* nor *thirty* : this understanding is the same *everywhere*; it has no numerical determination [. . .] My understanding is only mine to the extent that it is that of my neighbour; and the multiplicity of identity disappears *insofar* as every understanding implies and realises all the others.' (p. 530) But alas, anyone who has had experience of combative groups which form themselves 'as molten' knows that a unity of agreement of this kind is a mere figure of speech. [15]

14. *Conclusions*

We are now in a position to shed a little light on the question posed at the beginning of this examination of the concept of alienation which is found in the *Critique* − which means, in effect, that we can reveal the equivocal nature of the concept and of the set of meanings which this underlying equivocation produces in the full context of the work. It is an equivocation which faithfully mirrors that which is fundamental to Sartre's position in relation to the complex of problems brought about by his attempt to re-think the relations between Hegelianism, existentialism and Marxism.

The following points have been established as basic to Sartre's position on alienation: 1) alienation has its foundation in the particular *statut* of the relations between man and the world; 2) this is the *statut* of a consciousness inseparably tied to a materiality in a relationship of reciprocal and insuperable ontological incompatibility; 3) to the alienating necessity which the material world brings with it to the detriment of consciousness, there corresponds the necessity of de-alienation which consciousness brings with it to the detriment of matter; the relationship between the two is inversely proportional and irresoluble.

The alienating action of the material world on consciousness begets an opposition of consciousnesses which struggle among themselves on the material foundation provided by diffused scarcity. The action of this multiplicity of consciousnesses on the material is de-alienating when it takes the form of a resolution of multiple consciousness in the unity of the group. Since the 'presence' of the material world is an ineliminable *statut*, it means that on the political and historical plane the dilemma between alienation and de-alienation can never present itself in the form of *alternatives,* but only in that of *alternation.*

The ontological status of *alternation* is at the root of the equivocation fundamental to Sartre's position. It is very well expressed at the point where Sartre, after having questioned whether his position involves a return to Hegel, answers: 'Yes and no.' (p. 285) For Marx, de-alienation simply involves a change in the basis of the relations between man, the Other and natural reality. For Sartre it implies, at the most, the suppression, in the form of interiorisation, of the objective side of this relationship. The existentialist impossibility of this suppression has the effect of making Sartre turn on the one hand back to Hegel (in demanding the suppression) while on the other hand remaining faithful to Marx (in recognising its impossibility). *Sartre is right when he rejects the 'ease' with which alienation in Marx comes to be suppressed (i.e., the identification of this with the suppresssion of its capitalist basis), but he is wrong in believing that the way of rendering de-alienation less easy lies via a return to the Hegelian identification between alienation and objectification – the only deviation from this path being the existentialist recognition of the impossibility of a conclusive reabsorption of the object in the subject.* In other words, Hegelianism existentially decapitated of its optimistic outcome – that is to say, existentially corrected *from within* – does not constitute a possible corrective to the insufficiencies of Marxism because these have their source in positions which presuppose our going beyond the Hegelian framework and its conception of man as self-objectifying, self-alienating consciousness.

On the historical plane, the equivocation of Sartre's stance produces an ambiguous situation in that the movement of his thought is made to depend on the extent to which scarcity is ineliminable. Very generally, one can say that since it is scarcity which renders reciprocity inhuman (p. 208), the restoration of relations of reciprocity to their humanity, which is the objective of the socialist revolution, calls for the elimination of scarcity. Looked at in this way, scarcity takes on a contingent character. (pp. 200-2) On the other hand, since it is through scarcity that the relation of alterity impinges on social man, and this relation is founded in the *statut* itself of human reality insofar as this is a relation to materiality, scarcity can be seen as 'the necessity of our contingency and the contingency of our necessity.' (p. 202)

In this sense, Sartre sees scarcity as 'the fundamental relation of *our* History.' (p. 201) By insisting as he does on the fact of its being 'ours,' Sartre hopes to leave the way open to conceiving a surpassing of 'our History' (which then becomes a prehistory in Marx's sense); but on the other hand, the inclination to make *Capital* simply a denunciation of a particular moment in the relations of scarcity, which are by their nature of a kind to extend to all History (p. 224), including that of the present socialist countries (p. 219), allows the bedrock of 'necessity,' on which scarcity as the foundation of 'our History' rests, to remain visible beneath the appearance of 'contingency.' In fact, with the disappearance of scarcity, 'our very character as *men* would disappear and with it the singularity of our History. So that any man alive today must recognise in this fundamental contingency the necessity (imposed on him over thousands of years, and very directly today) of his being exactly that which he is.' (p. 201)

In this way, a fully socialist society, in the sense of one that had definitively eliminated the burden of scarcity from human relations of reciprocity, ends up being 'idealist' to the extent that scarcity reveals itself not only as contingent, but as the necessity of this contingency. Thus for us a society of this kind remains beyond our experience and comprehension:

As soon as there will exist *for everyone* a margin of *real* freedom beyond the production of life, Marxism will have lived out its span; a philosophy of freedom will take its place. But we have no means, no intellectual instrument, no concrete experience which allows us to conceive of this freedom or of this philosophy. (p 34, PM)

APPENDIX 1

Existentialism and Marxism*

1

The dialogue between existentialism and Marxism was initiated in France in the particular cultural and political climate that established itself immediately after the war. Its first relevant texts were *Existentialism and Humanism* by Sartre (a lecture delivered in 1946 and which, in presenting existentialism as a humanism *engagée*, appealed to Marxism to interpret its own commitment as that of a humanism freed of every materialist dogma) and *Humanism and Terror* by Merleau-Ponty (which appeared in 1947 with the significant subtitle, *Essay on the Communist Problem*). [1]

The last important text of what was by then an extended dialogue is the shorthand report of the *controverse* which occurred in Paris on 7 December 1961 — before a spectacularly large, public audience — between the existentialists, Sartre and Hyppolite, on the one hand, and the orthodox Marxists, Garaudy, Orcel and Vigier, on the other. [2] Unfortunately, one voice was missing, and that was of a principal participant in this important political and cultural interchange — an interchange, which in the course of its almost 20 years history had been rich in unpredictable volte-faces and bitter confrontations that had occurred, as it were, in symphony with the internal and international events accompanying it and which it entered into with impassioned commitment. The missing voice, of course, was that of Merleau-Ponty, who a few months previously, on 4 May, to be precise, had died suddenly at the age of 53. His intervention would have been of great interest, since his book *The Adventures of the Dialectic* (1955) posed for the first time the problem of the relations between existentialism and Marxism in terms of the dialectic. [3] Moreover, *The Adventures*, in the extreme harshness of its attack on Sartre's articles on *The Communists and Peace* (which appeared between 1952 and 1954 in *Les Temps modernes*),

* From: *Rivista di filosofia*, LIV, 1963, pp. 164-190

highlighted the point of friction between two lines of approach, the one, with its foundations quite close to Marxism, adopted by Merleau-Ponty himself, the other adopted by Sartre, at a greater distance from it. The symmetrically opposite directions in which they tended find their ultimate expressions respectively in Merleau-Ponty's last book *Signs,* and Sartre's *Critique de la raison dialectique,* both of which appeared in 1960. [4]

But the expression 'dialogue between existentialism and Marxism in France' needs to be made more precise in three important respects. The first concerns the term 'dialogue.' One should remember that the debate has never taken the form of a confrontation of two opposing positions. There were, in fact, several levels of discourse, important enough in themselves to render the dialogue incomprehensible unless their various influences are taken into account. One of them we can define generically as 'liberal.' Its case was well presented by Raymond Aron, who had at one time been close to Sartre. (It was he, who in 1932 on returning from Berlin, spoke with him for the first time of phenomenology and the German Kierkegaard-*Renaissance* and who also played a part together with Merleau-Ponty in the original editing of *Les Temps modernes.*) Aron subsequently became sufficiently distant from Sartre for us to find him writing in 1956: 'My ideas are opposed to yours in every respect.' [6] In his book, *The Opium of the Intellectuals* (1955), Aron made a profound attack on the positions of *Humanism and Terror,* [7] and it would seem with some success — at least if one is to give any credit to Simone de Beauvoir, who in her article 'Merleau-Ponty et le pseudo-sartrisme,' written in defence of Sartre (who did not himself reply) against the attack on him in *The Adventures,* charged Merleau-Ponty with having made Aron's thesis his own. [8]

A second, rather more important and insidious voice in the discussion can be identified as coming from the Marxist but non-communist sector of French culture. This is not a reference, as might be imagined, to the politically organised sector of right-wing socialist opposition to the PCF, but rather to the disorganised and fluid grouping of intellectuals and politicos who gave birth to a left-wing opposition, for the most part of Trotskyite inspiration. One of these, for example, was Claude Lefort, who in *Les Temps modernes* attacked the thesis maintained by Sartre in *The Communists and Peace* regarding the relations between proletariat and party, accusing it of counter-revolutionary Stalinism. [9] Another was Naville who defended the Marxist position in the discussions that followed the 1946 lecture *Existentialism is a Humanism,* and who can be found ten years later levelling the same charge of ultra-Bolshevism as Merleau-Ponty levelled against Sartre in *The Adventures.* [10] We should look at the accusation of Trotskyism levelled by Lukács against Merleau-Ponty in his book *Existentialisme ou marxisme?* (1947) [11] from this angle. The basic thesis of the Trotskyites is this: the ground for an encounter between existentialism and Marxism can only be Trotskyism, and never the Stalinism of the PCF.

A third and notably important voice was that of the Catholic left. When Sartre arrived in Paris in 1925, to attend the *Ecole Normale Supérieure,* he came into contact with Mounier. An intelligent biography of Sartre has made the following comment on Sartre's decisive change after the war: 'between the vocation of a Gide and that of Mounier – he had been quite familiar with the latter – Sartre has chosen Mounier.' [12] Now, Mounier, even in 1947, had held that 'the conciliation of Marx with Kierkegaard' signalled the destiny of future philosophy.' [13] In what subsequently developed, however, one should keep in mind Sartre's prophecy in 1956 of a 'living Marxism' and not 'an open Marxism as *Esprit* would like.' [14]

The last disconcerting and enigmatic voice is that of the 'memory' of Paul Nizan. A contemporary of Sartre and Merleau-Ponty at the *Ecole Normale Supérieure,* Nizan concealed beneath the provocative appearance of the dandy a very aware and enduring participation in the tensions of his time. Coming from a religious background, he joined the PCF in 1927 (at the time when Sartre had become bored with hearing nothing but politics)[15] to leave it in contempt in 1939, on the occasion of the Russian-German treaty; shortly afterwards, he died at the front. In 1931 Nizan had published *Aden Arabie,* which denounced colonialism as the true face of capitalism. In 1960 the book was republished with Sartre as editor and the latter provided a long preface in which the idealised figure of his misunderstood friend is reinvoked in terms of bitterest self-criticism, (while Nizan was consummating his fleeting drama, Sartre 'apolitical and reluctant to make any commitment' – as he says of himself in the preface [16] – had but recently published *La Nausée*) and of exasperated defence against the infamous charges with which the PCF sought to bury Nizan's memory. Sartre sees in Nizan the incarnation of a revolutionary force and moral inflexibility lost forever in the compromises of the post-war period:

> His death marked the end of the world. After him the Revolution became constructive, the Left assented to everything, until one day in the fall of '58 it expired, murmuring a final 'yes.' Let us try to recall the time of hatred, of unappeased desire of destruction . . . [17]

It is enough to ponder on the pages in the *Critique* where the class struggle is given the extremist and menacing form of class hatred, in order to comprehend the influence of Nizan on the development of Sartre's thought. But does the Sartrean Nizan really correspond to the actual Nizan? Shortly before his death Merleau-Ponty returned to the figure of Nizan, looking at him in terms of the preface to *Aden Arabie* in which, he says, 'Sartre has for the first time adopted the tone of despair and rebellion.'[18] For Merleau-Ponty Sartre's re-evocation is an 'extraordinary rediscovery of the lost other.'

Nizan already knew what Sartre said much later. In the beginning is not play but need. We do not keep the world, or situations, or others at the length of our gaze like a spectacle; we are intermingled with them, drinking them in through all our pores. We are what is lacking in everything else; and within us, with the nothingness which is the centre of our being, a general principle of alienation is given. Before Sartre, Nizan lived this pantragicism, this flood of anguish which is also the flux of history.[19]

Nizan's limitation, concludes Merleau-Ponty, was the inverse of Sartre's: in 1939 he discovered the positive meaning of Sartre's reservations and non-commitment, that is to say, of the value of refusal and of the critical spirit.[20]

The second way in which the expression 'dialogue between existentialism and Marxism in France' needs to be made more precise concerns the national restriction of 'in France.' It should be noted, in fact, that another country on at least two occasions impinged upon the dialogue with significant effect: Hungary. The first occasion was the appearance of Lukács' work *Existentialisme ou marxisme?*; the second was the Hungarian revolt and the publication in *Les Temps modernes* of several articles on the revolt itself. These came out in a special number introduced by Sartre's article 'The Spectre of Stalin,'[21] which was destined to have great importance for the subsequent evolution of his political thought.

Lukács exercised an influence on French existentialism in two opposing directions, which are consecutively and respectively reflected in his writings which appeared before and after his passive acceptance of the condemnation of *History and Class Consciousness*, published in *Pravda*, 25 July 1924. The 'Western Marxism' – condemned by *Pravda* – with its polemic against the 'vulgar materialism' of Engels and the technicist determinism of Bukharin, gave rise to a discourse which French existentialism could not but take into account in its approach to Marxism. The methodological formulation which Weber (Lukács' teacher) had given to the problems of Marxism was still able to function as a *trait d'union* between existentialism and Marxism in 1955 when Merleau-Ponty devoted an entire chapter of *The Adventures* to 'Western Marxism.' But everything changed with the events of 1924, and *Existentialisme ou marxisme?*, which appeared in France in 1947, is one of the exemplary texts of the sectarian dogmatism of 'Eastern Marxism.' Existentialism is denounced in it as a hotch-potch, as the ideological crisis of the bourgeoisie in the epoch of imperialism, as the philosophical expression of fascism.[22] All the same, its judgement on Merleau-Ponty is much more benevolent than that on Sartre, even if it does accuse him of Trotskyism. As far as Sartre is concerned, Lukács' book produced only sarcastic reactions, and still does so in the *Critique*. [23] The only effects it produced on the world of French culture was those of encouraging a more sectarian communist theory. So that even as late as 1954, when Sartre had gone off to Vienna at the invitation of the communist leaders, J. Canapa branded him 'the philosopher of Saint-Germain-des-Prés,' and 'the intellectual-*flic*' – and thus earned for himself a description – by Sartre – as 'a man whose insolence is matched only by his own servility.' [24] This state of affairs within the cultural environment of the PCF was due, according to Sartre, to the fact that among French communists, 'the best keep quiet, and the silence is filled with the chattering of imbeciles.' [25] Relations between Sartre and the intellectuals of the PCF improved progressively as the years went by, to the point where Sartre was able to write: 'it is twelve years now that we have been debating with the communists, at first violently, later in friendship.' [26] All the same, as late as 1961, in a letter to Garaudy (who was one of the protagonists of the 'entente'), Sartre reproached the Marxists with coming to him 'with their arms laden with flowers and their heads full of wisdom.' [27]

The Hungarian revolt was a major counter-blow to relations between existentialism and Marxism in France. Without it one cannot explain Sartre's movement from the quasi-Stalinist positions of *The Communists and Peace* to the 'critical' stance adopted in the *Problem of Method* (1957). The article, 'The Spectre of Stalin,' which headed the special number of *Les Temps modernes* devoted to the Hungarian revolt, is an attack of unheard of violence against the Stalinism that prevailed both before and after the revolt, and above all on the mystificatory attitude of the French communists regarding the nature and the protagonists (who for Sartre were the workers, socialists but not Stalinists,) of the revolt. Merleau-Ponty, who for his part, in *Humanism and Terror,* espoused an explicit adhesion to Marxism as representing universal liberation in revolution, became disheartened after the Korean war by the nationalist orientation of international communism and came increasingly to adopt the role of third party to the dispute. Hence we have the paradoxical situation whereby the indignation of an almost communist Sartre in regard to the Soviet intervention is countered by the 'realistic' judgement of an almost anti-communist Merleau-Ponty. The effect was to provoke from Sartre the despairing observation: 'If the USSR is worth neither more nor less than capitalist England, then, in truth, there is nothing left for us but to cultivate our garden.' [28]

The third and most important element calling for precision concerns the semantic definition of the terms 'existentialism' and 'Marxism.' The particular difficulties encountered in the attempt to specify any kind of homogeneous *corpus* of existentialist doctrine have already been made abundantly clear. And yet the specification seems unavoidable if one wants to pose the problem of the confrontation between existentialism and Marxism at the theoretical level. All the more so in that the same issue presents itself no less seriously for Marxism. No one would maintain today that there exists a unitary and coherent body of Marx-Engels-Lenin-Stalin-Khruschev doctrine. Everyone today rejects the attempt to make Marxism correspond to the linear and coherent development of Soviet political events, through a development that was likewise linear and coherent. After Khruschev's seizure of power, not even the most dogmatic Stalinist would feel like subscribing to what Lukács wrote in *Existentialisme ou marxisme?*: 'the individual attitude in regard to the USSR becomes the touchstone not only in all questions of politics but also in problems of ideology.' [29] Thus it was that even the theorists of absolute truth were forced to bite on the bitter fruit of heresy.

But the situation was very different when Lukács' book posed the problem of the relations between existentialism and Marxism in terms of an alternative between the bloc whose theory and practice was that of Marxism's absolute truth, and the mere ideological 'truth' of existentialism as representative of the crisis of bourgeois society in the age of imperialism. It then seemed clear that existentialism had but two paths open to it: either to accept its own condemnation by renouncing any attempt to dispute with Marxism on equal terms, or else to establish the existentialist problematic as a critical tool for demolishing the bloc of adherents to the theory and practice of the absolute truth of Marx-Engels-Lenin-Stalinism. The French existentialists naturally opted for the latter alternative. Since it suddenly became quite clear that the Marx whom the dogmatists opposed to existentialism was in reality an Hegelianised Marx, Wahl, Hyppolite and Kojève directed their study of Hegel towards an existentialist reading of the young Hegel which skillfully exploited all the hermeneutic repertory proferred by that *Hegelrenaissance* in which Croce discerned an 'existentialistic renaissance' of Hegel. [30] In this way, existentialism tended to play a bridging role between the young Hegel and the young Marx, something previously put out of court by the study of the systematic and reactionary Hegel, whose inheritance was willingly ceded to the dogmatic Marxists. But given this basis it became almost impossible to regard Engels as the faithful interpreter of Marx; and even less possible to count all that had passed from Engels into Leninism and into Stalinism as, without qualification, Marxian. Thus, in a note prefacing the second edition of *Materialism and Revolution* (1949), Sartre wrote:

> Since I have been reproached with bad faith in not citing Marx in this article, let me make it clear that my criticisms are not directed at him but at the scholastic Marxism of 1949; or, if you prefer, at Marx as seen by Stalinist neo-Marxism;

and in the *Critique*, alluding to *Materialism and Revolution*, he declares his target there to have been Engels rather than Marx. [31]

The dialogue between existentialism and Marxism took the form, then, as much in Sartre as in Merleau-Ponty, of a rediscovery by existentialism of 'authentic' Marxism. But a formulation of this kind, if it were not to resolve itself in a convenient evasion, had to settle accounts with the practico-political dimension of what presented itself under the name of Marxism. There were two parties in France proclaiming themselves to be Marxist, the communist party and the socialist party, while the world at large was becoming increasingly divided up into communist and anti-communist blocs. In their movement towards Marxism, the existentialists had no option but to transform their theoretical evaluation of Marxism into a criterion of personal choice within the arena of practical politics. In brief, existentialism very soon came to distinguish between Marxism as: 1) the political bloc of the Marxist forces in their struggle against the anti-Marxists; 2) as the Marx-Engels-Lenin-Stalin doctrinaire bloc; 3) as the 'authentic' Marxism which was to be rediscovered. It should be kept in mind that the PCF adhered very closely to the Soviet political and ideological bloc, with the result that the dialogue between existentialism and Marxism in France frequently took place in an atmosphere of violent polemic and bitter intransigence on both sides (more in reaction on the part of existentialism, than on its own initiative).

The examination of the connexions and mutual determinations between these three dimensions of Marxism would call for a lengthy and detailed work, out of place in the present context. It would, however, constitute a very useful field of investigation and verification of the possible influencing relations which get established between theory and 'situation' in a particular state of historical tension. Here we shall limit ourselves to some general observations. The French communists in general have subscribed to the view that Marxism is represented by the Soviet political bloc and on this pretext credit themselves with being the orthodox expression of its corresponding ideology. From this point of view they have denounced existentialism's claim that this official ideological bloc must be countered by an insistence upon rediscovering 'authentic' Marxism, as a bourgeois expedient. Their maestro is the Lukács of *Existentialisme ou marxisme?*, at least up to the point of de-Stalinisation. The non-communist Marxists (for the most part Trotskyites) encouraged the existentialistic attempt to counterpose an 'authentic' Marxism to the Stalinist ideological bloc, but were not disposed to follow the existentialists in the 'existential' formulation which they tended to give the dialogue with Marxism.

The attitude of the existentialists has varied considerably depending on the different situations in which Marxism in its three instances has been found operating. The only uniting factor in it has been its repudiation of

Marxism as an ideological bloc claiming to represent absolute truth. But even in this respect, we find some pretty complex nuances of tone. It should not be forgotten, in fact, that the Soviet political bloc made the justification of the infallibility of its own political practice dependent on the absolute validity of the ideological bloc whose custodian and interpreter it declared itself to be. Now, to the extent to which the existentialist approach to Marxism took the form of a political option (even if only a momentary and conditional one) in favour of the Soviet political bloc, the polemic against the ideological bloc and its dogmatic pretences was attenuated or disguised in order not to weaken the political action which the USSR or the PCF were involved in at that particular moment. The most important documentation of this attitude, which was very complex and rich in undercurrents, is to be found in Sartre's articles *The Communists and Peace,* where he supports the thesis that the party of the working class can never be wrong. Hence the accusation of ultra-Bolshevism levelled at Sartre by Merleau-Ponty, and his bitter observation that the Sartrean theory of the 'chief' evoked 'painful memories.'[32]

Sartre had written those articles, however, in a situation that was quite specific in regard to the history of the French proletariat. On 28 May 1952, the PCF had organised a big demonstration of workers against the visit to Paris of the American general, Ridgeway. The workers refused to demonstrate; not only that, but on 4 June following they refused to strike for the release of Duclos, arrested in the course of the failed demonstration. This sensational rupture between the proletariat and the PCF was greeted by the right-wing press as a 'working class victory,' and the Trotskyites found in it a confirmation of their theory of the ultimate validity of working class 'spontaneity.'

From the existentialist point of view the Trotskyite thesis ought to have found significant agreement. Instead, Sartre, by now convinced that the only *politically effective* proletarian force rested with the PCF, came to adopt positions even more extremist than those of the PCF's own theorists, denying that there was anything problematic about the relations between the working class and the PCF. Sartre's subsequent writings have not confirmed this radical stance, though perhaps it finds a veiled continuity in his subsequent interpretation of Marxism as the philosophy of the working class in the period of its struggle for emancipation. If, as the *Critique*[33] asserts, a philosophy besides being totalization of knowledge, a method, regulative idea, a community of language, is also 'an offensive weapon,' then it is not clear why this weapon should not come to be disguised, hidden, and transformed according to the changing circumstances through which the struggle for emancipation passes. Furthermore, in one of the first things written by Sartre on the relations between existentialism and Marxism, namely *Materialism and Revolution* (dating to 1946, but reaffirmed in 1960 in the *Critique)*[34] the problem of materialism is already being posed in terms not of truth and falsity, but rather of revolutionary efficacy. Philosophy, it is claimed, assumes a materialist basis when it aims for a decisive change at the practical level: that is how it was with Epicureanism, with the Enlightenment and with Marxism. The explanatory technique of the *per causas* reverses the optimistic formulations of the *per fines* technique, which typifies those philosophies for which the world is quite in order. All the same, Sartre rejects the 'myth of materialism' because *today* it is no longer equal to the revolutionary tasks which the communists persist in wanting to entrust to it. Today, the liberation which socialism offers to the masses as the objective of its own revolutionary humanism, presupposes conceptual tools which are incompatible with the metaphysical materialism implicit in the materialistic myth.

The evolution of Merleau-Ponty's position in regard to the three instances of Marxism that presented themselves in France was in noticeable contrast to that of Sartre at the time, since it proceeded from a point of closest proximity to Marxism but ended up at a point of maximum distance; whereas with Sartre it was rather the reverse. Sartre's support for Marxism (much like Merleau-Ponty's at first) never went further than that of a fellow-traveller, because there was never any point at which his adhesion to the Marxist political bloc was accompanied by an adhesion to the ideological bloc, in regard to which Sartre insisted upon the necessity of a rediscovery of authentic Marxism – as the *Critique* testifies to even today. Merleau-Ponty moves, by contrast, in *Humanism and Terror,* from a preferential choice in favour of the Marxist political bloc.[35] For him both blocs were expressions of violence, but in the Marxist bloc the violence is turned towards a definitive dissolution of the conditions which render *any* violence possible. His preferential choice for the Marxist political bloc was therefore able to overcome the supposed obstacle of the incompatibility of the Soviet ideological-political bloc with authentic Marxism (this being in Trotskyite fashion, held to lie in the international and universal nature of the revolutonary proletariat). The weakness of this identification (which, at heart, was an identification of Stalinism with Trotskyism) was bound to become even more apparent as the communist political bloc gradually came to reveal its nationalistic nervature. The effect of this was to make the two opposing blocs, the Marxist and the anti-Marxist, increasingly take on the appearance, in Merleau-Ponty's eyes, of being equipped with a preconstituted set of preferential values. Hence his ever-increasing loss of faith in revolution as universal catharsis, and his ever more 'sceptical' evaluation of the double standard of assessment which the two blocs applied to the particular historical situations they confronted. He says:

We are also against abstract morality. That is why we do not go along with the anti-communists, who judge communism without considering the USSR's problems. Still, values must be recognizable in their appearance at a given time. That is why, not recognizing those of Marxist humanism in today's communism, we are not Communists. [36]

2

It was within this perspective of the diverse play of influences between the communist political bloc, the Marxist ideological bloc and the need for a rediscovery of an authentic Marxism, that the debate on the dialectic, in which the theses of the orthodox Marxists such as Garaudy, Orcel and Vigier were opposed by those of the more or less orthodox existentialists such as Sartre and Hyppolite, took place. Garaudy was a member of the 'politburo' of the PCF, and director of the 'Centre for Marxist Studies and Research.' An upholder, in the initial stages of the meeting-cum-collision with the existentialists, of the most rigid orthodoxy put out by the scientistic, Stalinist press (witness Sartre's witty portrait of him in *Materialism and Revolution,*[37]) he subsequently became one of the protagonists of a thaw in the cultural cold-war, without deviating, however, except verbally — as we shall see in the present debate — from his original assumptions. Orcel and Vigier were two Marxist scientists.

The *controverse* concerned the following question: 'Is the dialectic only a historical law, or also a law of nature?' Or rather, what is most striking in the report on the debate is the fact that it was held without any previous agreement and was hence subject to growing equivocation throughout its course as to what was meant by 'dialectic.' The fact that the two parties were in agreement in recognising the existence of a dialectic in history in no way implied they had an agreement on what was to be meant by the term: even this apparent, general agreement served only to obscure the equivocations.

As it was, in introducing the debate, Orcel offered a very vague definition of the dialectic as 'the science of universal connexions.' Speaking after him, Sartre proposed instead a notion of the dialectic that, for all its apparent candour, in reality concealed all the problematic features of the confrontation between existentialism and Marxism. The existential solipsism of his earlier style had led Sartre to devalue the synchronic as much as the diachronic dimension to relations with the 'other' — to devalue, that is, the original nature of relations with society and with nature as much as their rationality and their meaning as historically developed. But to the extent to which, in his post-war works, existence became increasingly freed of its wholly fantastic isolation in the exceptional and the incommunicable, the principal problem of Sartre's philosophy became not that of the individual but that of the *whole,* in the sense of being the problem of a totality in which the individual finds himself placed within the perspective of the *totalized,* while yet preserving his own particularity as *totalizing* existent.

In this way the problem of the dialectic became for Sartre the problem of the 'totality' as the synchronic and diachronic dimension of the mode of being of human existence, as historicity which totalizes and is totalized at one and the same time. 'The fundamental category of historical being and of the thought of that being is the category of totality. This was Hegel's discovery.'[38] With the passage to Marx, there emerges, according to Sartre, the principle of the irreducibility of being to thought, and 'the key of the historical dialectic' assumes the form of a principle according to which the relations of production form a whole. Sartre accepts this principle and infers from it the *true* 'historical materialism': I say 'true' because Sartre specifies that 'since this whole (the relations of production) is founded on the fact that man, himself, as biological individual, is a whole: need, work, enjoyment in historically given conditions,' the outcome is that 'it is on the human totality of each individual that the totality of the economic and of production ultimately rests.'[39] The ultimate foundation, then, is the *mode of being of man* (existence); hence the wholly particular nature of Sartre's dialectic and his constant rejection of the assimilation of *this* historical materialism to 'dialectical materialism.' So that we are given a materialistic theory of the (existential) dialectic accompanied by a rejection of dialectical materialism.

It is quite clear that Sartre's adoption of this stance — which represents a very summary version of the theses upheld in the *Critique* — ought to have provoked a suspension of the debate on the issue of whether or not the historical dialectic can be extended to include nature, in favour of posing the preliminary question of the specificity and the foundations of the dialectic in general, or, if you like, it ought to have demanded, as a condition for pursuing the debate, that an agreement be reached on the sense to be given the term 'dialectic.'

Instead, Garaudy, who spoke after Sartre, restricted himself to observing in opposition to him, that 'the category of totality is certainly of capital importance ... but it is not enough to define the historical dialectic,' and furthermore, the Marxist inversion of Hegel is not to be summed up in the idea that 'knowledge ceases to identify itself with being.'[40] Thereafter his argument took the form of a wide-ranging argument *ad hominem,* in which, quoting various passages of Sartre's *Critique,* he hoped to demonstrate how, if Sartre was to be consistent in his declarations, he would have to extend the dialectic to include nature.

For his own part Garaudy insisted upon the following thesis: 'there exists a material in itself (before us and outside of us); it has (always before us and outside of us) a structure; the sciences prove that this structure is dialectic.'[41] In this way he imagined that he had rescued the dialectic (and its laws) from every *a priori* and metaphysical contamination, thus conferring on them 'heuristic value.' But when it came to exhibiting the proof that the *sciences on their part* demonstrated the existence of an in-itself and of its dialectical structure, Garaudy (completely disregarding the methodological caution that for centuries has been displayed in relation to the very possibility of any such 'scientific' demonstration) had nothing better to offer than: 'certain features common to all the sciences from the eighteenth century onwards: a) every inertia is relative; everything is in motion; b) in every case of motion what occurs is not the simple re-arrangement of immutable elements, but the appearance of something new; c) this appearance of the new permits us to date things.' [42] In brief, to the extent to which they give the lie to mechanistic materialism, the sciences testify to the dialectical structure of reality:

> The reduction of the higher to the lower is merely a definition of mechanistic materialism. The property of the dialectic is precisely that the whole is other than the sum of its parts; and this is true at every level. [43]

We shall not pursue here the line followed by Sartre's all too obvious objections regarding the theological nature of this 'scientific' conception of the dialectic, but rather the line of our own fundamental objection, by asking whether, even if we admit the way in which, in general, the sciences testify 'at every level' to the qualitative excess of the whole over its parts, this excess is sufficient to provide us with a definition of 'dialectic' which satisfies even the most elementary terminological presuppositions of the question at issue, above all in regard to its very apparent historico-cultural references?

But let us analyse Vigier's intervention. As a trained scientist he had the merit of bringing to philosophy the frankness and candour which the philosophers themselves had lost through original sin. Sartre had admitted that with reference to nature one could speak of a dialectic only by analogy; but in so doing, he left the decision as to the employment of the term, to the scientists. Vigier, in effect, said: 'Good, here I am, a scientist!' And then gave a "philosopher's" talk. For Vigier, the dialectic of nature 'rests in the idea of history, of evolution, of development,' which we find in Heraclitus and Darwin. By contrast, the anti-dialectical conception *par excellence* is that of the constant presence of primary elements. When it came to giving a somewhat more precise definition of what it is that makes history, evolution and development 'dialectical', Vigier appealed to that law of the transformation of quantity into quality, of which Engels had given us 'examples which remain classic, such as the transformation of water into steam.' [44] The idea that natural reality progresses through 'qualitative leaps' is for Vigier also the fundamental dialectical idea, on which it is possible to build a whole theory of the diversity of ontological levels, as much of inorganic nature as of organic and social life. Thus, he says, 'Marx applied, to the study of the history of man, the same procedure which the entomologist uses in his study of ants or bees where individual fluctuations are neglected.' [45]

The merit of these assertions by Vigier was that they exposed, as Hyppolite[46] was quick to point out, the attempt to historicise nature as in reality concealing the attempt (or even effecting it) to naturalise history. For while it was true that Vigier rejected a mechanistic determinism, he did so only to substitute for it a determinism even more forceful in that it operated on the *substance* itself of things, rather than at the phenomenal level.

> I believe (he says) that whatever the area of consideration, the problem posed for knowledge is always the same: to understand the profound nature of the movement of things, not in terms of inert materiality subjected to external laws, but in terms of deeper internal necessities in which the laws reduce themselves to properties of things in their dynamic movement.[47]

This states the matter clearly, and allows us to establish once and for all that to speak of the 'dialectic' as a 'universal law' means:

1. Making affirmations about reality that are *necessary*.
2. Maintaining that these assertions have their necessity in the 'deeper *internal* necessities' of things.

So it was that just as the discussion was drawing to a close, with Vigier's contribution, there emerged the problem with which it ought to have begun, that of the meaning of 'dialectical.' Garaudy realised the profound and serious implications of Vigier's discourse and hastened to make some reparation in his concluding statement. In order to evade the all too easy accusation of naturalistic determinism he declared emphatically: 'Such an idea is not in the spirit of any Marxist . . . The passage from capitalism to socialism is not a process of natural history.' [48] It is true that one could counter such a remark with what Marx himself wrote in this respect: 'Capitalist production begets, with the inexorability of a law of Nature, its own negation.'[49] But that is not what counts. There is no guarantee, in fact, that such statements in any sense adequately represent the true historical significance of Marxism. The problem, rather, is precisely that of the *compatibility* between what, as Garaudy put it, 'is intended' by Marx and/or the Marxists and the categorical and syntactic structure in which it is presented. It is in terms of this compatibility that the problem of the dialectic should by rights be posed. And it is above all within the

framework of those terms that the problem of the dialectic presents itself
as a problem of 'essence' or of the significance of the dialectic in the
framework of Marxism and socialism in general.

Garaudy fully realised how matters stood when, in his final very brief
intervention, he posed the problem of the dialectic as the problem of the
'necessity of history,' and meant the problem of 'necessity' to be seen as
the problem of the 'differing senses' of 'necessity.' But a problem of this
kind, which is the nucleus within the complex of categories relating to the
dialectic and as such determines the subordinate question of whether or
not the dialectic extends to include nature, cannot be confined (as, in
effect, it was) to a post-script. Garaudy, however, did distinguish between
two 'different senses' of 'historical necessity.' Let us hear what he said:

> But when Marx speaks of the *necessary* laws of capitalism, when, for
> example, he studies, in *Capital,* the laws of accumulation of capital, he
> shows that by virtue of alienation and of the fetishism of the market,
> certain of the processes of capitalist development resemble processes of
> natural history. But when Marx says, and we say, that the coming of
> socialism is *necessary,* the term necessity takes on another meaning. It
> means just this: that the contradictions of capitalism are such that their
> solution is possible only through the agency of socialism. [50]

This distinction between the two meanings of 'necessity' suggests the
following comments:

   A. That in the second case 'necessity' does not have the character of
natural necessity can mean two different things: 1) that the coming of
socialism is not predetermined in space and time in the manner of a natural
fact (and thus history can 'fester' for a long time, as Lenin put it); 2) that
socialism will come increasingly to present itself to man as something *to be
chosen* in order for him to realise himself as man.

   B. On the hypothesis of the first meaning, (**A.1.**) the
impossibility-of-not-being of the socialist future has a necessity *identical* to
that of the natural event. That we cannot give a definite point in time for
its occurrence merely loads the temporal necessity with an obscure
metaphysical fatality (provided, that is, we are not dealing here with the
kind of expdient which Weber claims the Hebrew prophets had resort to
whenever their prophecies failed to be realised at the time predicted).

   C. In consequence, the sole alternative to natural necessity, which is
to say, the sole way of conceiving the advent of socialism in a way which
rescues it from natural necessity, lies in denying that it has the character
belonging to a natural event of impossibility-of-not-being, while leaving
on one side the problem of the extent to which its spatio-temporal moment
can be determined.

   D. But the outcome of this is a radical and explicit denial of the

principle that Vigier had maintained lay at the foundation of the dialectic
— the principle according to which at all levels of reality there prevails 'a
profound internal necessity, in which the laws reduce themselves to
properties of things in their dynamic movement.' In one respect the
doctrines of Marx and Vigier are at the antipodes to one another: for
Marx, socialism is something in virtue of which man must *recognise himself*
as man, for Vigier it is something in virtue of which man must *refuse to
recognise himself* as man in order to become aware of his kinship to the ant.

    E. The establishment of socialism is something which concerns the
future of man, and the future of man (and therefore man himself) loses all
meaning if it is conceived as *impossibility-of-not-being,* as a necessity of
nature (always allowing what in itself is dubious enough, that such a
necessity exists in 'nature'). The future of man has the mode of
possibility-of-being; it is a case of 'in certain conditions, yes, in others, no';
in other words, it is impossible to exclude the *conditioning* and the *choice* of
conditions from the mode of being of man. The horizon of the possibility
of choice is certainly not limitless, but neither is it non-existent.
Kierkegaard in his time pointed out that the category of possibility is the
'weightiest.' If one strips this weighty quality of any romantic
assumptions, it becomes clear that its *weight* lies more than anywhere in its
negative and *limiting* implication — that is, in its sense of 'conditioning.'
Looked at in this way, man is a being subject to the 'removal' or, in the
reverse case, 'restitution' of his own possibilities. But this presupposes that
man is a being *constituted* by possibility and that in and through these
possibilities his very being is at stake. It follows from this that even if
possibility is constantly increasing its 'weight' as a result of the progressive
limitation of possibilities (which can happen, for example, by virtue of the
particular set of conditions and constitutive factors of a given social basis),
it will never be able to transform man into a being whose mode of being is
the *impossibility-of-not-being* of natural necessity. To deprive man of every
possibility is to suppress him and thus transform him into a natural event.
To sum up: there is no means of passage between possibility and necessity.
In other words, *possibility is not a type of necessity* (as Garaudy would have
it be when he made the possibility of socialism a certain type of
'necessity').

3

If these comments are correct, the problem of the essence of the dialectic
(which determines the problem of its extension) is transformed into a
problem concerning the connexions between *dialectic, necessity and
possibility.* One initial gain seems clear: if there is no means of passage
between possibility and necessity, and thus no compossibility of the two, it
will be absolutely impossible for any 'dialectic of possibility' to co-exist

with a 'dialectic of necessity.' If by 'dialectic' is meant the sequence of historical events in their diachronic and synchronic dimensions, it must be said that there can be no dialectic save that of possibility. At times the possibilities seem so stringently conditioned and possibility thus so weighted that the illusion arises that a realistic and 'hard' philosophy must speak of necessity. In reality the category of necessity is the most *airy and mystificatory.* And Marx saw this quite clearly when he claimed that the fundamental mystification of classical economy lay in its transformation of the laws of capitalism into *necessary laws.* Those who interpret the Marxist dialectic as a dialectic of natural necessity would do well to reflect on this point.

But although the only real dialectic is the 'dialectic of possibility,' the established use of the term since Hegel's day has been that of a 'dialectic of necessity.' Hence the endless equivocations the term allows in post-Hegelian and even in contemporary thought, which are such as to make it seem reasonable to suggest that we abandon such a prejudicial term in the interests of clarifying philosophical discourse. [1] The equivocation is rooted in Hegel himself. In fact for him the term is used to signify: a) the *necessity of the connexions* between the finite moments that the intellect limits itself to distinguishing; b) the *necessary* connexion between the moments themselves. But the *necessity of a connexion* has no right to be equated with a necessary connexion; in fact the necessity of the connexion leaves open an indefinite number of possible connexions, while the admission of a necessary connexion is equivalent to the exclusion of any alternative.

Hegel's greatness lies in his having made it clear that the rationality of historical understanding in every case posits the necessity of the connexion. But what characterises the Hegelian dialectic when taken as an organic whole is that it ultimately interprets the necessity of the connexion between historical elements as the necessary connexion of the elements themselves. The incompatibility of the two concepts of the dialectic (as 'dialectic of the possible' and 'dialectic of the necessary') was recognised and confronted by Hegel in the form of an assimilation of the necessity of connexion to necessary connexion.

All the same, the basic ambiguity in Hegel's concept of the dialectic cannot help but continue to have its effect in subsequent thinking, and particularly in Marx. Norberto Bobbio has made the acute observation that two different meanings of the term 'dialectic' can be traced in Marx; [2] it stands on the one hand for the correlation of opposites and, on the other, for their synthesis. In the first sense — it is easy to find evidence for it — necessity does not appear except as reciprocity of relations, i.e. as necessity of connexions; in the second sense, by contrast, it appears as necessary connexion. It is quite clear that the collection of concepts which go to make up the dialectical armoury are inscribed within wholly divergent syntactical contexts depending on which of these two senses is involved. One might take, for example, the category of 'totality' on which Sartre lays such weight. Where the dialectic is taken as meaning necessary synthesis of opposites, this category succeeds to the title of *apodicticity* as being the final unity of reality with itself (as takes place in Hegel). But if the dialectic is taken as correlation of opposites, necessity does not express anything except a *formal* determination, and the totality appears under the title of *problematic* unity (in the Kantian sense). It is only in this second sense that one can speak, as Sartre does, of a 'totality' such that 'on the human totality of every individual' must depend every other totality. And it is only on the basis of a problematic totality of supersession of opposites that the 'dialectic' can strip itself of all the characteristics of natural necessity and allow, as Garaudy sees it doing, for the intervention of man's intelligence and projects.

But are the two dialectics, which we encounter in Marx in the form of two differing techniques of investigation, compatible? Or is it the case, as in Hegel, that the incompatibility of the two dialectics takes the form of an assimilation of the dialectic of possibility to the dialectic of necessity? The question can also be posed in the following way: has Marx introduced into the Hegelian conception of the dialectic innovations which render an alternative to the Hegelian conception possible? One can grasp the bull by the horns by interpreting the two dialectics as purely methodological. But was this what Marx took the dialectic to mean, and is it compatible with his thought in general? It is certain that the ordering of opposites on the basis of the negation of the negation, which is required by the dialectic of necessary connexions, renders the principle of problematical reciprocity void and meaningless and dissolves the *formal* necessity which regulates it in *real* necessity or in the necessity of content in which history as uni-directional sequence of events consists.

The left Hegelians insisted at length on the distinction that can be made in Hegel between a reactionary system and a progressive dialectic. But, in reality, the dialectic of necessary connexions presupposes the complete idealisation of content. One can make necessary assertions about things only if one has previously assimilated them in the order and connexion of ideas. This does not lead, be it noted, to an intellectualist liquidation of Marx's thought. In fact, two questions always remain open. 1) does the true and proper meaning of Marxism lie in the necessaristic *Weltanschauung* or rather in the introduction of historical materialism as the process of historical interpretation?; 2) if we insert historical materialism into the necessaristic *Weltanschauung,* that is, if we make it into a unique and absolute principle, does it enrich or impoverish its ability to explain things?

If we look closely, one thing seems clear — that if the 'bearer of the dialectic' (to use Marx's expression in the *1844 Manuscripts*) is man, and if the mode of being of man is a finite possibility-of-being, it will never be legitimate to extend the dialectic beyond being that of the possible, or a dialectic of the 'necessity of *connexions*' which bind men to men and to nature.[53] It follows from this that a dialectic of '*necessary* connexions,' or a dialectic of the real necessity of things in themselves, can only take its starting point from an absolute real, from being insofar as it is necessary being. One can arrive at absolute necessity only by setting out from absolute necessity. And, in effect, for Hegel, history is 'a tragedy which the Absolute plays out with itself.'[54] Finiteness, progress, rationality, time and man appear here to us as mystification; so too does the dialectic – and hence the need to remove and annihilate it – of problematical reciprocity, of necessary connexions, of real possibility, which constitutes the foundation of those determinations.

From this point of view one can measure the whole greatness and historical significance of Heidegger's late philosophy. It is, no more nor less than Hegel's, a *dialectical* theorisation of the Absolute, or – as he puts it – of Being in so far as it is Being. I say 'dialectical' because even in Heidegger's late work Being is/has a necessary structure (*Geschick des Seins*) in which consists its *essentially historical* nature and the foundation of every history. For Heidegger too, then, history is a tragedy which the Absolute plays out with itself. But Heidegger's greatness rests in the fact that in his thought the *tragedy remains a tragedy right to the end*; there is no 'happy ending' to it, and no devices which would rescue man, reason and time from that final catastrophe to which they are destined right from the start.

If the *point of departure* has to be not man but Being, if historicity is to be understood as a constitutive character of things in their structure, if dialecticity constitutes the necessary law according to which this structure makes itself historical, if, that is, philosophy must adopt the point of view of the Absolute in so far as it is Absolute, then the true and genuine dialectic is that of Heidegger, a dialectic in which the finite (and thus man) waits upon the Absolute only to hear the sentence with which the Absolute proclaims the nullity of that very waiting. So that history is not progress but indifference, reason is a term of derision in Roman commercial parlance, the word is a *fatum* of being; the event is the *Gleich-Zeitigkeit* of being.

It is from this standpoint that Heidegger maintains, and absolutely coherently, that Nietzsche, the prophet of the 'eternal return of the same,' is the philosopher who brings our epoch to its close or at least concludes that era of metaphysics which had come to its full maturity with the work of Hegel and Marx. Heidegger professes a high opinion of Hegel as being 'the only Western thinker who conceived the history of thinking thought.'[55] But he nonetheless maintains that Hegel's thought falls *within* the history of metaphysics since the Hegelian dialectic, with its subjectivism, presupposes that unconcern with being which characterises the entire history of metaphysics up until Nietzsche. The existentialistic experience leads Heidegger to de-mystify the Hegelian procedure by clarifying the way in which a philosophy that concerns itself with the movements of the Absolute can only culminate in the self-recognition which the Absolute *already* implies of itself — that is, in the annulment of philosophy as *human knowledge.* Heidegger's stance is not subject to the criticisms which Hegel made of Schelling's philosophy in the celebrated pages of the *Phenomenology of Mind.* His point of view is not that of the un-knowing of the night in which all cows are black, but rather that of a knowing for which *all cows are the cows which they are* — that is, of a knowledge in which there is no 'holy terror' of mediation, but the simple recognition that the mediation is that of the Absolute with itself, and the acceptance of the consequences which follow from this right to the end. The principal consequence is that if the dialectic is the mediation of the Absolute with itself, the thinker who summarises and brings to its conclusion the whole course of romantic speculation on the dialectic is Nietzsche, the prophet of 'the eternal return of the same.'

From this angle it is also interesting to look at Heidegger's stance in relation to Marxism. Heidegger refuses to examine Marxism from the standpoint of an alternative between 'materialism' and 'spiritualism.' Modern materialism, according to him, does not consist in the materialist assertions of this or that philosophy but in a technicist degradation of the relations with Being, which today characterises even spiritualistic philosophies. A dialogue with Marxism, to be 'productive,' must start from the problem of the original historic nature of Being and from the connected problem of alienation as 'forgetfulness' of Being. Heidegger says:

> Since Marx, in his recognition of alienation, penetrates an essential dimension of history, he puts himself beyond all other historiographic conceptions. But since neither Husserl, nor, to my way of thinking, Sartre hitherto, have recognised in being the essentiality of what it is to be historical, phenomenology as much as existentialism have not installed themselves in that dimension within which a productive dialogue with Marxism alone becomes possible. [56]

One notes that for Heidegger the idea of alienation 'which Marx took from Hegel in a significant and essential sense,' [57] is the Marxist equivalent of that 'forgetfulness' of Being by virtue of which the Hegelian dialectic falls within the history of metaphysics, a history to which Nietzsche provides the prophetic conclusion.

Only by reconquering the sense of Being as the eternal return of the same will it be possible to remove that 'forgetfulness' of being which is alienation and carry the de-mystification of the dialectic to its end point, thus restoring to it its authentic meaning as 'tragedy which the Absolute plays out with itself.' [58]

4

From the point at which we have arrived, we can draw the following conclusions in respect of the Paris debate on the dialectic:

1. The discussion as to whether or not the historical dialectic extends to include nature was vitiated by a non-univocal use of the term 'dialectic.'

2. Those upholding the existentialist side regarded the dialectic as connected with the mode of being (possibility-of-being) of man as finite and conditioned existence; those on the Marxist side regarded the dialectic as connected instead with the mode of being (necessary-being) of the *whole* as the unitary and omnicomprehensive reality in which man re-enters as a simple *part*. On one side, then, a dialectics of real possibility, on the other a dialectics of real necessity, the two *radically incompatible*.

3. The matrix of the equivocal use of these two meanings of 'dialectic' is Hegelian thought, in which one finds: a) the dialectic as *necessity of connexion* of opposites (reciprocity and universal correlation); b) the dialectic as *necessary connexion* of opposites (uni-directional historical ordering of content).

The necessity of connexion is in no way equivalent to a necessary connexion, since the necessity of connexions only implies a *formal* and *heuristic* prescription (equivalent to: 'the connexion is there; look for it') and leaves the horizon of *possible* connexions open, while necessary connexion concerns content, in the sense of its being the negation of any other alternative (equivalent to: 'here is the connexion').

To the necessity of the connexion there corresponds a dialectic of real possibility, to the necessary connexion a dialectic of real or metaphysical necessity. The incompatibility between the two types of dialectic takes the form in Hegel of a mystificatory resolution of the dialectic of the possible in the dialectic of the necessary.

4. The two dialectics are to be met even in Marx's thought where their incompatibility takes the form of an unresolved juxtaposition.

5. The position of the Marxists participating in the debate, and particularly that of Vigier, was Hegelian in type; it tended towards dissolving the dialectic of the possible in the framework of a dialectic of metaphysical, omnicomprehensive necessity. Garaudy's attempt to introduce two types of meaning of 'necessity' is unacceptable, because in one case it is a matter of 'limited possibility' and in the other of the 'necessity of things.' And between the possible and the necessary there is

neither any means of transition nor common genus, but pure and simple incompatibility.

6. The dialectic of the necessary connexion of the whole in the unconditioned unity of Being is 'a tragedy which the Absolute plays out with itself' and where it has found its demystified form, and thus its genuine and exemplary one, in the Heideggerian theory of the necessary epocality of Being in so far as it is Being.

7. The term dialectic is unusable when it is not accompanied by a specification of its meaning in regard to the fundamental alternatives mentioned above.

APPENDIX 2

The concept of 'alienation' in existentialism*

1. The Terminology

It has been noted that the problem of alienation, at least in the form and meaning which it has in our culture today, found its first systematic formulation in Hegel. This original formulation is accountable for certain of the lexical and semantic ambiguities which still affect the problem today. Hegel, and Marx after him (but in a different context), used the terms *Entäusserung* and *Entfremdung* with such finely drawn distinction as to render then ultimately synonymous. It is common practice to translate the first by 'alienation' and the second by 'estrangement,'** but then, under the thrust of Hegelian theory, we end up by designating the loss of self in something other, in which properly speaking estrangement consists, by the term 'alienation.'

Whether or not we accept the Hegelian theory, which originates in the Enlightenment, of the notion of alienation, it cannot be denied that in Hegel's use of the term *Entäusserung* (and even more in that of *Veräusserung*, which plays such an important role in the *Philosophy of Right*) there is the echo of the contractual notion of alienation as *cession*, partial or total, of the self. Now, it is very important to keep in mind that this contractual notion of *Entäusserung-Veräusserung-alienatio*-cession is not necessarily connected with the meaning of *alienation-Entfremdung*-loss of self in other, which we are now in the habit of conferring on the Italian term *alienazione*, and even more on the French *aliénation*. Therefore, to

---

* From *Rivista di filosofia*, LIV, 1963, pp. 419-45.
** Italian 'alienazione' and 'estraniazione.' There can hardly be said to be any very common practice among English translators. Thus, M. Milligan (*Economic and Philosophical MSS of 1844*; cit.) translates *Entfremdung* as 'estrangement' and *Entäusserung* as 'alienation' (or 'externalisation'); T. Bottomore (*Karl Marx Early Writings*) claims that Marx does not distinguish between the two terms and translates both as 'alienation' (or 'estrangement'). D. McClellan *(Karl Marx Early Texts)* and L. D. Easton and K. H. Guddat *(Writings of the Young Marx)* translate *Entfremdung* as 'alienation' and *Entäusserung* as 'externalisation.' The different policies of the English translators are a clear reflection of the problems of translation discussed by Chiodi. (Trans.)

take *Entäusserung* and *Entfremdung* as so closely synonymous that their meanings converge in the one term 'alienation,' is equivalent to a tacit recognition of the validity of the Hegelian formulation of the problem of alienation, thereby discounting from the start the Enlightenment formulation which rests on the contrast between 'cession' (*Entäusserung*) and 'estrangement' *(Entfremdung)*. Later on we shall see in what way Marx goes beyond the Hegelan position.

With a view precisely to extricating ourselves from such a wholly equivocal situation, we shall in what follows reserve the term 'alienation' for the latter meaning (*Entfremdung-alienation*-loss of self in other), while we shall indicate the first meaning (*Entäusserung-Veräusserung-alienation*) by the term 'cession.' For the contractualists, the departure from the self in the sense of ceding something of one's own to another is so little a loss or diminution of the self as in certain cases rather to signify an enrichment of the self and an advantageous 'bargain.' Only in certain cases, and under certain conditions, can cession assume the character of alienation; and even in these cases, it does not exclude the possibility of reappropriation. Most importantly, this latter is never understood in the sense of a state of non-cession that has to be reinstated but rather in that of a renewed and different (made under different conditions) cession. Even when the character of inevitability, and thus of necessity, comes to be attributed to cession, such a necessity is not understood as the mode of being of an alienating exteriority opposed to freedom as interiority. A 'necessary' cession is not for that reason an alienating one; the alienating character of the cession depends exclusively on that which one cedes as opposed to that which one obtains in compensation. For example, the cession of self and property to an absolute sovereign is alienating because it cedes too much and one receives so little in return. Clearly the same cannot be said of that cession from which Rousseau's social contract originally derives, given that in that 'each uniting himself with all, is obedient only to himself, and remains free as before.'[1]

To interpret cession as being in every case alienating is to assume that the alienatory nature of the cession can be determined without considering the *other* term of the contractual relation – which is to say, that it can be determined from the moment of the simple externalisation of self on the part of the person making the cession and of the rupture that this implies with his original wholeness. In other words, cession and alienation only coincide on the hypothesis of a coincidence between objectification and alienation. Now it is known that the main point of the view of alienation presented by Marx in the *Economic and Philosophical Manuscripts of 1844* is contained in the rejection of this coincidence. Objectification is alienation only in determinate conditions which are to be historically discovered and not metaphysically defined once and for all. From the terminological point of view it has to be remembered that the quasi—interchangeability of *Entäusserung* and *Entfremdung*, which one meets in Marx no less than in Hegel, does not have the same implications in the former's work as it does in the latter's. In Hegel the identification of *Entäusserung* (cession) with *Entfremdung* (alienation), two concepts which the contractualists have always kept well distinct, is significant to the extent that, given the identification of cession with de-subjectification, the identity between *Entäusserung* and *Entfremdung* implies the identity of objectification and alienation. By contrast, in Marx the denial of the identity of objectification with alienation means that the identification between *Entäusserung* and *Entfremdung* ceases to be meaningful in terms of any content it implies and becomes a matter merely of terminological use. The role that the denial of the identity between cession and alienation plays in the contract theory of the Enlightenment is here played by the denial of the identification of objectification on the one hand with *Entäusserung-Entfremdung* on the other. It seems, then, that the *conceptual structure* of the Marxian theory of alienation is closer to that of Enlightenment contractualist theory than to that of Hegel.

It is true that Marx derived his inspiration from Hegel, but it is nonetheless true that right from the beginning he had seen the Hegelian theory of alienation to be a product of alienation itself.

2. *Alienation and Alterity*

In the most general way, alienation can be defined as the process whereby someone or something (for Marx, nature itself can be involved in the process of human alienation) is constrained to become other than that which it properly is in its being. This 'becoming other' at times takes the form of a 'feeling other' (as in the Heideggerian notion of *Unheimlichkeit*, and in the psychopathological forms exposed by Jaspers in his early work and by *Daseinsanalyse*). This 'feeling other' is in fact always a mode of being and not a mere perception. [2]

Insofar as it implies a 'becoming other,' the notion of alienation presupposes therefore, in every case, that of 'alterity,' and it is always bound to a particular interpretation of this. But we should at this point specify how it is that at this most general level the notion of alienation does not necessarily carry with it a negative significance. In this connexion, in fact, one comes up against three differing positions:

A. *Alienation as positive quality.* This is the position typical of mystical thought, according to which alienation coincides with ecstasy as the supreme moment of man's fulfillment.

B. *Alienation as negative quality.* This position is best exemplified in Marx. It is also shared in general with existentialism. The friction between Marxism and existentialism arises here over the question of the means and limits by and within which alienation can be removed.

C. *Alienation as positive and negative quality at the same time.* This is the typical Hegelian position. Marx had fully realised it when he asserted that in Hegel 'this externalisation of consciousness has not merely a negative but a positive significance.' [3] Insofar as it is being-other, alienation is negativity, but insofar as it is a presupposition of its own negation it is something good and positive, the reasserted unity of the for-itself. For Marx, this Hegelian dialectic of *et-et* is possible only as mystification. It presupposes, in fact, that alterity and the object are not real but only apparent, i.e., 'nullity.' This mystification of the object is possible, for Marx, only when the subject is subjected to a double process of alienating abstraction: of real man in simple consciousness, and of consciousness in absolute consciousness knowing itself. At this point Marx says:

> Consciousness, then, knows the nullity of the object (i.e. it knows the non-existence of the distinction between the object and itself, the non-existence of the object for it) because it knows the object as its *self-alienation*; that is, it knows itself – knows knowing as the object – because the object is only the *semblance* of an object, a piece of mystificaton, which in its essence, however, is nothing else but knowing itself, which has confronted itself with itself and in so doing has confronted itself with a nullity. [4]

According to Marx, then, the positive aspect of alienation found in Hegel is equivalent to that alienating mystification on which his theory of alienation depends.

3. *Alterity and Alienation in Existentialism*

A general feature of the existentialist point of view is its denunciation of the mystification implicit in the Hegelian dialectic of the *et-et*, and this holds also insofar as the theory of alienation is concerned. The adherence to 'real man' in place of the mystified man of mere consciousness, the reafirmed reality of the other as against its reduction to an appearance, the finite point of view (whether individual or social), and the de-mystification of the concept of relations are so many bases established in the common battle waged by existentialism and Marxism against Hegelianism. Only in its latter-day romantic convolutions (those of Heidegger, for example) does existentialism lead to an alignment with the third of the positions examined above, because it interprets alienation and de-alienation alike as necessary modes of being of absolute being. [5]

In its original, most typical inspiration, existentialism: a) vindicates the finite point of view; b) declares the other to be an effective reality; c) considers the relationship of alterity to be original, essential and ineliminable. The Marxist principle, according to which man cannot enter into an authentic relationship with himself except on condition of entering into a particular relationship with others, is held by all the existentialists as well. But while for Marx the other always takes the form of a verifiable alterity (society, nature as the realm of man), existentialism, at least in its primitive form – the second generation calls for a quite separate treatment – has revealed a tendency to individuate and isolate a privileged sector in the generic relation of alterity, within which the relation to the other takes the form of a relation between the finite and something which the finite is not, that is, something which in a generalised and neutralised fashion could be called the trans-finite. Instances of this are Kierkegaard's God of faith, Jaspers' *Umgreifende,* Heidegger's Being, Marcel's Mystery: in all these cases one is confronted with a relationship of alterity which is ontologically privileged by virtue of its 'non-verifiability,' and thus conditions other relationships. There are two consequences of this, which make themselves felt throughout the whole history of existentialism: 1) the relation to the finite other is demoted to the second rank; 2) there is a devaluation of the diachronic dimension in the relation to the finite other, and thus of the incidence of history in the process of de-alienation.

As far as the first point is concerned, it is essential, however, to remember that the relation to the trans-finite other does not take the form, as it does in Hegel, of a resolution of the finiteness in the process through which the trans-finite realises itself. This kind of resolution presupposes, in fact, that the relation to the finite is none other than the *appearance* of the relation of the trans-finite to itself; it presupposes, that is, that the other is 'nullity' and the relationship one of self-revealing identity, while – as we have seen – the irreducible reality of the other and the ineliminable originality of the relationship of alterity are two irrevocable tenets of the existentialistic formulation.

Given all this, the privileged status of the relation to the trans-finite other and the consequent demotion of the relation to the finite other have the effect of creating in existentialism an insuperable cleavage of human reality between an ineliminable state of fact and an unattainable state of right, between ontic actuality and ontological destination. This insuperable cleavage gives the character to what existentialism theorises as 'the human situation.' It is therefore at the heart of this theory, both in its constants and in its variations, that we must look for the notion of 'alienation' as it is revealed in the various currents of existentialist thought. Among the positions common to them all, three are particularly significant: 1) alienation is a feature of the human situation itself; 2) the state of alienation is ineliminable; 3) the ineliminable nature of alienation is connected to the factual elements conditioning the human situation (the body, need, nature etc.).

4. *Alienation and Situation*

For Kierkegaard the paradoxical nature of the human situation consists in the fact that man, whose destiny lies in his relationship to God, encounters a *de facto* alienation in social and mundane relations. This formula is repeated not only in Jaspers and Marcel but also in the early Heidegger, where nothingness plays the role of the trans-finite other which religious existentialism attributes to God. This is the whole root of Kierkegaard's polemical attack on the 'crowd,' of Jaspers' against 'the existence of the mass,' of Heidegger's against 'being-together,' of Sartre's assertion that 'the other is the secret death of my possibilities,' [6] and of Marcel's declaration that 'Everything which exists in society besides the individual translates itself into the minus sign.' [7]

Nor should the theme of co-existence which recurs to some degree in all the existentialists deceive us. When Heidegger affirms that the *Sein* of existence is co-original with *Mit-sein*, when Marcel states quite explicitly: 'I should be inclined to contend that existence can only be attributed to others, and in virtue of their otherness,' [8] and Jaspers: 'Not only do I not in fact exist for myself alone, but I myself cannot form myself as I without forming myself and developing myself together with others,' [9] one is dealing with assertions that must be placed within a common perspective on the human situation, one which sees its character as that of being afflicted by a paradoxical conjuncture between relations to the finite other and to the other as trans-finite. Co-existence belongs to the facticity of the human situation: it is true that existential facticity is ontologically loaded, but this is a case of an ontological quality whose sign is negative, and it is in this that its ineliminable character of alienation lies.

Without anticipating what we shall say later about de-alienation, it is quite clear that it is just this insuperable quality of the alienating cleavage by which the human situation is afflicted, which pushes those forms of existentialism in whose theory it forms a part towards fictitious alternatives, such as revolt in the absurd or *amor fati*; these are the kind of alternatives which open the way to those evasions in pure consciousness that are the presupposition for so many of the romantic forms which characterise existentialism's decline into religion or despair.

5. *The Ineliminability of Alienation*

For Hegel, 'this alone is the true nature of the finite, that it is infinite and rids itself of itself in its being' [10] In Hegel, the relation between finite and infinite is nothing but the 'appearance' of the infinite to itself. For existentialism, by contrast, this relation is the original and ineliminable mode of being of the first reality: existence. Enmeshed within this, then, is the double relationship to the trans-finite other and to the finite other. As the relation to the trans-finite other, existence tends towards liberation from its own alienation; as relation to the finite other it is ineluctably tied to it.

From this perspective a brief comparison of existentialism with

Hegelianism and Marxism may be illuminating. Both these latter theories, unlike existentialism,[11] conceptualise alienation as removable once and for all. But in Hegelian theory, alienation can be removed only by removing objectification, that is, by removing existence itself as the finiteness of the relation, and this is due to the fact that it is the relation itself which is alienating. For existentialism too, the relation to the finite is alienating as such, but this relation cannot be removed because it coincides with existence itself. For its part, Marxism has in common with Hegelianism the belief that it is possible to remove alienation once and for all, but in common with existentialism, it preserves the relation to the finite. Alienation is merely a determinate historical basis of this relation and can thus be removed while conserving the relation. In other words, in Marxist theory alienation is not an ontological feature of existence, but only a moment in its history; hence, the way in which Marxism has constantly accused existentialism of mystically reifying what is only a determinate moment of history.

At first sight it seems, then, that Marxism constitutes the simultaneous and complete supersession of both Hegelianism and existentialism. From this point of view, existentialism is the living embodiment of the Hegelian crisis which is yet to be brought to its ultimate conclusion. The positive aspect of this crisis is then to be found in its vindication of the irreducibility of existence as relation to the finite other, while its negative aspect is to be identified in its romantic, residual adherence to the irrevocable nature of the relation to the trans-finite other. In this perspective existentialism might be seen as a Marxism still lacking its Feuerbachian mediation, that is, still waiting for its theory to be freed of the notion that the relation to the trans-finite other is a real relation.

But is Marxism really a supersession of Hegelianism in every aspect? What is the impact on this problem of the common doctrine that alienation is removable once and for all? There is no doubt that this doctrine inscribes itself in the conception of history as a process of deliverance and liberation, of 'self-production' of human reality, which Hegelianism and Marxism can proclaim in opposition to the value attached by so much of metaphysical existentialism to the extra-historical 'instant' or the 'eternal return' of history. All the same, it seems legitimate to ask: What will there be to history once alienation has been removed? For Hegelianism the answer is easy because history closes in the coincidence of history with itself. But this solution cannot operate for Marxism, in which the 'bearer' of the dialectic is finite man. What will be the mainspring of history when, with the removal of economic alienation, every other form of alienation is removed?

At this point the Marxist theory of alienation reveals certain ambiguities of major relevance. In one aspect (A) it presents itself as the outcome of a scientific analysis of a complex of socio-anthropological phenomena which are linked to a determinate mode of production. In another (B) it assumes the character of a metaphysical prophecy to the effect that alienation will disappear once the advent of communist society has removed the cause of economic alienation.

Even if one confines aspect (B) to romantic eschatology and retains only aspect (A), the ambiguities are not finished with, because within (A) we have the alternative of either (A.1.) seeing the Marxist theory of alienation as the simple denunciation of a phenomenon termed 'economic alienation,' together with a suggestion as to the techniques for its removal (the passage from a capitalist to a communist economy) — and in this case one would leave the problem of the continued existence of other forms of alienation wholly undetermined, and thus too the problem of their possible connexion with economic alienation; or else (A.2.) seeing in the Marxist restriction of the theory of alienation to an examination of economic alienation, an explicit recognition of the assumed inexistence of other forms of alienation deserving of investigation.

Thus three possible interpretations of the Marxist theory of alienation present themselves: 1) it is the outcome of an enquiry which neither in its assumptions nor its predictions transcends the sphere of the verifiable (A.1.); 2) it is the implicit negation of the continued existence of other forms of alienation (A.2.); 3) it is the assumption that economic alienation is the metaphysical principle of the causation and removal of every other form of alienation (B).

Depending on which of these points one takes as pivotal, the relations between Marxism, on one hand, and Hegelianism and existentialism, on the other, are altered. It seems, in fact, that Marxism can present itself as superseding the existentialist position that alienation is ineliminable (in a recovery of the Hegelian position of its definitive eliminability) only on the basis of the theses of 2) and 3), that is, only on the basis of an arbitrary assumption or an unverifiable hypothesis. It seems hazardous, therefore, to maintain that Marxism, in this respect, surpasses existentialism, if in order to do so one needs to have recourse to the procedures typical of that Hegelianism against which existentialism provides a critical bastion.

6. *Alienation and the Trans-finite*

We have already seen how, at least for primitive existentialism, alienation constitutes a feature of the human situation as such. Since to speak of situation means speaking of finiteness, existentialism shares with Marxism, against Hegelianism, a theorisation of alienation from the standpoint of the finite. But existentialism and Marxism diverge strongly in the way they interpret the finiteness of man's situation. In both conceptions, finite situation is seen as coincident with the possession of historical nature. But for Marxism, the human situation is historical in the sense that in every case it exists as a basis to be overcome in time; while for existentialism, the historical quality of the situation is identified with its insuperable structural circularity. From this standpoint, Marxism charges existentialism with metaphysical reification of the human situation, with a failure to place its character as momentary conjuncture in perspective, with having an inadequate foundation for thinking history in general. 'There is no human situation in general,' objected Naville against Sartre in the discussion which followed his lecture 'Existentialism is a Humanism,' and which marked the beginning of the dialogue between existentialism and Marxism in France.

Is it possible to claim that the existentialist conception of the human situation, and thus its thesis that alienation has a structural character, relies on having established the characteristics of the finite human situation from the starting point of its relations with the trans-finite? In other words, can one say that the difference between the Marxist and existentialist conceptions of the human situation relies on the fact that for the latter the crisis of Hegelianism has not yet been weathered for lack of a critique and expulsion from its theory of the Hegelian notion of the infinite real? At first sight it seems natural to answer yes. But one could ask whether the notion of alienation itself is conceivable from the point of view of a finite which founds itself upon the unqualified rejection of all reference to the trans-finite. Put more explicitly, one can ask whether it is the case that the Marxist theory of alienation operates at the Feuerbachian level, which is marked by the disappearance of any reference to the trans-finite, or whether it supersedes that level and thus recovers, at a different level, the concept of the trans-finite. In other words, does Marxism, in placing alienation within a historical perspective, rely on Feuerbachian positions, or does it rather correct Feuerbach by means of a recourse to Hegel?

The issue is an important one because if one has to answer in favour of the second hypothesis, the insufficiencies of the existentialist notion of alienation would relate not to the fact of its having posed the problem of alienation in the form of a problem of the relationship between finite and trans-finite, but rather to its *particular* way of posing this problem; and this then becomes a question in itself that has to be raised in the course of any enquiry into alienation.

Now existentialism's particular way of posing the problem of the relation between finite and trans-finite is in terms of *oppositions in mutual implication*. Finite and trans-finite oppose each other and imply each other at one and the same time, in a manner that is paradoxical and from which there is no escape. This conception has the advantage of rescuing the finite from the resolution in the infinite which the Hegelian type of mediation involves, but it has the disadvantage of safeguarding human finiteness only on condition of making it the negative and factual implication of the positive trans-finite. The alienating character of the human situation comes in this way to be identified with its impassable *factuality*. The finiteness of situation is saved from mystification in the infinite, but only on condition of being opposed to the latter, outside of time and history, in a way that renders its factual present an insuperable alienation.

7. The 'Beautiful Soul' and the 'Ugly Soul'

The merit of existentialism's particular conception of alienation is that it effects a confluence of the *two* features seemingly indispensable to the escape from the mystification of Hegelian theory: a) the irreducibility of the finite; b) the indispensability for the finite of its relationship with the trans-finite. A theory of alienation which brings about, as does Hegelian theory, a resolution of the finite in the trans-finite renders de-alienation of the finite impossible, unless it is negated in the trans-finite. On the other hand, it is difficult to see how a conception of the finite which adopts the presuppositions of a materialistic naturalism − which is what Marxism appears to be to some − can establish, on the basis of the negation of any relation to the trans-finite other, even the simple distinction between alienated and de-alienated finite. The existentialist demand for a conception of the finite such that it is in relation to the trans-finite but persists nonetheless as finite, therefore seems well-grounded. It is known that this demand found its fundamental categories in the twin notions of *project* and *possibility*.

But primitive existentialism has not succeeded in making these two categories the spearhead in creating a genuine crisis for Hegelianism and has ultimately remained the prisoner of an Hegelianism which is rejected but not removed. Thus the demands for the irreducibility of the finite and for the indispensability of the relation to the trans-finite − which are validated in terms of the Hegelian problematic of absolute necessity − have remained as oppositions existing nonetheless conjointly and giving rise to a model of mutually implicating oppositions the locus of whose categories is *necessity as impossibility*. The finite relation to the trans-finite is necessary but impossible, de-alienation is necessary but impossible. Existence comes to be the necessary self-projection of an impossible possibility. If one remembers that for Hegel existence was the self-projection of necessary possibility − the apparition of the infinite in the finite − it becomes clear that primitive existentialism remains a prisoner of the Hegelian problematic of absolute necessity. In fact, to transform de-alienation, as existentialism does, from 'necessary possibility,' which is what it is in Hegel, into 'impossible possibility,' is equivalent to inverting Hegel from within while remaining his captive. To say that de-alienation is an impossible possibility, as does existentialism, is indeed equivalent to saying the opposite of what Hegel says when he states that de-alienation is necessary possibility, but only apparently − because in both cases the possible is dissolved in its opposite, the necessary. To say that the finite is necessarily de-alienation, or else to say that it is necessarily alienation, means saying that in every instance the finite is necessarily that which it is or else that it expresses the impossibility of being anything other than that which it is: that it is impossibility and not possibility. In the last analysis, for Hegelianism as much as for primitive existentialism the finite is necessarily alienation, but Hegelianism, in that it is a philosophy of the infinite, comes to rid itself of the finite and with it of alienation also. While for primitive existentialism – which remains faithful to the exigence of the finite's irreducibility, but at the same time still imprisoned in the Hegelian schema of categories for which the finite is necessarily that which it is, namely alienation – the irreducibility of the finite takes the form of the ineliminability of alienation.

In primitive existentialism, finite and trans-finite counterpose each other in their implication of each other as irreducible entities. But one is not dealing here with a pre-Hegelian position deficient in mediation. One is dealing, rather, with a position that arises on the ground of the critique of Hegel and of the function he attributes to mediation in being the process of reduction of finite to infinite. One is dealing, that is, with a position which arises out of a rejection of the Hegelian mediation in so far as this resolves itself in the reduction of the finite upon the appearance of the infinite.

By vindicating in this way the irreducible persistence of the finite, while at the same time conceiving it, in Hegelian fashion, as alienation, existentialism attaches itself to a 'figure' of existence whose form is symmetrically opposed to that of the Hegelian 'Beautiful Soul,' and which might be defined as the 'Ugly Soul.' The Beautiful Soul, Hegel tells us, 'lacks the force of alienation'; the 'Ugly Soul' of primitive existentialism, in contrast, lacks the force of de-alienation; furthermore, the Beautiful Soul in Hegel 'is deprived of effectivity,' while the Ugly Soul is irretrievably cast down and lost in the impassable effectibility that derives from its actual finiteness. [12]

8. *Alienation, Production and Technique*

It is not surprising that the identification of alienation with impassable actuality is that much more marked the sharper the religious character of the particular existentialist current of thought. But the identification is to be met with even in the so-called atheist existentialists: one finds it, for example, in the Heideggerian notion of *Verfallen* and in Sartre's *facticité du pour-soi*. The identification of facticity with alienation produces three effects: 1) the state of alienation becomes insuperable; 2) alternatives within the state of alienation are equivalent; 3) the praxes and techniques for modifying the internal relations of the alienated situation are devalued.

It is quite clear that the second and third points restate the Hegelian theses to the effect that objectification is equivalent to alienation, with the difference, however, that for Hegel, it is possible to remove objectification (at the end point of the process) and thus alienation along with it – while for existentialism, which denies that there is any end to the process, because it rejects the idea of a conclusion in infinity, the state of alienation takes on the form of a tragic destiny, simultaneously both unacceptable and insuperable.

Looked at in this light, existentialism can be seen as denouncing alienation while at the same time recognising that, as it is a state of *fact,* there is *nothing to be done.* Hence the devaluation of praxis in general and of labour in particular, not to mention of the techniques of projection and transformation.

The technical world as such, and hence any mode of production, are in themselves alienation. This existentialist conception has given support to directly opposed politics: on the one hand to a pro-Marxist existentialism, which at one and the same time recognises the effect and endorses the persistent denunciation of the state of the alienation which attaches to the present system of capitalist production; on the other hand to a liberal and neo-capitalist politics which acts as the justification of the persistence of the state of alienation under any system of industrial production, whether it be capitalist or socialist. This explains Garaudy's indulgent treatment of the theory of alienation subscribed to by a religious and right-wing existentialist such as Gabriel Marcel and explains the accusation of incoherence made by Aron against Sartre (and against *Esprit*) for their acceptance of the Marxist theory of the definitive removal of the worker's alienation in capitalist society. [15]

The Marxist and existentialist theories of alienation are, in truth, closely bound by their common denunciation of alienation as *economic and social fact.* But with existentialism one is dealing with a fact whose 'facticity' expresses a metaphysical, and thus ineliminable, dimension of human existence. In this respect the existentialist position is subject to the criticisms of classical political economy made in the *Economic and Philosophical Manuscripts of 1844*; that is to say, it 'presupposes as fact that which must be explained.' Classical political economy, in its assumption that the relationship between the worker and his product was immutable, concealed the fact that the nature of alienation lies in its being the particular characteristic of a specific form which this relation can assume. Neo-capitalism, for its part, seeks to go beyond Marxism by assimilating capitalism and socialism under the concept of the industrial society and in this way attempts to recover the typically existentialist theory of the persistence of alienation in any industrial society, a persistence which thus frees itself of the burden of 'scandal' and 'denunciation' which in existentialism it has carried with it.

9. *Hegelianism, Existentialism and Marxism*

From what we have said so far, it is fairly clear that an analysis of the notion of alienation held by existentialism can only be made if it is constantly held in the context both of Hegelianism and of Marxism. For the most part the attempt has been made to see the terms of reference of this context as providing a logical or historical ordering in accordance with a linear sequence of development or one of direct supersession. Löwith, for example, has seen in existentialism and Marxism two parallel manifestations of the dissolution of Hegelianism. Lukács, by contrast, has seen Marxism as the legitimate heir of Hegelianism and has confined existentialism to the margins of history as being the retrogressive and expedient ideology of the bourgeois class in its decline. Other Marxists deny that there is any direct continuity between Hegelianism and Marxism and would want to insert between them a necessary, even if ideal, existentialist moment. Others again have recognised in Marxism the form that Hegelianism must take in order to answer its existentialist critics. Latterly, existentialism has been seen by Sartre as the necessary internal moment of any Marxism which does not want to lose its nature in 'voluntaristic idealism.' [14]

There are many reservations which can, and must, be made when it comes to such schematic alignments of doctrines which have frequently sprung up in wholly divergent historical situations. But the reservations diminish in proportion to the extent to which the 'theories' are the product of a fairly homogeneous and recurrent historical context. It is certainly not by chance that Hegelianism, existentialism and Marxism re-enact themselves in a complementary fashion even in the most diverse cultural contexts. Existentialism has played a major part in the dissolution of Hegelianism in Italy just as the most recent crisis of existentialism in Germany has reintroduced Hegelian currents and positions. The existentialist crisis of Hegelianism has often been, even in Italy, a bridgehead to Marxism, just as the crisis of Hegelianised Marxism has recently (in Poland after 1955) taken the form of a revival of the issues at stake in existentialism.

This complex of incompatibilities and implications which for more than a century has linked Hegelianism, existentialism and Marxism is one of the most interesting cultural features of our time, even if it seems to give rise to a sort of recurrent checkmate in thought and history. It does not, in fact, seem easy to confine this conflict to the timeless and directionless tensions in terms of which Kant was wont to resolve all such conflicts in his good-natured referral of their proud antagonists to the court of critical reason – the reason being, even if there were no other, that a problem that relates to whether or not alienation is removed on passing from capitalist to communist society affects us in a very different manner from the problem of the infinite divisibility of matter as conceived by metaphysics. Nevertheless, the sage of Königsberg has one teaching which should not be lost sight of in the present issue, and that is that where we have a situation of irresoluble conflict the error attaches to something common to both contestants. We shall devote the last paragraphs of this enquiry into alienation to a clarification of this negative factor common to Hegelianism, existentialism and Marxism. We shall proceed from the standpoint of an existentialism which presumes that it has found, in its own internal capacity for self-correction and development, the ground for going beyond both the deficiencies of primitive existentialism and the element common to the 'dialectical' clash between Hegelianism, existentialism and Marxism.

10. *The Infinite and the Finite Point of View*

These are the salient features of the Hegelian theorisation of alienation: 1) the protagonist of alienation is the Spirit in its unique and absolute subjectivity; 2) alterity is only 'apparent'; 3) the relation is provisional; 4) objectivity coincides with alienation; 5) history is the progress which leads from the necessity of alienation to the necessity of de-alienation. Primitive existentialism, if considered more in its polemical intent than in its theoretical achievements, sustains a point-by-point opposition to Hegelianism: 1) the protagonist of alienation is man in his finite concreteness; 2) alterity is real; 3) the relation is a permanent structural feature of human and extra-human reality; 4) departure from the self is not necessarily alienation; 5) alienation is necessary and de-alienation impossible.

In its attack on the point of view of the infinite, existentialism's fundamental acquisition rests on its vindication of the relational structure of man's being. To exist is to *ex*-sist, it is project, the relation to the other, and it is so in its being, that is, from the time when it is to the time when it no longer is. This position it also fully shares with Marxism, for which human finiteness signifies an original and ineliminable relation to society and nature. Even for Hegel the spiritual reality is a 'being outside of itself,' but it is not the case that it has an *original* and *ineliminable* character: from beginning to end the Spirit is in itself; the departure from self, alterity, the relation, objectification, are positive features only to the extent to which they are there in order to be removed.

The fundamental corollary, and thus the most visible token, of a conception which adheres to the finite point of view is therefore the denial of the identity between objectification (as the issuing 'outside of self' on the part of the subject) and alienation, in the same way that the interchangeability of alienation and objectification announces the implicit assumption of the infinite point of view. The two counterposed positions become even clearer in the theorisation of de-alienation; on the latter view de-alienation always takes the form of a return to subjectivity as pre-relational interiority, for the former it takes the form of a transformation on a *global* scale of the relational basis. In the first case the relation of alterity is something provisional and instrumental in respect to the subjective pole which constitutes its *foundation*; in the second, the foundation is a problem *internal* to the relation itself, and has in some way to involve both poles. In the first case de-alienation is substantially a problem of pure and simple awareness in subjective consciousness; in the second it is a problem of the awareness on the part of the subjective consciousness of the task to be undertaken at the objective pole of existence.

11. *Existentialism and Hegelianism*

The spearhead of existentialism's attack on Hegelianism lies in its defence to the bitter end — one might say at all costs — of the structural (thus original and ineliminable) nature of the relationship of alterity. Hence its rejection of the mediation used by Hegel as the instrument for reducing one pole (the objective) of the relation to the other (the subjective).

But this defence to the bitter end is characterised by the fact that it is played out *within* Hegelianism and the categorial scheme that provides the Hegelian framework. Let us briefly examine the last of the characteristics listed as typical of the Hegelian position, that is the thesis according to which history is the necessary progress which leads from alienation to de-alienation. According to Hegel the historical process takes place through a succession of mediating relations whose purely instrumental and provisional function is proved by their disappearance in the final moment of the de-alienating return of the Spirit to itself. If a defence to the bitter end of the relationship of alterity is made *from within* this formulation, by way of transforming it from something instrumental and provisional into something original and definitive, a series of consequences follow which in their conjunction clearly define the positions inherited from Hegelianism by primitive existentialism (i.e., its negative burden): 1) alienation remains, as it does in Hegel, a negative state; 2) de-alienation, while continuing to be demanded, is recognised as impossible because in the Hegelian framework in which it is offered to us, it would require the elimination of the relationship of alterity; 3) history, from being necessary progress, becomes necessary regression, expressed in the eternal return of alienation to itself; 4) the ultimate point reached by the historical process, at which for Hegel finite and trans-finite coincide, is defined by the impossibility of their fusion (not by their mutual exclusion).

Alienation thus preserves the character of ontological necessity which it possesses in Hegelianism; but while in the latter this ontological necessity encounters a further ontological necessity for de-alienation, in existentialism the necessity of de-alienation is inverted into a declaration of its impossibility. This is because in the Hegelian framework in which primitive existentialism continues to find its bearings, the admission of de-alienation would imply the reabsorption in the unity of the spirit of that relationship of alterity whose defence to the bitter end constitutes the very rationale of the existentialist polemic. In Hegelianism alienation constitutes a sort of original, relational state of fact which is taken up and resolved in the process of de-alienation, which finds its conclusion in a unitary and conclusive state of right. Existentialism, in declaring the relationality original and at the same time insuperable and making that declaration *within* Hegelianism, finishes by bringing about the coincidence, in Hegelian fashion, between that relationality and the factual state, between originality and facticity. De-alienation then becomes a rightful state foreseeable and foreseen, but unobtainable in fact. Thus Hegelianism becomes the paradise lost of an existentialism which has opened its eyes on the human situation. The whole Hegelian patrimony (albeit mystified) of the supersession of the factual by the rightful situation and of the positive nature of history as the rational locus of this supersession is thus forsaken.

The ambiguity of this situation comes to light particularly in relation to the concept of objectivity. On the one hand, existentialism, in defending the relationality of existence, can hardly do otherwise than defend its ex-centric and exterior quality. Yet on the other hand, by interpreting originality as insuperable facticity, it preserves all the Hegelian nostalgia for subjective interiorisation, while the impossibility of this being realised is laid at the door of the tragic *factuality* of the human situation. This explains why existentialism, although insisting at heart on the interpretation of existence as co-existence and as being-in-the-world, finishes up by recognising in these two characteristics the sign of its inauthenticity. *The declared identity between relational facticity and inauthenticity is the modality in which primitive existentialism repeats the Hegelian identification of objectification with alienation.*

12. *Absolute Necessity as the Presupposition Common to Hegelianism and Primitive Existentialism*

The existentialist problematic is dominated, then, by a radical and ineliminable tension within it between the necessities of a rigorous theorisation of its own original assumption, constituted in the defence at all costs of the structural relationality of existence, and the fatal deformation to which this theorisation is subjected by virtue of its being elaborated within the Hegelian framework of categories. Hence the subsequent development of existentialism must choose either to further the defence of the structural relationality of existence by making this the spearhead of a crisis for the Hegelian categories or else to carry on the crisis of Hegelianism only within its own categorial plane, thus perpetuating its global structure in a process of radicalisation whose only positive aspect lies in the exposure of its mystificatory nature which it must implicitly make.

Italian existentialism, in resolutely opting for the first alternative, has made it clear that concepts such as those of relation, project, co-existence, being-in-the-world, to which prmitive existentialism appealed, could not have been made to function as articulating categories from the finite standpoint as long as they were made to operate on the categorial plane of necessity which Hegel, with extreme coherence, had placed at the base of the infinite standpoint. As long as the vindication of the relational structure of existence was given its validity within the Hegelian categories of necessity, existentialism would never be able to be other than an inverted Hegelianism. The Hegelian absolute necessity was thus revealed as the *axis* around which the recurrent inversions of Hegelianism in existentialism and of existentialism in Hegelianism, or Hegelianised Marxism, rotated. Hence the imperative of discovering a different level of categories which could function validly as the authentic foundation of the finite standpoint, a level on which the relational structure of existence might find its *raison d'être* in its own renewed status as possibility and not in its inversion in the necessity of fact. Only on this condition can the relational structure come to be defended to the ultimate without its being metaphysically sealed in a present from which history and future were excluded.

This supersedes the alternative — created by the contrary implications of primitive existentialism and Hegelianism — between a relational structure that can only preserve itself by enclosure within an ahistoric present, where the prospect of what should be by rights is dissolved in the repetition of what is in fact, and a relational structure which by moving towards a future authentic transformation in accordance with what should be by rights, must negate itself as such in the unrelated unity of absolute reality. Only a categorial level at which the intransigent defence of the relational structure can find its basis in the renewed status of the possibility of the structure itself appears to offer the means of rendering the finiteness of existence compatible with its historical nature.

13. *Alienation and De-alienation in the Existential Structure*

With regard to the problem of alienation, the most direct consequence of this new point of view lies in its rigorous negation of the thesis generic in primitive existentialism, according to which the relational structure of existence itself expresses a *state* of alienation. If one accepts this thesis, which Hegelianism deduces from the myth of the unity of the real, one can no longer escape the alternatives which it brings about *within* Hegelianism between the ineliminability of alienation and its elimination through the suppression of the relation itself in the final unity of reality with rationality. The relational structure of existence is not a state of alienation, above all because *it is not a state.* If by state one means, as one must, a mode of existence of reality, the relational structure of existence cannot in any instance constitute a state because its mode of existence is not reality but possibility. The structure is not a state. Rather, one finds it passing through a variety of states, each one of which expresses its own real possibility. There are several important consequences of this which are relevant to our problem – the state of alienation, in fact, 1) does not concern the structure of existence, but a determinate historical situation; 2) it is not determinable once and for all and *a priori,* but only by means of a specific enquiry; 3) it constitutes a possibility constantly open as much to its removal as to its re-establishment; 4) it places existence in a global context.

It follows from this, first of all, that the structure of existence, in constituting an articulation of the possible, does not carry with it any guarantee that alienation is either definitively insuperable or definitively removable. Alienation and de-alienation are states of reality, and as such do not fall under the *direct* dominion of philosophy – whose concern is with the possible – but rather under that of the human sciences in general from whose techniques of verification the necessary is excluded in so far as it is unverifiable. Assertions such as the following: 'alienation will never be able to be definitively removed because . . .' or else, 'alienation can be definitively removed if . . .,' only make sense if taken as equivalent to: 'alienation is a possibility to which human reality is always subject,' or else, 'an uninterrupted commitment towards the removal of alienation is compatible with human reality.'

The same can be said in respect of the global nature of the state of alienation. Marxism's great merit has been its insistence upon this primary character of the phenomenon of alienation: it is the whole of human reality which is at stake in it, and thus – because of its original relationality – society and nature itself. It is not possible to condemn one sector of human reality (the economic, for example) to alienation while saving the rest in the name of its presumed hegemony or self-sufficiency. Equally it is not possible to save an individual man or a class of men while abandoning the rest to a state of inhumanity. When the bell tolls, it tolls for each and everyone. One cannot remain a man and at the same time look with indifference upon the dehumanisation of another man or of a part of ourselves.

But Marxism has believed that this global quality can and must be rooted in a necessary unity, which it identifies in the economic structure. Here what is being questioned is not the efficacy of such an interpretation of Marx's thought in putting paid to idealist beliefs, still less its fidelity to the spirit, and even the letter, of Marxist thinking. What counts is the fact that a conception of this kind is obedient to the Hegelian formulation of the problem of alienation (except that it substitutes the world of the economic for the world of the spirit in the role of unifying principle). In this way, it allows Hegel's prophecy to the effect that alienation can definitively be removed to be reinstated, while at the same time creating, with its metaphysical simplification, insurmountable difficulties for any Marxist approach to the problem of alienation as it affects the sectors and institutions whose practices are (relatively) autonomous of economic conditions.

14. *De-alienation and Normativity*

All the same, the appeal to a single principle, which is common to both Hegel and Hegelianised Marxism, conceals a dimension of the theory of alienation which cannot be disposed of simply by attributing it to the metaphysical nature of such theoretical exercises. The 'singular principle' is, in fact, entrusted with the function of being that *constraint* upon the finite without which alienation becomes inconceivable. In fact, if the finite point of view is equivalent to a pure and simple vindication of *Selbständigkeit* of the finite as such then it is impossible to see how alienation and de-alienation could be given any meaning (that is to say, to what they could refer). This point is the spearhead of Marx's criticism of Feuerbach, and the weakness of a certain existentialism in which absolute freedom goes along on an equal footing with the equivalence in status of possibilities.

If alienation and de-alienation are to be something more than mere words concealing what is on the best hypothesis only an innocuous 'interior' adventure, two quite specific conditions must be fulfilled: a) that alienation be the outcome of a real constraint, that is, of an external one exercised upon the finite; b) that de-alienation be the result of activating a *project* of real transformation — that is to say, of one that is carried out in the real world (of nature and society) — on the part of the finite. It seems, therefore, that a theorisation of alienation from the finite point of view demands the admission of a trans-finite something which exercises a real constraint upon the finite, yet is nonetheless removable on the initiative of the finite itself. Without the constraint there is no alienation, without its removal there is no de-alienation.

The trans-finite, then, is to be interpreted in such a way as to render the constraint and its removal equally possible. And in fact, Hegel conceived the Spirit, the Infinite, as the 'principle' as much of alienation as of de-alienation, but he did so from the point of view of the Infinite — that is, in a mystificatory manner from the standpoint of the finite — since the removal of alienation coincides with the annulment of the finite itself. Hence primitive existentialism's reaction, which was to salvage the finite by denying the possibility of de-alienation, and hence, above all, the necessity, if the finite point of view is to be made authentic, of interpreting the trans-finite in such a way that *in its mode of being* the effects produced by the constraint upon the finite are rendered compatible with its removal through the work of the finite itself.

The effect of all this is that it becomes impossible for the trans-finite to oppose itself to the finite as a principle which by virtue of the constraint either determines it, or directly suppresses it, on the basis of the necessity of its unitary constitution. The mode of existence of the trans-finite cannot consist in a necessitating unity but must consist in an articulation that allows for possibilities. The order which it installs cannot be that of a univocal determination but must rather be that of an *equilibrium of conditions* which vary with the variations in the coefficients of adversity and/or in the initiatives which from time to time come into play. The only *unitary* factor is the articulation of the relational structure, the only *necessary* one the problematic nature of its changing determinations.

The trans-finite is thus constructed in such a way that it includes in its own structure of constraint the possibility of an initiative for its removal on the part of that same finite upon which the constraint is being exerted. Such a structure, which is the same as the structure of existence seen *a parte obiecti*, does not carry with it any condemnation to perpetual alienation nor any guarantee of definitive de-alienation. It does nothing more than express the human situation as one 'condemned,' not already to absolute freedom, but to an alternative and to action. Even if the *state* of alienation is a durable one, consolidated in time and hardened in institutions founded upon violence or mystification, it remains always a *state* – that is, a historical determination of the human situation which includes, in its very structure, the possibility of an initiative for its removal. On the other hand, de-alienation is nothing other than the outcome of the removal of a determinate *state* of alienation, following upon the initiative of a human reality whose structure, once again, is such as to include the constant possibility of a relapse into the same state of alienation or of a collapse into another, and even worse, one.

In other words, a philosophy which takes the finite point of view to its conclusion is not in a position to point out for man any principle which functions as an infallible norm for discovering human alienation or as an instrument for definitively removing it. But that does not imply that philosophy is reduced to impotence. On the contrary, philosophy is reduced to the impotence of the *post factum* when it assumes the point of view of the infinite, according to which history resolves itself – as Marx in the *Holy Family* accused Hegel of resolving it – in a movement of the absolute Spirit accomplished unconsciously and in the ignorance of men.

In assuming the point of view of the finite and recognising with absolute rigour the categorial level of the possible which it demands, philosophy finds itself constrained to leave the domain of *necessary reality* to the consolation or mortification of pure speculation, and the domain of *effectual reality* to the specific researches whose appropriate techniques allow them to determine the limits of their own field of 'reality.' Philosophy is not concerned directly with reality but with possibility. And it would be gravely restricted if possibility constituted a merely accessory determination of reality. But if, by contrast, one understands reality as 'presence' (the 'present' of the possible), philosophy comes to acquire, with regard to the various fields of 'reality' and their practices, an ineliminable role in its existence as conscious awareness of the *conditions,* and thus of the *limits,* of their constitution and of their *human* significance.

There is no doubt that the relations which bind men to society and to nature are 'real' relations and as such are exposed to precise techniques for assessing and correcting them; but to the extent to which these real relations constitute the outcome of a project in which the very humanity of man is at stake, they attack and compromise philosophy. The latter becomes, then, the guardian not of the reality of being, but rather of the humanity of man. Insofar as it is a guardian, it is itself implicated in the situation and threatened by it; but its task cannot go beyond exposing the danger and inviting action.

The danger consists in the dehumanisation of man – that is, in the loss of the possibilities which give him definition throughout the constantly changing circumstances of the historical situation. The only form that philosophy can assume is that of promoting the maximum development and enrichment of human possibilities in any given historical situation. In the last analysis, human alienation consists in a coercive subtraction of possibilities. Philosophy cannot function as a de-alienating technique except on pain of itself falling into alienation. Its very anguish is the reason for its greatness.

Notes to the Text

Preface

1. J.-P. Sartre, *Words* (London, 1964), p. 171. English translation by Irene Clephane of *Les Mots*, (Paris, 1964). For an assessment of the book which appeared after the Italian translation cf. E. Paci, 'Le Parole', *Aut aut, 82*, July 1964, pp. 7-17.
2. Sartre, *Words*, p. 83.
3. J.-P. Sartre, *The Problem of Method* (London, 1963), p. 28. English translation by Hazel E. Barnes of *Question de méthode*. *Question de méthode* is the prefatory essay to *Critique de la raison dialectique*, Tome 1, (Paris, 1960), and the only part of that work at present available in English translation. See translator's note p. vi of this volume.
4. M. Merleau-Ponty, *The Adventures of the Dialectic* (London, 1974), p. 151. English translation by Joseph Bien of *Les adventures de la dialectique* (Paris, 1955).
5. This is the basic criticism levelled by H. Lefébvre against Sartre's latest philosophy. He places Sartre, together with Merleau-Ponty, with those philosophers who 'force us to reconsider the classic philosophical categories dialectically.' ('Critique de la critique non critique,' in *La nouvelle revue marxiste*, (1961), no. 1, p. 61.) Cf. also by H. Lefébvre 'Philosopie et politique. Questions à Roger Garaudy, Jean-Paul Sartre et Jean Pierre Vigier,' in *La nouvelle revue marxiste*, (1962), no. 3, pp. 78-85. J. Houbart's book on Sartre, *Un père dénaturé*, (Paris, 1964), is merely a confused and vulgar *pamphlet* conducted from the standpoint of a misunderstood dialectical materialism. It is said in it that Sartre 'starts off from socialism to arrive at the confessional' (p. 57) and , of course, that he is a lackey of the French bourgeoisie (p. 169).

Chapter I

1. G. Lichtheim, 'Sartre, Marxism and History,' in *History and Theory*, III, (1963), no. 2, p. 22.
2. S. de Beauvoir, *Force of Circumstances*, (London, 1966), p. 5. English translation by Richard Howard of *La Force des choses*, (Paris, 1963). For a reconstruction of Sartre's itinerary in regard to political and philosophical

problems, and their reflection in his literary work, cf. F. Jeanson, *Sartre*, (Paris, 1966).

3. S. de Beauvoir, *The Prime of Life*, (London, 1962), p. 429. English translation by Peter Green of *La force de l'âge*, (Paris, 1960).

4. de Beauvoir, *Force of Circumstances*, p. 5.

5. J.-P. Sartre, D. Rousset, G. Rosenthal, *Entretiens sur la politique*, (Paris, 1948). Sartre prophesies here that the antithesis between freedom and authoritarianism will be overcome in a movement towards the 'concrete freedom' of socialism. (pp. 101-2).

6. *Les Temps modernes*, nos. 129-30-31, (1956-7), p. 696.

7. de Beauvoir, *Force of Circumstances*, p. 7.

8. J.-P. Sartre, *The Transcendence of the Ego*, (New York), p. 105. English translation by Forrest Williams and Robert Kirkpatrick of *La transcendance de l'Ego*. This work first appeared in *Recherches philosophiques*, (1936-7), but was written in 1934.

9. 'Matérialisme et révolution,' *Les Temps modernes*, I, nos. 9–10, (1946). The English translation is by Annette Michelson and is included in J.-P. Sartre's *Literary and Philosophical Essays* (New York, 1955).

10. Sartre, *Les communistes et la paix*, English translation by Irene Clephane, (London, 1969).

11. Perhaps the earliest anticipation of the *Critique* was in 1946, when Sartre wrote: 'Someday I am going to try to describe that strange reality, History, which is neither objective, nor ever quite Subjective, in which the dialectic is contested, penetrated and corroded by a kind of anti-dialectic, but which is still a dialectic.' J.-P. Sartre, *What is Literature?*, (New York, 1965), p. 30. note. English translation by Bernard Frechtman with an introduction by Wallace Fowlie of *Qu'est-ce-que la littérature?* (Paris, 1947).

12. Sartre, *Question de méthode*.

13. A. Gramsci, *Il materialismo storico e la filosofia di Benedetto Croce*, 6th. ed., (Turin, 1955), pp. 94-6.

Chapter 2

1. J.-P. Sartre, *Being and Nothingness*, (London, 1957), p. 73. English translation by Hazel E. Barnes of *L'être et le néant*, (Paris, 1947).

2. M. Heidegger, *Being and Time*, (Oxford, 1967), p. 254. English translation by John Macquarrie and Edward Robinson of *Sein und Zeit*.

3. Heidegger, *Being and Time*, p. 227.

4. Of the social realism traditional to Marxist aesthetics, Sartre has declared: '. . . every human being, and particularly the artist, since our special concern is with him at the moment, is all of humanity. I hope to reinforce this idea ultimately in the second volume of the *Critique de la raison dialectique*.' ('Sartre parle . . . ,' in *Clarté*, (1964), no. 55, p. 42.)

5. J.-P. Sartre, *Being and Nothingness*, p. 615.

6. Sartre, *Being and Nothingness*, p. 627.

7. Sartre, *Being and Nothingness*, p. 239.

8. Sartre, *Being and Nothingness*, p. 248; cf. p. 221 sqq.

9. Sartre, *Being and Nothingness*, p. 251.

10. Sartre, *Being and Nothingness*, p. 245.

11. R. Garaudy, *Perspectives de l'homme*, (Paris, 1961), p. 102.

12. Sartre, *Being and Nothingness*, p. 429.

13. Heidegger, *Being and Time*, p. 89. On the problem of the relations between consciousness and existence in Marx, cf. Chap. 6, note 9.

Chapter 3

1. Garaudy, *Perspectives de l'homme*, p. 112.

2. Garaudy, *Perspectives de l'homme*, p. 113.

3. Sartre, *Being and Nothingness*, p. 239.

4. Garaudy, *Perspectives de l'homme*, p. 113.

5. Garaudy, *Perspectives de l'homme*, p. 112.

6. J. Kopper emphasises the critical aspect of Sartre's revision of Marxism, maintaining that Sartre's attempt combines the fundamental points common to the first two Kantian critiques. ('Sartres Kritik der dialektischen Venunft,' in *Kantstudien*, (1961-2), no. 3, p. 371).

7. *Geschichte und Klassenbewusstsein* (Berlin, 1923); English translation by Rodney Livingstone, (London, 1971).

8. G. Lukács, *Existentialisme ou marxisme?*, (Paris, 1961), p. 224.

9. The story of Lukács' relations with existentialism has appeared even more complex than one might have believed since the republication of his early pre-Marxist works, *Die Theorie des Romans*, translated into English as *The Theory of the Novel*, by Anna Bostock, (London, 1971); *Die Seele und die Formen*, (Neuwied, Luchterhand, 1971), translated into English as *Soul and Form* by Anna Bostock, (London, 1974). Those attest to an existentialist phase in Lukács' formation, directly preceding the Kierkegaard–Renaissance (see the accurate and full account given by Cesare Pianciola in *Rivista de filosofia*, (1964), no. 1, pp. 88-96). It is significant, moreover, that a Marxist such as J. Michaud expresses his views on *History and Class Consciousness* as follows: '. . . the bible of the French existentialists – repudiated by its author.' *Teoria e storia del 'Capitale' di Marx*, (Milan, 1960), p. 15, note.

10. M. Merleau-Ponty, *The Adventures of the Dialectic*, p. 31. In the Epilogue to this work Merleau-Ponty starts by assuming that according to every 'dialectical' conception of revolutionary activity, 'the very nature of revolution is to believe itself absolute and not to be absolute precisely because it believes itself to be.' (p. 222) The myth of the absolute supports and corrupts the 'dialectical' conception of the revolution. The true humanist transformation must denounce mythology and take account of the relative value of every change, of the basic ambiguity of the historical process. It is by starting from this basic ambiguity that the authentic dialectic comes to be understood in the framework of the relative and not of the absolute. From this point of view, dialectic and revolution are rendered incompatible: 'There is no dialectic without opposition and freedom, and in a revolution opposition and freedom do not last long.' (p. 207) Soviet communism of the present day has itself renounced the myth of revolution being the eruption of the absolute and has confirmed the maxim that 'all revolution is relative . . . and there are only *progresses.*' (p. 223) These same convictions are to be found in the last of Merleau-Ponty's works to appear during his lifetime, where only a 'genuine dialectic' is admitted – that is, one that places both means

and ends on the same relative level, e.g., by criticizing Stalinism from the standpoint of the non-existence of the absolute, and not from that of a degenerate absolute. Merleau-Ponty, *Signs*, (Evanston, Ill., 1964), p. 299. English translation by Richard C. McCleary of *Signes* (Paris, 1960).

11. For a critique in depth of Sartre's concept of the dialectic from the point of view of the social sciences cf. G. Gurvitch, 'La dialectique chez J.-P. Sartre,' in the work of the same author, *Dialectique et Sociologie*, (Paris, 1962), pp. 157 sqq.; Cl. Lévi-Strauss, *The Savage Mind*, (London, 1966), pp. 245–69. English translation of *La pensée sauvage* (Paris, 1963). R. C. Kwant has also insisted on the difficulty of making the dialectical passage from individual to history in the *Critique*, see 'Het marxisme van Sartre', in *Tjischrift vorr Philosophie*, (22 Jaargang, Leuwen, 1960), p. 660.

Chapter 4

1. K. Jaspers, *Philosophy*, Vol. II, (Chicago, 1970), p. 108. English translation by E. B. Ashton of *Philosophie* (Berlin, 1932).
2. Sartre, *Being and Nothingness*, p. 531.
3. Sartre, *Being and Nothingness*, p. 506.
4. Sartre, *Being and Nothingness*, p. 498.
5. K. Marx, *Economic and Philosophical Manuscripts of 1844* (MEGA I, 1, 3, p. 167). English translation by Martin Milligan (New York), p. 188.
6. W. Dilthey, *Gesammelte Schriften*, VII, p. 135.
7. It is interesting to note that back in 1946 Sartre was defining History as 'that strange reality [. . .] which is contested, penetrated and corroded by a kind of anti-dialectic but which is still a dialectic,' Sartre, *What is Literature?*, p. 30, note.

Chapter 5

1. G. Lichtheim, 'Sartre, Marxism, and History,' in *The Concept of Ideology and other Essays*, (New York, 1967), p. 240.
2. G. Lapassade, 'Sartre et Rousseau,' in *Les études philosophiques*, (1962), no. 4, p. 517.
3. This is the thesis maintained by Galvano Della Volpe in *Rousseau e Marx*, (Roma, 1962), 3rd. ed., pp. 67 sqq.
4. Lichtheim, 'Sartre, Marxism, and History,' p. 235.
5. The 'ethical,' according to the *Critique*, 'is nothing other than praxis enlightening itself on the basis of given circumstances.' (p. 208) The irreducibility of doing, the identification of man and praxis, constitute the 'only profound novelty of Sartre's current thought' according to Pierre Javet, 'De *L'être et le néant* à la *Critique de la raison dialectique*' in *Revue de Théologie et de philosophie*, (1961), no. 1, pp. 54-5. M. Dufrenne also emphasises the positive sense of the continuity between *L'être et le néant* and the *Critique*, in *Esprit*, (April 1961), pp. 676-77.
6. Lapassade, 'Sartre et Rousseau,' p. 515.
7. A. de Waelhens, 'Sartre et la raison dialectique,' in *Revue philosophique de Louvain*, t. 60, no. 65, (February 1962), p. 85.
8. J. C. Michaud expresses himself as follows on the Sartrean theory of

scarcity: 'When Sartre repeatedly defines the realm (of political economy) as being that of "scarcity" he is much closer to Pareto and Marshall than he is to Marx.' (Michaud, *Teoria e storia del 'Capital,'* p. 37, note.) For A. de Waelhens also, the Sartrean concept of scarcity is to be placed 'at the antipodes' of Marxism (de Waelhen, *Sartre et la raison dialectique*, p. 85.) For A. Patri, it is a case rather of a tactical reversal of the classic Marxist theory of surplus production, inserted into 'the global strategy of contemporary Bolshevism' for the conquest of the developing nations, i.e., being applied to a situation of scarcity ('Le marxisme existentialisé,' in *Preuves*, (1960, August), p. 68.) Abstracting from questions of 'strategy,' it is beyond doubt that the Sartrean foundation of economy is more nearly linked to the problems of socialism in the developing nations than to those in the industrialised countries. Even Sartre, who sees in Marxism a theory of relative scarcity of a kind that allows its extension into a theory of scarcity in general (p. 224), is inclined to place socialist economy beyond this 'great watershed,' which separates classical from neo-classical or modern economics. By locating the problems of Marxism beyond this 'great watershed,' that is, by displacing them from the area of production into that of needs and the choice of the means of their satisfaction, Sartre has found an economic terrain on which it is easier to found a conception of the dialectic which rests on individual choices and on the original struggle between man and man (rather than between classes in an already evolved system of production). This explains why Sartre's theory of alienation is presented more in the form of a denunciation of the techniques of 'extermination' (as the way of dealing with the insufficiency of production) than in the form of a theory of the extraction of surplus-value. This obviously connects with Sartre's tendency to make alienation a permanent state – the precise reason for this being that it is bound to a human 'situation' of original scarcity and not to a provisional state of scarcity which arises with the phase of capitalist production (as is Marx's way of seeing the matter). For this reason, even if Sartre locates his conception of political economy on the terrain of the (marginalist) notion of scarcity, the sense in which he accepts the term and the consequences which he derives from it in the political sphere, do not allow us to place his economic thinking in an anti-Marxist context (whether pre- or post-Marx). The purpose of his operation is not to place himself within the confines of marginalist theory in order to use the theory of utility-value as an instrument for evading the political consequences which Marx had drawn from the labour theory of value, but rather to use the idea of scarcity as a means of deriving a *theoretical radicalisation and historical amplification* of the Marxian theses. (One need only note the thoroughness of Sartre's rejection of the market-economy which has been the corollary of marginalist theory.) For a history of the idea of *rareté* cf. E. Roll, *History of Economic Thought*, 3rd. ed., (London, 1954); E. James, *Histoire de la pensée economique au xxe siécle*, (Paris, P.U.F., 1955). For an examination of the theory of *scarcity* from a Marxist point of view, cf. V. Vitello, *Il pensiero economico moderno*, (Rome, 1963); C. Napoleoni, *Il pensiero economico del 900*, (Turin, 1963, 2nd. ed.).

Chapter 6

1. MEGA, 1,1,3, pp. 160 sqq; *Economic and Philosophical Manuscripts*, p. 179.
2. MEGA 1, 1, 3, pp. 154–155; *Economic and Philosophical Manuscripts*, p. 179 sq.
3. 'Kierkegaard ... is certainly not a philosopher,' Sartre, *The Problem of Method*, p. 10. A judgement which echoes that of Heidegger: 'Kierkegaard is no thinker, but a writer on religious affairs.' Heidegger, *Holzwege*, (Frankfurt a M., 1950), p. 230.
4. S. Kierkegaard, *The Concept of Dread* 2nd. ed., (Princeton, 1957), p. 73, translated by Walter Lowrie.
5. MEGA, 1, 1, 3, p. 153; *Economic and Philosophical Manuscripts*, p. 173.
6. Kierkegaard, *The Concept of Dread*, p. 74.
7. S. Kierkegaard, *Diario* (Brescia, 1948-53), II, p. 575. (English translation, *Journals and Papers*, by Howard V. Hong and Edna H. Hong (Indiana, 1967)).
8. Sartre, *Being and Nothingness*, p. 375.
9. The extent to which Sartre's position here diverges from that of the 'Marxism of Marx' is made clear in the following passage from the *Economic and Philosophical Manuscripts of 1844* where the criticism that Marx directs against Hegel is to a significant degree valid for Sartre too: 'The *estrangement*, which therefore forms the real interest of this alienation and of the transcendence of this alienation, is the opposition of the *in itself and for itself*, of *consciousness* and *self-consciousness*, of *object* and *subject* — that is to say, it is the opposition, within thought itself, between abstract thinking and sensuous reality or real sensuousness. All other oppositions and movements of these oppositions are but the *semblance, the cloak, the esoteric* shape of these oppositions, which alone matter, and which constitute the *meaning* of these other, profane oppositions. It is not the fact that the human being *objectifies himself inhumanly*, in opposition to himself, but the fact that he *objectifies himself* in *distinction* from and in opposition to abstract thinking.' MEGA I, 1, 3, pp. 154-5; Eng. trans., p. 173. Merleau-Ponty in *The Adventures of the Dialectic* asserts: 'Marxism needs a theory of consciousness [...] It is towards this theory that Lukács was leaning in his book of 1923.' (Lukács, *Existentialisme ou marxisme?*, p. 41). But there are many possible 'theories of consciousness,' and they include that maintained by Lukács in 1923, which he himself subsequently recognised was flawed by the 'Hegelian error' of identifying alienation with objectification, cf. Lukács, *Arguments*, no. 5, (1957), and no. 20, (1960). But the identification of alienation with objectification is the typical corollary of every theory of alienation which takes consciousness to be a subject metaphysically privileged in respect of the object, this latter being, as such, alienation demanding to be removed (even by terroristic methods). In the political context such a position gives rise to Hegelian absolutism, to Stalinism, and also, alas, to the Sartrean theory of the chief. It is certainly not by virtue of a 'theory of consciousness' of this type that the crisis of Stalinism in Poland has brought about 'a sudden eruption of existentialist influence' (A. Schaff, *A Philosophy of Man*, (London, 1963), p. 11.) Schaff writes: 'This applies particularly to the

capital discovery by Existentialism of the existence of conflicting moral situations, a discovery which delivered a death blow to the idea of an absolute morality and to the oversimplified moralising connected with it. And it applies in the sphere of politics as well.' (Schaff, *A Philosophy of Man,* p. 6.) Another Polish philosopher writes of the drama implicit in our constant need to take moral decisions while nonetheless remaining wholly in ignorance of their consequences. See L. Kolakowski, *Marxism and Beyond,* (London, 1968) part two, esp. pp. 174-5. English translation by Jane Zielonko Peel. The attack on the Sartrean theory of consciousness continues to be of a Stalinist type if it has the sense of a demand for the resolution of human multiplicity in the absolute, however that absolute is understood. It must rather have the significance of a demand for a deeper rooting of consciousness in existence, that is in the mode of being of 'real, corporeal *man,* man with his feet firmly on the solid ground,' of man whose own moral or physical being is not the instrument whereby he achieves de-alienation. For a Marxist critique of Sartre's theory of consciousness, cf. F. Valentini, 'Sartre e il marxismo,' in *Aut aut,* no. 51, (May 1959), pp. 189-94; A. Sabetti, 'Le *Questions de méthode* e l'esistenzialismo marxista,' in *Societa,* XVI, no. 6, (Nov.-Dec.), pp. 1199-1225. Cf. also the position taken by N. Badaloni, who accuses Sartre's latest theory of 'running the risk of exchanging the concept of alienation for that of real objectivity' (*Marxismo come storicismo* (Milan, 1962), p. 236), and M. Alicata's preface to the collection of Sartre's work which appeared in Italy under the title *Il filosofo e la politica* (Rome, 1964). Alicata calls for a frank discussion between Marxism and existentialism that would escape the alternatives of threats or blandishments which typify the Stalinist political culture. (An amusing example of this was recently provided in the article by Leo Figuères, 'La lotta ideologica in Francia,' in *Problemi della pace e del socialismo,* (January 1963).) On the question of the relations between existentialism and Marxism presented in Sartre's latest work cf. also A. Patri, 'Le marxisme existentialisé, in *Preuves,* (Aug. 1960), pp. 63-69; L. Sève, 'Jean-Paul Sartre et la dialectique en 1960,' in *La Nouvelle Critique,* (1961), no. 123, pp. 78-100; U. Compagnolo, 'N'est pas marxiste qui veut,' in *Comprendre,* 1961-2, no. 23-24, pp. 201-7; S. Kruithof, 'Sartre en het marxisme,' in *Dialog,* 1960-61, pp. 41-60. Alessandro Pellegrini has an interesting hypothesis according to which in order 'to understand the Jansenist, and even Manichean aspect of Sartre's thought,' we must 'perhaps consider the conception of his literary work more than his political ideas.' A. Pellegrini, 'Sartre oggi' in *Il ponte* (1959), no. 4, pp. 474-79.

10. The 'tragic' character of the conception of history to be found in the *Critique* has been emphasised by Nicola Petruzzellis, 'Dal gruppo alla storia secondo Sartre,' in *Rassegna di scienze filosofiche,* (1963), no. 1, p. 1. Cf. by the same author 'G. P. Sartre tra filosofia e ideologia,' *Rassegna di scienze,* (1962), no. 1, pp. 1-27; 'La materia e la prassi nella *Critica della regione dialettica,*' (*ibid.,* 1962, nos. 3-4, pp. 269-85); 'La genesi fenomenologica del diritto secondo G. P. Sartre,' *Rassegna di scienze,* (1963), no. 4, pp. 299-312.

11. The global dimension which history assumes in Sartre's thought has led Cl. Lévi-Stauss to assert that Sartre conceives history in the same way as

primitives conceive the eternal past, that is, mythically. Lévi-Strauss, *The Savage Mind*, P. 254.

12. Sartre, 'Merleau-Ponty vivant,' *Les Temps modernes*, nos. 184-5, 1961.

13. Cf. Sartre's address to the world Congress for disarmament and peace (Moscow, 9-14th July, 1962), included in J.-P. Sartre, *Il filosofo e la politica*, pp. 239-48. It is not clear, however, how Sartre can reconcile 'peaceful co-existence' (the title of his paper is 'Peaceful and Cultural Co-existence') with the 'Manichean' character that the *Critique* confers on the political struggle. In this connexion, Sartre's interview in *Le Monde*, 18 April 1964, with Jacqueline Piatier, is significant. In it he asks: 'What does literature mean in a world where there is hunger?' and declares 'Faced with a dying child, *La nausée* has no importance.' For Sartre's most recent attitude in regard to the problems of literature, cf. the two interviews he gave to *Polityka* (7 July 1962), translated into Italian in *Contemporaneo*, (September 1962), pp. 3-10, and to *Clarte'* (March-April 1964), pp. 42-47.

14. Cf. Sartre, *Il filosofo e la politica*, p. 205.

15. Moreover, empirical sociology knows no groups of the Sartrean type. Thus M. Olmsted in his book *The Small Group*, (New York, 1959), reaches the conclusion that the primary group always has a 'competitive' structure (p. 18), and draws upon the results of research initiated by C. Cooley (*Social Organisation*, New York, 1909): 'It is not to be supposed that the unity of the primary group is one of mere harmony and love. It is always a differentiated and usually a competitive unity, admitting of self-assertion and various appropriative passions.' (pp. 23–24). B. Malinowsky writes to the same effect, *Sex and Repression in Savage Society*, (London, 1927): 'Human sociality is always a combination, a dove-tailing of legal, political and cultural functions. It is not a mere identity of the emotional impulse, not a similarity of response to the same stimulus, but an acquired habit.' (p. 191) By contrast, Sartre has found support in the field of social psychology from D. Anzieu, who claims to find of 'a convergence between the process of genesis and transformation of the group which Sartre analyses at the level of pure intelligibility, and the observations of social psychologists on artificial groups in accordance with the *T-group* or group diagnostic technique.' ('Sur la méthode dialectique dans l'étude des groupes restreints,' in *Les études philosophiques*, (1962), no. 4, p. 502); also by D. Anzieu, 'A propos du fonctionnement des groupes humains,' in *Bulletin de Psychologie*, XV, (1962), no. 9, pp. 441-52. Cf. also G. Gurvitch, *Dialectique et Sociologie*, pp. 157 sqq.; Cl. Lévi-Strauss, *The Savage Mind*, pp. 245 sqq.

Appendix 1

1. J.-P. Sartre, *Existentialism and Humanism*, (London, 1948). English translation by Philip Mairet of *L'existentialism est un humanisme* (Paris, 1946); M. Merleau-Ponty, *Humanism and Terror*, (Boston, 1969). English translation by J. O'Neill of *Humanisme et terreur*, (Paris, 1947).

2. J.-P. Sartre, R. Garaudy, J. Hyppolite, J.-P. Vigier, J. Orcel, *Marxisme et existentialisme, controverse sur la dialectique*, (Paris, 1962).

3. Merleau-Ponty, *The Adventures of the Dialectic* (Paris 1955; London, 1974).

4. Sartre, *Critique de la raison dialectique*; Merleau-Ponty, *Signs.*
5. Cf. de Beauvoir, *The Prime of Life*, p. 118.
6. *Les Temps modernes*, no. 123, (1956), p. 1522.
7. R. Aron, *The Opium of the Intellectuals*, (London, 1957), p. 115 sq. English translation by Terence Kilmartin of *L'Opium des intellectuels*, (Paris, 1955).
8. *Les Temps modernes*, no. 114-15, (1955), p. 2116.
9. C. Lefort, 'Le marxisme de Sartre,' in *Les Temps modernes*, no. 89, (1953), pp. 1540 sqq.
10. *Les Temps modernes* no. 123, (1956), p. 1508.
11. Lukács, *Existentialisme ou marxisme?*, (Paris, 2 ed., 1947, 1961), pp 187, 221, 228.
12. R.-M. Albérès, J.-P. Sartre, (Paris, 5th ed., 1960), translated by Wade Baskin, (London, 1964), p. 132.
13. E. Mounier, *Introduction aux existentialismes*, (Paris, 1947), p. 90.
14. *Les Temps modernes*, no. 122, (1956), p. 1160.
15. de Beauvoir, *The Prime of Life*, p. 3.
16. P. Nizan, *Aden Arabie*, translated into English by Joan Pinkham, (New York, 1968), p. 18.
17. Nizan, *Aden Arabie*, p. 51.
18. Merleau-Ponty, *Signs*, p. 23.
19. Merleau-Ponty, *Signs*, p. 27.
20. Merleau-Ponty, *Signs*, p. 32.
21. *The Spectre of Stalin*, English translation of *Le fantôme de Staline*, by Martha H. Fletcher with the assistance of John R. Kleinschmidt, (New York, 1968).
22. Lukács *Existentialisme ou Marxisme?* pp. 28, 61. The relations between Weber, Lukács and Merleau-Ponty in regard to Marxism are analysed in depth by Pietro Rossi, *Storia e storicismo*, (Milan, 1960), see particularly pp. 169-215.
23. Sartre, *The Problem of Method*, pp. 21, 28, 37, 53, 136.
24. *Les Temps modernes*, no. 100, (1954), pp. 1724-25.
25. Sartre, *Situations* III, (Paris, 1949), p. 225.
26. *Les Temps modernes*, no. 129-30-31, (1956-57), p. 696.
27. To be found in Garaudy, *Perspectives de l'homme*, p. 113. The ideological sectarianism and the imputation of bad faith, which have been the inevitable accompaniment, whether of the trials of the Inquisition, or those of Moscow reappear in the part devoted to Sartre of Leo Figuères' article, 'La lotta ideologica in Francia,' which appeared in the January, 1963 issue of *Problems of Peace and Socialism*, the international communist review. Sartre is described there as not only an ideological, but a political enemy of communism, who is to be distinguished from the 'spokesmen of American anti-communism' only because he pursues his ends 'by more subtle means.' Perhaps this article reflects disappointment over what Adam Schaff, the Polish communist theoretician, has recently termed the 'eruption' of Sartrean existentialism in Poland (although the phenomenon is not only a Polish one) which began with the de-Stalinisation of 1955-57. Schaff does not conceal the very close connexion between the ideological and political crisis of Stalinism and the undervaluation produced by it of the problems of the individual, and particularly of the problems of the *conflict* between individual

and society, to whose reinstatement existentialism owes its 'sudden and tremendous appeal' in the climate of Marxist Poland; nor does he conceal the *positive function* of the existentialist problematic in having recalled Marxism to the necessity of a theoretical and political re-examination of such problems, if it really wants to liberate itself from Stalinism. Schaff, *The Philosophy of Man*, p. 11. Rather than make this re-examination of the problems of the individual, which existentialism has proposed that Marxism should do, Figuères prefers to have recourse to what Sartre has branded 'the terroristic practice of liquidating individuality.' This is an ideological and political manifestation, unfortunately, of a distortion of Marxism of the kind that Lukács himself has termed 'voluntaristic idealism.' Cf. Sartre, *Problem of Method*, p. 28.

Figuères' thesis has been firmly rejected (from a standpoint of personal loyalty to Sartre) by Cesare Luporini in the article 'Sartre e i communisti,' which appeared in April 1964 in the review of the PCI *Critica marxista*. It is not possible to expound here, let alone discuss, Luporini's arguments. To put them very generally, he holds that Sartre, *Les Temps modernes*, no. 81, (1952), pp. 19, 57, as much as Merleau-Ponty, *Signs*, p. 299, has frequently opposed to the sectarianism of the PCF, the demands for ideological renewal and for 'tolerance' made by the PCI. Luporini cites the stance taken up by Togliatti at the 10th Congress of the PCI, where he favoured 'tolerance towards anyone who sincerely, in the cause of development rather than in the service of reactionary forces, and at the cost of personal suffering, torments himself in the pursuit of truth.' The ultimate problem, however, lies in seeing whether this 'tolerance' takes the form of an ethical or dianoetic virtue; whether, that is, it expresses simply a moral 'condoning' by someone in possession of truth for someone in error, or whether it is the recognition of the fact that intellectually this opposition itself cannot be sustained.

28. *Les Temps modernes*, no. 129-30-31, (1956-57), p. 678.
29. Lukács, *Existentialisme ou marxisme?*, p. 224.
30. B. Croce, *Indagini su Hegel e schiarimenti filosofici*, (Bari, 1952), p. 70
31. Sartre, *Situations* III, p. 135; and *The Problem of Method*, p. 34.
32. Merleau-Ponty, *The Adventures of the Dialectic*, p. 151. From their respective Marxist and Catholic standpoints, F. Valentini and N. Petruzzellis arrive at substantially negative judgements on the fruitfulness of the encounter between Marxism and existentialism. For Valentini the ahistoric role that existentialism grants to consciousness means that it has nothing to teach Marxism; F. Valentini, *La filosofia francese contemporanea*, (Milan, 1958), pp. 92-97, 175-80. For Petruzzellis, existentialism merely introduces an 'ambiguous and fanciful stance' into the conflict between capitalism and Marxism, 'G. P. Sartre tra filosofia e ideologia,' in *Rassegna di scienze filosofiche*, XV, (1962), p. 27. Valentini's comments on the evolution of Sartre's thought — which at the time had scarcely been delineated — do, however, open up the prospect of a discourse which must take into account the very valuable research which Valentini has devoted to clarifying the negative aspects of French existentialism. Important comments on the relations between existentialism and Marxism are to be found in F. Battaglia, 'Existencialismo y marxismo', *Revista de estudios politicos*, vol. XXXIII,

(1950), pp. 13-27 and in L. Pareyson, *Esistenza e persona*, 2 ed., (Turin, 1960), pp. 175-86 (a work referring to a series of studies by A. Del Noce, of which cf. A Del Noce, 'La non-filosofia di Marx e il communismo come realtá politica,' in *Atti del congresso intern. di filosofia*, (Rome, 1946). (Cf. also P. Scarpelli, *Esistentialismo e marxismo*, Turin, 1949); A. Santucci, *Esistentialismo e filosofia italiano*, (Bologna, 1959), pp. 288 sq.; C. Vasoli, *Tra cultura e ideologia*, (Milan, 1961), pp. 59-78, 129-95, 511-20; E. Garin, *La cultura italiana tra '800 e '900*, (Bari, 1962), pp. 229 sqq.

33. Sartre, *The Problem of Method*, p. 6.
34. Sartre, *The Problem of Method*, p. 34.
35. After Merleau-Ponty's death, Sartre gave an account, from his own point of view, of the complex history of his relations with his lost friend: Sartre, 'Merleau-Ponty vivant,' *Les Temps modernes*.
36. Merleau-Ponty, *Signs*, p. 323.
37. *Situations* III, pp. 214-5.
38. Sartre, et al., *Marxisme et existentialisme*, p. 3.
39. Sartre et al, *Marxisme et existentialisme*, p. 5, for this and the preceding passage. For a commentary on the most recent positions adopted by Sartre cf. the issue of *Aut aut*, no. 51, (May 1959), devoted to Sartre, with contributions by P. Caruso, E. Filippini, U. Segre, C. Bo, E. Paci, F. Valentini, G. Morpurgo Tagliabue, O. Borrello. *Aut Aut* no. 82 (July 1964) is also devoted to Sartre's latest work and includes contributions by E. Paci, G. Daghini, A. Bonomi, M. Maggiò, P. Caruso.
40. Sartre, et al., *Marxisme et existentialisme*, p. 27.
41. Sartre, et al., *Marxisme et existentialisme*, p. 35.
42. Sartre, et al., *Marxisme et existentialisme*, p. 33-4.
43. Sartre, et al., *Marxisme et existentialisme*, p. 41.
44. Sartre, et al., *Marxisme et existentialisme*, p. 60.
45. Sartre, et al., *Marxisme et existentialisme*, p. 73.
46. Sartre, et al., *Marxisme et existentialisme*, p. 46.
47. Sartre, et al., *Marxisme et existentialisme*, p. 73.
48. Sartre, et al., *Marxisme et existentialisme*, p. 91.
49. K. Marx, *Capital*, I, p. 715.
50. Sartre, et al., *Marxisme et existentialisme*, pp. 91-2.
51. N. Abbagnano, 'Quattro concetti di dialettica,' *Studi sulla dialettica*, (Turin, 1958), p. 17. Franco Fergnani, in his pertinent study of the *controverse* we are examining here, has proposed that the term 'dialectic' be used in the sense of a 'family of conceptual structures' on the model proposed by L. Geymonat, *Studi per un nuovo razionalismo*, (Turin, 1954), pp. 228 sq., in respect of the notion of 'cause.' Fergnani's proposal finds its limit in what he himself recognizes – that the constitutive concepts of this family are 'profoundly different and irreducible to each other.' 'Un dibattito sulla dialettica,' in *Il pensiero critico*, (1962), p. 18. Among the most recent writings on the dialectic cf. the work by Mario Rossi, *Marx e la dialettica hegeliana;* L. Colletti, 'Dialettica scientifica e teoria del valore,' which prefaces E. V. Ilyenkov, *La dialettica dell'astratto e del concreto nel Capitale di Marx*, (Milan, 1961); N. Badaloni, *Marxismo come storicismo*, (Milan, 1962); G. Della Volpe, *Rousseau e Marx*, 3rd ed., (Rome, 1962); N.

Merker, *Le origini della logica hegeliana*, (Milan, 1963).

52. Abbagnano, 'La dialettica in Marx,' *Studi sulla dialettica*, pp. 230 sqq.

53. Departing from an alignment that was originally existentialistic, Enzo Paci now confronts the re-thinking of the Husserlian 'dialectic' in a Marxist light. From among many papers, those which seem particularly significant are: 'L'ultimo Sartre e il problema della soggettivita' in *Aut Aut*, no. 67, (1962), and those presented at the conference on *Il significato dell'uomo in Marx e Husserl*, held at Prague, 24 October 1962, *Aut Aut*, no. 73, (1963), pp. 10-21. On the concept of the dialectic in Sartre and Merleau-Ponty cf. the studies by G. Semerari included in *Da Schelling a Merleau-Ponty* (Urbino, 1962), particularly pp. 317 sqq. On the relations between Merleau-Ponty and Sartre cf. A. Bonomi, 'La polemica con Sartre,' in *Aut Aut*, no. 66, (1961), pp. 562-67.

54. In M. Rossi, 'Articolo sul diritto naturale,' *Marx e la dialettica hegeliana*, I: *Hegel e lo Stato*, (Milan, 1960), pp. 216, 339.

55. Heidegger, *Holzwege*, p. 298.

56. Heidegger, 'Brief über den Humanismus, in *Platons Lehre von der Wahrheit*, (Berne, 1947), p. 87.

57. Heidegger, *Brief über den Humanismus*, p. 87.

58. Heidegger has made the observation on the celebrated *11th Thesis on Feuerbach* that thought can change the world only on condition that it finds itself in the correct relationship with Being, (*Kants These über das Sein*, (Frankfurt a M. 1963), pp. 6-7.)

Appendix 2

1. Cf. Rossi, *Marx e la dialettica hegeliana*, pp. 124-31, 298-302.

2. Cf. 'Filosofia dell'alienazione e analisi esistenziale,' by P. Filiasi Carcano and others, *Archivio di filosofia*, (Rome, 1962).

3. MEGA, I, 1, 3, p. 160; *Economic and Philosophical Manuscripts* p. 179. (See the Eng. translator's note on terminology p. 58-9).

4. MEGA, I, 1, 3, p. 163; *Economic and Philosophical Manuscripts*, pp. 183-4. Since alienation can take on a positive character it can obviously be equated with the objectification which is precisely a positive, because structural, condition of the realisation of man. But the equivalence between alienation and objectification is the fundamental corollary of every philosophy, such as Hegel's, which theorises alienation from the starting point of a subjectivity of the spirit which it takes to be an original reality. In this case, de-alienation calls for the removal not of a determinate object, but of objectivity as such, i.e. for the recognition of its *nullity*. Again, in the *Economic and Philosophical Manuscripts of 1844*, Marx says: 'As we have already seen, the appropriation of what is estranged and objective ... means equally or even primarily for Hegel that it is *objectivity* which is to be annulled, because it is not the *determinate* character of the object, but rather its *objective* character that is offensive and constitutes estrangement for self-consciousness. The object is therefore something negative, self-annulling —a *nullity*. This nullity of the object has not only a negative but a *positive* meaning for consciousness ...,' MEGA I, 1, 3, pp. 162-63; *Economic and Philosophical Manuscripts*, p. 183.

The attempt to dissolve, or at least to attenuate as far as possible, the quite clear-cut distinction made by Marx between 'objectification' and 'alienation' is now widespread and has often been made for quite diverse reasons. The point of convergence of such attempts, however, is a 'renaissance' of Hegelianism. They are made in answer to what are basically two demands: 1) to enlarge the role of 'consciousness' in the process of de-alienation by making alienation an aspect of objectification consisting in the departure outside of self on the part of consciousness. Taken to its extreme, this position involves the lapse into 'voluntaristic idealism' of which Sartre accused its major defendant, Lukács (apropos of this, Lukács' declaration thirty years later in *History and Class Consciousness* is illuminating: 'In the treatment of alienation I have repeated the Hegelian error which consists in identifying alienation with objectivity in general.' J. Gabel, *La fausse conscience, Essai sur la reification*, (Paris, 1962), note 4, p. 15); 2) to enlarge the understanding of the concept of alienation in Marx and to deny the subordination of every form of alienation to the economic. The limit to this demand — it emerges quite transparently in J. Hyppolite, *Studies on Marx and Hegel*, English translation by J. O'Neill, (New York, 1969) — lies in its compromising of the possibility of de-alienation. This is effected by means of an existentialist reading of Hegel and an Hegelian one of Marx, in which the indistinguishability of alienation and objectification is ascribed to the 'human situation.' In whatever way we might want to view these 'demands,' the conceptual instrument with which they are made to hold good, i.e. the distortion of the Marxian opposition between objectification and alienation, does not appear acceptable. On the one hand, there is a rich and precise body of texts opposing it; on the other, it is in contradiction with the historical and ideological essence of Marxism, for which de-alienation presents itself as a task of political and economic transformation; from the point of view of (1), however, this task runs the risk of being resolved in a purely conscious operation; from the point of view of (2) it becomes straightforwardly impossible, or anyhow, useless. On the other hand, since Stalinism's banner in the cultural field and its means of ideological monopolisation of Marx's thought has been its repudiation of every amplification or integration along these lines, we can specify the cultural location, and thus the limitations, of such polemical attitudes as those found in an article by Giulio Preti, 'Un concetto da chiarire: alienazione', *Il filo rosso*, I, no. 1, (1963), in which alienation is declared to be 'a *moral, not political* problem,' and the socialist world is seen as 'the passage to a world of greater emancipation . . . that takes place only dialectically, and not *in fact* and *in itself*: because in fact, and in itself, it is precisely the world of greatest alienation.' (p 29) A position in some respects analogous is to be found in the long chapter, 'Pour une théorie de l'aliénation', in the book by André Gorz, *La morale de l'histoire*, (Paris, 1959), which reflects the Sartrean theses of the *Critique* — whose inspiration is also a merciless anti-Stalinist polemic — on the re-evaluation of the subjective and conscious factor in the process of revolution. The limit of such a position is made clear in Gorz's assertion that 'The revolution is the historical *Instant* in which the force of humanity triumphs over inhuman powers . . . So that, on pain of being a failure, the communist revolution cannot, must not, result in substituting a communist *system* for a capitalist *system*; because to speak of a system is to speak of the alienation of free praxis ...' (p. 153) An article by Umberto Eco, 'Del modo di formare come impegno sulla realtà,' *Menabò,* 5, (1962), p. 198-237, is also for the most part devoted to the problem of the relations between objectification and alienation. Eco also proposes to amplify the concept of alienation, but he maintains that Marx himself 'has a glimpse of the possibility of this persistence of a dialectic, once economic alienation has been eliminated.' (p. 206) Eco's position has been criticized from a Marxist point of view by Alberto Asor Rosa, 'A proposito del *Menabò 5*: Ancora su industria e letteratura,' *Mondo Nuovo,* IV, 20; as also that of Preti by Gianni Toti 'Non perdere il filo, rosso o no,' *Il Contemporaneo,* VI, 60, pp. 90-98. Some important comments concerning the meaning of 'alienation' are to be found in Nicola Badaloni's note, 'La parola "alienazione", *Rinascita,* XIX, no. 7. (16 June 1962), p. 32, the occasion for which was the debate promoted by *Espresso* on the meaning of the term. Badaloni underlines the difference between objectification and estangement but believes it opportune to recognise two different senses of 'alienation' in the two terms. It seems to me that if one does so, one runs the risk of compromising the clear-cut Marxian opposition between objectification (which *as such* is never alienation) on the one hand, and alienation-estrangement on the other.

5. 'Perhaps every salvation which does not issue from the source of the danger itself is doomed to fail,' says Heidegger commenting on the lines of the Romantic poet, Hölderlin: 'There, where is the danger, there springs salvation.' Heidegger, *Holzwege,* p. 273.

6. Sartre, *Being and Nothingness,* p. 264.

7. G. Marcel, *Being and Having,* (London, 1965), p. 203. English translation of *Etre et avoir,* (Paris, 1935).

8. Marcel, *Being and Having,* p. 113.

9. K. Jaspers, *Vernunft und Existenz,* (Munich, 1973), p. 60.

10. G. W. F. Hegel, *Jenenser Logik, Metaphysik and Naturphilosophie,* (Leipzig), p. 31.

11. The argument that where Hegel differs from Marx is in interpreting alienation in such a way that it can never be definitively removed is the product of a mere equivocation. Since, even if it is true that for Hegel alienation is not removed with the removal of a determinate basis of the Subjectivity-objectification relationship (for Marx its basis is bourgeois society), it is nonetheless true that alienation is fully removed in the conclusive dissolution of objectification in Subjectivity which brings the process whereby alienation first arose to its end point. It does not seem possible, therefore, to appeal to the 'existential drama' in Hegel in order to declare him more existentialist than Marx, as Hyppolite does, *Studies on Marx and Hegel,* pp. 116-7. History for Hegel is 'a tragedy which the Absolute plays out with itself'; the tragedies which a finite being plays out *with itself* are already, in reality, comedies with happy endings — all the more reason for those which the *Absolute* plays out with itself being so.

12. G. W. F. Hegel, *Phenomenology of Mind,* (London, 1931) p. 667 sq., cf. p. 251, p. 675. For the connexion between the 'Beautiful Soul' and 'alienation'

in Hegel cf. Eco, *Menabò*, 5, p. 206.

13. Cf. Garaudy, *Perspectives de l'homme*, pp. 137-52, 315; R. Aron, *The Opium of the Intellectuals*, p. 66 sq.

14. An analogous function in regard to Marxism is entrusted to the Husserlian phenomenology by Enzo Paci. Paci writes: 'Husserl has ignored the basic problems of the economy, and in this, as in other respects, he must be corrected by Marx. But it is indisputable that the Husserlian critique of the objectification or alienation of the sciences appears to us today as being on the same level as the Marxist critique of the fetishism of commodities, while, in its turn, the formalistic scientism and the alienation which Marxism can produce within itself, can be made known only be means of Husserl's methodology.' E. Paci, 'In un rapporto intenziale,' in *Questo e altro*, no. 2, (1963), p. 28.

Index of Names